Castle on a Cloud

Castle on a House © Copyright 2005 by Paul Chambers

All rights reserved. No part of this work may be reproduced or stored in an information retrieval system (other than for purposes of review) without prior written permission by the copyright holder.

A catalogue record of this book is available from the British Library

First Edition: December 2005

ISBN: 1-84375-235-2

This is a work of fiction. Names, characters, places and incidents are the product of the author's imagination or are used fictitiously, and any resemblance to any actual persons, living or dead, events, or locales is entirely coincidental.

To order additional copies of this book please visit: http://www.upso.co.uk/paulchambers

Published by: UPSO Ltd
5 Stirling Road, Castleham Business Park,
St Leonards-on-Sea, East Sussex TN38 9NW United Kingdom
Tel: 01424 853349 Fax: 0870 191 3991
Email: info@upso.co.uk Web: http://www.upso.co.uk

Castle on a Cloud

by

Paul Chambers

UPSO

This story is dedicated to the memory of my wife, Joan

Thanks are due to my daughter, Julie,
for her help in editing this book

1

WHAT? NO HOBBITS?

This word processor screen is blank, Den.
   You're talking to yourself again, Paul. Of course it's blank. You haven't started typing yet. You know – the story of Paul Dennis Potts.
   I'm worried, Den.
   What about now? Let's just get cracking, eh? We've done a sort of outline.
   That's why I'm worried. We don't have one hobbit in the whole book; we've got no wizards either.
   We're going to have a Grand Panjandrum, aren't we?
   That's not the same, Den, Harry Potter and the Grand Panjandrum doesn't have that intriguing ring about it.
   Funnily enough, Paul, it does. But we're not going to have a bloody Harry Potter!
   I'm worried about that as well. Plus we haven't catered for one earthquake or a single iceberg.
   You'll want to put an ocean liner in the book next!
   No, not necessarily. But we haven't got a gunfight in a corral, or a murder in a cathedral, or a detective with a magnifying glass, or any cops, or any robbers. We could have a murder at the wedding, eh? 'Murder in the church!' That would beef it up a bit.
   Look, Paul, people are getting fed up to the teeth with violence. Let's have a story about ordinary folk. I thought we'd agreed that.
   I'm having second thoughts though, Den. Here's an idea, what about man-eating plants?
   No!
   Terrorists?

No! We hear enough about them on the telly.

What about swearing? These days, all books have swearing in them, Den.

Well, we'll have a bit, not much mind. But I've just had a brilliant thought, Paul. We could start the book with this conversation we've been having.

Are you mad, Den? People would read the first page and put it straight back on the shelf.

No, no. We could tell them some of the fascinating things that *are* in the book.

Like what? Like Paul Potts went to the grocer's?

No. Like there's real life, there's love, there's heartache, there's sorrow, there's humour, there's tragedy.

Hey, we don't want much of that. Tragedy's sad.

There'll be fun too; and people. Some ordinary people, some special.

Like Paul Potts and Joan?

Well, Joan was special. I'm not sure about dithery Paul Potts. Anyway why do you keep saying Paul Potts? Why don't you say Paul Dennis Potts?

What's that got to do with anything? Anyway, what about sex, will that be in the book?

Oh, aye, Paul. There'll be oodles of sex, but our readers will have to use a lot of imagination.

They won't have much of that. Not our readers.

What a thing to say! You'd be surprised.

OK, OK, we'll give it a go. Let's start typing.

2

HONEYMOON HOTEL

"He thinks he's the Grand Panjandrum." That was elder brother, Don, complaining about me to young Cecil, those childhood years ago. It was the day I'd walloped him 10-0, that day we played headies in our backyard. It was a funny thing, he never played headies again. Not with me, anyway.

But Grand Panjandrum? A person of great power? Perhaps I was he! Hadn't I made a dream come true?

Clickety-click, clickety-clack. The train picked up speed, rattling over the points as it pulled out of York Station – destination 'Sunny Scarborough' – but wet and windy Scarborough was the forecast for this weekend in the March of 1948.

The locomotive strained and puffed noisily as it crossed the bridge over the Ouse, but soon the flat terrain allowed it to gather momentum. We looked out of the rain-flecked window. The fading light unveiled a sombre scene of lowering clouds, with bare trees swaying in the wind.

Yes, *we* looked out – Joan Speed and Paul Dennis Potts. No – correction – Joan Potts, that was her name now. As from today.

We'd snaffled a 'No Smoking' compartment, but yet there was a lingering smell of stale tobacco. I snuggled up to Joan, resting my head on her shoulder. Her nearness, her perfume, dispelled that tang of fustiness. I took her hand and settled to contented meditation.

Why would any girl with a decent name like Speed, a name she'd borne for twenty-two years, agree to change it to Potts? Especially to Mrs Pee Potts! I smiled inwardly. Only some girl who was in love with this Potts guy. Not just any girl mind, but a tall, pretty lass with soft brown hair, laughing eyes and dimpled cheeks. Oh! And don't forget her voice, a voice that was filled with melody.

OK, I was a goner, but so was this girl sitting by my side. It must be love; surely she wouldn't marry a guy just for his four pounds ten a week? No, no. Not even if he had good prospects. I patted my breast pocket. Yes, the marriage certificate was still there, I bet the ink was hardly dry yet.

"What have you lost?" Those soft tones never failed to please.

"Just checking, love."

The train seemed to be beating out a rhythm now – 'derri-de-dum-dum', 'derri-de-dum-dum', 'Mister-and-Miss-us', 'Mister-and-Miss-us', taking Mr and Mrs on their two-night honeymoon.

"What the heck," I'd said, in a rare moment of abandon. "OK, Joan, we might not be flushed, but let's go for it!"

Grand Panjandrum, though? Mm, yes, I suppose the Grand Panjandrum was already at work. Who spotted this empty compartment, eh? There were plenty of passengers on the train, mind, but these other people were just humdrum shoppers, not happy honeymooners. Workaday shoppers returning from trips to York or Leeds. I guessed they'd spent not only money, but clothes coupons, curtain permits, even furniture vouchers. This civvy life that I'd returned to almost two years after the end of the Second World War was still swimming in tokens.

For a while I just held Joan's hand. Happy to relax after the hoo-ha of the church wedding and the commotion at the slap-up, two-shillings-a-head reception at swanky Borders Cafe in Coney Street. A reception financed by Joan's well-paid dad. Engine-driver, dad. It was swanky alright – we even had table napkins and side plates. Plus two knives, two forks, and three spoons. I'd done well there; out of that collection I'd just the one spoon unused.

But commotion? Commotion and confusion. Scores of Joan's relations were milling about in the cafe: her mam and dad, brother and sister, uncles, aunts, cousins, second cousins, even a grandma thrown in for good measure. The whole palaver had been a big blur to me.

Hmm, no big blur for Joan, though, me having just one relation from hometown Gateshead in the melee – brother Don. I grant that Dad had a valid excuse to be missing (dead for some nine years), but Mam absent, just because she was a Catholic born of Irish immigrant parents? OK, she was distraught at my getting wed in a Protestant Church and thus bringing ignominy on the family, but was that reason enough? (Mind, I had a hunch that she prayed nightly, pleading with God not to let my fall from grace reach the ears of the parish priest.) None of my aunts or uncles was there. Well, they wouldn't be would they? They were Catholics too. Aye, just brother Don, for support.

Not even younger brother Cecil was there. Aye, I'm sure Cecil would have come, but he was away at Oxford. No, no, not to the University, just doing his National Service in the RASC. Of course luckless, lame, absent-minded eleven-year-old brother Stephen was not at the wedding, he was back home with his Mam. In a huff because he'd missed the express train ride to York.

Yes, Mam had graciously allowed me one concession; tubby, elder brother Don was to be my best man. Genial, garrulous, brother Don. Gee thanks! Mam.

No matter, the wedding was over now, the future belonged to us. We could start to work at living happily ever after.

It was then that a certain unease crept into my ruminations. Living happily ever after? We *would* have to work on that I suppose. But why had people been so sceptical?

"Why don't you wait until you can get a place of your own?" Mam had said, eager to cause any delay which might culminate in a wedding cancellation.

"Joan, luv, Paul, luv, why don't thees wait until ye have ye own house? Somethin' to rent even."

That was Joan's Mam, worried that her favourite daughter would be leaving her home in salubrious York for dubious accommodation in mucky Gateshead.

Her Dad was even more concerned about his little girl.

"Paul. Have ye considered lookin' for a job here in York? Aa believe ye could rent a house here, tha knows."

We'd listened to them – sort of – but had already agreed our future, not only when we became engaged, but in the scores of letters we'd exchanged during our two years apart; me in India, Joan in York. It was to be a future in Gateshead. My old boss had promised me significant promotion upon my demob. "Within months," he'd said. We wanted to be together – now. I had no doubts. We were in love. Too long had I been without her beside me. And Joan? Joan felt the same. Surely?

"Well, missus, you've gone and done it now."

Her lips brushed my hair. "I have that, hubby; it's awesome, isn't it?"

"Have you any regrets, Joan?"

"No, love. Not yet anyway."

She laughed, but was there uncertainty behind her avowal? Day one of a journey into the unknown?

The train slowed to a halt at Malton – next stop Scarborough. There were a number of people waiting to board. Hopefully, I crossed my fingers.

"Spread out, Joan, we don't want any pests in here."

Some hope. A trilby-hatted fellow, sporting an Errol Flynn moustache, peered through the corridor window. We hadn't spread out enough, because he turned and beckoned to hidden companions, slid open the door, and stepped to one side. Those hidden companions revealed themselves as they brushed passed him and bustled into our compartment.

First, a rosy-cheeked matron carrying a baby. She subsided on the seat opposite and commenced to rock her precious cargo. Second came a small laddie, waving a half-eaten toffee apple. This little blighter had the temerity to climb up on the seat beside me. I abandoned the spreading out plan and moved closer to Joan, as 'Errol Flynn' himself came in. I hoped 'Errol' would take the lad, plus his claggy fingers, onto his knee. But no! He shook his wet umbrella, sat down beside his wife, closed his eyes, and even before the guard had waved his green flag and blown his whistle, was snoring noisily.

Meantime, the sticky toffee apple was poised perilously close to my best double-breasted suit. My only suit apart from that demob issue – the suit that Joan hated. Danger was only averted when the big gobstopper disappeared into the laddie's mouth. I looked up, the mother had her eye on me, so I gave the little perisher what I hoped was a friendly grin.

The mother smiled, I returned the smile grudgingly. What right had this pesky family to invade our honeymoon privacy? Now she seemed to be looking at my shoulder, I turned my head – confetti on my jacket. What a giveaway! Hurriedly, I brushed it off.

Joan laughed, "We've been to a wedding in York." Then to me, "You've been standing too near the bride, Paul."

Quick thinking by Joan, but had her remark fooled the woman? I thought not when I saw her eyeing our luggage on the rack. I soon knew for certain it hadn't when the train came to a halt in Scarborough station. As I pulled down our cases and moved towards the corridor, there came a shout:

Castle on a Cloud

"Have a nice honeymoon!"

The wind, gusting through the station, caught Joan off balance as she stepped down onto the platform. She grabbed my arm. "You're always showing me up on trains," she chuckled.

"You don't mean when I proposed to you three years ago? That was romantic."

"Romantic to propose on a train rattling through Ferryhill Station?" she laughed. "In that crowded wartime coach?"

"You must admit it was different. That couple opposite nearly applauded when you said yes."

"We were young and daft then."

"Anyway, it was your fault today; you should have noticed the confetti on my shoulder."

"I was too busy looking into those clear blue eyes of yours, love!"

It seemed a flimsy excuse, even if I did have that skinny, Frank Sinatra look.

We passed through the station concourse, with its bogus posters of sunny Scarborough – sleek girls in swimsuits prancing in the sparkling sea. Out into the open, we were hit by a rainstorm, and Joan grappled with her umbrella. I was carrying the two weekend cases, hers, a spanking new present from her Dad, mine, a family heirloom made of stout cardboard, fraying at the corners and threatening to dissolve with damp. She tried to protect us both from the deluge, but with little success.

Dodging the elements by hailing a cab didn't seem an option to me. Four taxi rides in one day, even a wedding day, would be much too flamboyant. Four taxis? Before this day, a single taxi ride would have been one more than I had ever experienced.

"Are we going the right way?" I shouted.

"Yes," she cried, "it's in Trafalgar Square, 'Cherrytrees', near the cricket ground. I still remember being on holiday there with Mam and Dad before the war; Mrs Appleyard's, she's a homely woman."

"Is it far?" I bellowed, trying to make myself heard through another squall.

"Less than ten minutes, far enough in this weather," she shouted, grimly hanging on to a brolly that threatened to fly apart any second.

A wet ten minutes later, I thumped the big black knocker on the boarding house door. The bang reverberated like a big base drum. The noise scared the life out of me, but at first failed to produce a response from inside. A mini cascade sloshed over a broken gutter above the doorway. We hopped around trying to avoid the splatters.

"Come on, Mrs, let us in before we drown," I muttered.

The door opened. A tall, gaunt, sombrely dressed woman stood on the threshold. Her piercing eyes and hawk-like nose reminded me of the black kites, which had scavenged outside our Army mess-hall back in India. Those sinister birds would hover, and then, before we could get to the trash cans, would swoop low, their outstretched talons grabbing the leftovers from our tin plates. Ugh.

"Mrs Appleyard?" Joan asked, but looking puzzled as well she might. This woman didn't look the homely type to me. "We're the Potts."

The apparition spoke through thin lips. "Mrs Appleyard? She's not here any more. She's been dead nigh on two years." The tone was sepulchral; the meagre smile an obvious fraud.

"But your letter heading said 'Cherrytrees – Mrs Appleyard'."

"Oh, that! I'm just using up the old stationery. Waste not want not is my motto. You're soaking, you'd better leave your umbrella and your coats in the lobby here, I don't want you dripping all over the carpet. Then if you follow me, I'll show you your room."

I hung my demob raincoat and Joan's stylish, belted 'New Look' blue mac on a couple of rusting hooks. We treaded carefully behind her up a gloomy, dimly-lit staircase. She opened a door on the landing.

"You've got the best room; I've got it ready specially. I don't usually take guests until Easter, Scarborough's such a dead place in the winter. I don't know why you've come. It takes all sorts, I suppose. I'll leave you to settle then. High tea is at half past six."

She wasn't the only one who wondered why we'd come. Count me in, I thought, crummy place, eerie landlady. I closed the door to shut out the creepy creaking of her thick-soled shoes on the stairs.

"This is her best room? It's not Room 504, that's for sure," I said, tripping over a greyish rug and colliding with a moth-eaten armchair.

"She must have sold Mrs Appleyard's furniture; she's got this rubbish from some thruppenny-bit auction. Look at that dressing table, Paul! It's falling to bits. What on earth are we doing here?"

"But, Joan. It's not all gloom and doom. That's Yorkshire's ground isn't it?" I said, moving over to the window. "Pity it's not the cricket season, eh?"

"We didn't come here to watch cricket."

Castle on a Cloud

I sat on the bed and bobbed up and down. "That's very true, love."

"You and your one track mind."

One track mind? What other track would my mind be on? Tonight was to be our wedding night!

She sighed. "This is not the place I remember, Paul; perhaps I was looking through a child's rose-coloured spectacles. Mrs Appleyard was a lovely person with a smile a yard wide. Fancy that woman not telling me in her letter that she'd died! I wouldn't have booked here if I'd known."

"We'll just have to make the best of it. Ignore the grottiness, love. The good news is it's only for two days. Look, there's an electric fire." I pointed to the tinny looking object in the fireplace.

"Yes, I see, but only one bar. That's not going to throw out much heat, is it?"

"I'll just have to keep you warm, darling."

"You had better," she said, smiling ruefully as she opened her case. "I suppose I'll have to take this carrier bag down to Mrs Grumps, Paul. She'll want the ham and these eggs and the other things."

"Yes, it'll be better if you take them, being the woman, love. Don't look like that, Joan." I laughed. "Mind, I think your mam's given you plenty to bring, just for two nights."

"Well, it's better that Grumps doesn't get our ration books. Anyway, people don't provide landladies with coupons for short stays. I've told you that."

Alone now, I looked around. So this is a boarding house? I hadn't missed much in my youth by the looks of this place. Surely there must be better ones, though, otherwise people wouldn't bother with them.

My musing came to an abrupt end when a flustered Joan burst into the bedroom.

"What's the matter, love?"

"What's the matter? We didn't bring any tea, that's what's the matter. She noticed as soon as she emptied the carrier bag. 'Where's the tea, Mrs Potts? I said bring some tea'."

"Never mind, love, she won't throw us out. What's Grumps' name by the way, Joan?"

"Graves."

"By the look of her she'll be in one soon. Never mind, pet, you wouldn't please her if you'd brought a packet of Earl Grey."

She sighed, "Probably not, but I'm mad about forgetting it. Giving her the chance to moan."

"Come here and give us a cuddle, love; never mind Graveyard."

She looked at her watch. "There's no time for cuddles, Paul, I'd better get ready for this high tea affair."

Joan opened her case and scrabbled inside. She tossed a skirt here, threw a blouse there, like a conjuror who'd mislaid his rabbit. Except I'd never seen a magician pull a pair of interesting lacy knickers out of a suitcase before, not even at Gateshead Empire. But what was this all about?

"Oh, Paul! You won't believe this – I've forgotten towels!"

"Ee, what are you like! You could ask Graveyard for one, couldn't you?"

"No way, when I think about it she told us to bring towels and tea. I've got the coupons to buy towels, but it's Sunday tomorrow."

"I could take my vest off, we can use that," I joked.

Apparently I wasn't joking.

"We'll have to, that's the answer. That'll have to do – your vest!"

She perked up a bit, then. But only for a minute: "Oh, no! Guess what?"

"Don't say we haven't got any 'thingies'!" I gasped.

Her worried look returned as she slumped onto the bed. "You've got the 'thingies', I hope?" she cried.

I laughed, "I was just having you on, love."

"I wish you wouldn't upset me like that – for a minute I thought that you'd forgotten them. That would have put the kybosh on any hanky-panky tonight. We don't want any babies yet, pet. Anyway, this is more serious, we haven't got any soap!"

Soap! God! What had happened to her priorities? Then a flash of inspiration: "We have, I've got my shaving soap, Joan."

"Of course, you have! You're a darling. We'll have to make do with that. The main thing – we don't have to ask Grumps any favours."

Came time for high tea; the frugal helpings reminded me of the 18 months I'd spent in civvy digs at Mrs Crow's in York, I was in the Army Pay Corps then. That was before my posting to India. No doubt about it, 'Graveyard' was a Mrs Crow type, worse – at least in York I always got a smile with the skimpy portions. And why skimpy portions anyhow? At this rate the bagful of groceries we'd brought would have lasted a week. The dank empty dining room – all but one of the tables garbed with dust covers – reverberated with echoes of our voices. We

Castle on a Cloud

spoke in hushed tones. From the kitchen came what sounded like the wail of a banshee. It was only Graveyard, scolding some unfortunate. Some poor unfortunate. Her husband? A skivvy?

Upstairs again, Joan, bless her, was putting on a brave face. "Where should we go? It may be too late for the second-house at the pictures."

"We could stay in." I yawned. "I feel a bit weary."

She laughed. "No, Paul, I want to tire you out a bit. We'll go out. For a walk at least, I think it's stopped raining."

Down to the South Shore we trailed. Whoever had written our honeymoon script had blundered, blundered badly. Not only rotten digs, but no moon, no stars for us this night. I could dimly discern many fishing boats in the harbour; seemingly, few had ventured out to sea. We gazed out over the darkness and watched the foamy breakers pounding over the beach and onto the shore road.

Joan shivered as the wind howled. I felt rain on my face. "Come on, love, let's find a little pub and you have a whisky to thaw you out."

The warmth of the little inn was welcome after the rawness of the night. Joan settled into a corner seat by the cheery wood fire. Ordering the drinks at the counter, the red-faced landlord, of Falstaffian proportions, told me of his solution to the coal shortage – 'driftwood from t'beach'. Judging by the stormy waves we had seen breaking on the shore, there would be cartfuls of fuel for him in the morning.

Despite the cosiness of the pub, only a few locals had ventured out on this wet and windy night. "This place'll be crammed in t'summer," the landlord had said, "Scarborough's gettin' ower the war at last, tha knows."

The fire danced merrily, its warm glow in competition with Joan's eyes. The steam rose pleasingly from the two raincoats I'd slung on stools beside the hearth. The snug aura of the room was relaxing, inviting, tempting us to stay. I looked at my watch, and gave Joan an approving glance. We must go soon, though. I wanted her.

She sighed wistfully. "This is nice and cosy, I see they've got rooms, it's a pity we weren't booked in here. I don't fancy going back to Grumpyland."

I looked at my watch again. Checked it with the clock over the bar counter.

"It's half past nine, darling. It should be alright to go back now surely? It's a reasonable hour for a married couple to go to bed, isn't it?"

"You are impatient, love, what's the hurry?" she teased, "It's nice and warm in here."

"I'll give you what's the hurry. Come on, you wretch."

Cherrytrees seemed grimmer than ever after the homely pub, our room even more forbidding. I switched on the electric fire – there was a pop – then nothing.

Joan harrumphed. "Charming! Not even one bar! I'd better go and have a hot bath; that might warm me up. Let's have your vest, love."

I'd forgotten I was wearing our towel. I felt chilly after she'd disappeared. I pulled my pyjamas out of the case. Would I need them? Yes, at first, I thought – in that cold bed.

BANG! It was Joan, knocking the door off its hinges again.

Wow! Should girls wearing lacy blue diaphanous nighties go prancing around like that? I discerned all sorts of exciting nubile oscillations.

She slammed the door to and cried out; "That woman! Her and her hot water, it's lukewarm. I'm nithered. I haven't emptied the bath, Paul; it was starting to run cold. You'd better jump straight into it. Me, I'm going to bed before I freeze. A hot water bottle would be useful right now."

"Joan! Surely I'm better than a hot water bottle?"

She smiled ruefully and clambered into bed, "I'm hoping you are!"

I didn't stay long in the bath – the water was on the cold side of tepid. Moreover, I was inspired by a vision of Joan. Joan, in bed, arms outstretched, nightdress discarded, honeyed tones whispering, 'Come to me darling.'

Hurriedly, I dried as best I could on my now sodden vest – pulled on my pyjamas – leapt across the landing – barged into the bedroom. I felt like Charlie Chaplin in fast frame. Even more like Charlie, when, dashing to the bedside, the grotty rug skidded from under me and I ended up doing the splits.

Joan, nose peeping out of the covers, hooted with laughter. Joan who hated slapstick! Fickle creature.

And where were her open arms?

"Ooh! You haven't hurt yourself, love?"

"Thanks for showing concern," I said, getting up gingerly. "I think I've done my groin in."

"I'll cure that, love, come to bed."

Joan cuddled up to me, her cold feet on mine, her icy fingers inside my pyjama jacket, her freezing nose nuzzling into my shoulder. "It's getting warmer," she murmured, her hand stroking my hip.

"You're getting warmer, Joan. I'll shout out when you're hot."

I fumbled with her flimsy nightdress, and with her eager help, soon both that, and my pyjamas, were stuffed under her pillow.

"We don't want them on the freezing floor, Paul," she whispered. "We might need..." The rest of the sentence was unspoken as my lips found hers. For a brief moment, I tried to envisage a scenario where nighties and pyjamas would be required again, but without success. Unless the boarding house caught fire.

The transition from the cold to a comfortable warmth was most pleasant. A mutual desire for each other became dominant. Outside, the sky may have been starless and black, but inside, we made it to the moon.

We'd had two clandestine undress rehearsals for this, our wedding performance. Both had been hugely successful, but 'Opening Night' was something else. Bells were ringing, angels were singing, the small cast was in rapture. Surely, this show would run and run.

For an enchanted while we forgot everything but our affection, our desire for each other. Everything: our landlady, the cold, the rattle of the rain on the window and the howling of the wind down the disused chimney.

Our breakfast of boiled eggs and toast with weak tea, served by Graveyard, was a comedown of gargantuan proportions. We made the toast into little soldiers to make it go further; then it was out into another windy, rainy day. Another day in Scarborough in this weather would be drab. Another night, once we were in bed, I could handle.

I bought the 'Sunday People' to discover how Newcastle United had fared. Finding a shelter in Peasholme Park near the boating lake, I opened the paper with difficulty; the canopy was useless against the swirling wind.

"How did our team come on yesterday, love?" (The black and whites weren't just my team; they were 'our' team now!)

"I'm just trying to find out, Joan," I said, wrestling with the newspaper. "If they've won they'll be well in line for promotion."

"Just think, Paul, we'll be able to see them play all the top teams next season if they do go up." Was Joan to become a bigger United fan than me?

"Sheffield Wednesday could be a crunch game, we'll see that one," I said, trying to get the sport section under control. Suddenly, a severe gust blew the football page out of my grasp. I bounded to my feet, chased it across the path, then made a despairing dive. Too late! The precious newssheet soared skywards and then, catching a rare eddy, plummeted gracefully into the lake. Disturbed by the strange intrusion, a clutch of what were mallards, but for a fleeting moment, I thought may be pochards flying to eastern climes to breed, quit the scene with squawks, quacks and a flutter of wings. One thing for certain, they were bloody ducks. And whether they were mallards, pochards or even great-crested grebes mattered not one wit – they didn't rescue my newspaper. I watched with dismay as the sports page slowly submerged amid the ripples.

Joan tinkled with laughter, "I hope that doesn't mean that United's promotion hopes are going to be sunk!"

It would be a lie to say that I laughed at her silly remark. I was not amused. Did she not realise that all the newsagents were closed? They were open only for a few hours on a Sunday morning. It would be Monday before I would know United's fate. Most of this honeymoon wasn't living up to expectations at all.

Thank God for the wee small hours.

We had difficulty filling in our time that day. 'Sunny' Scarborough was like a ghost town. How glad we were of the shelters to help us avoid the showers. The underground Gala Land amusement park was closed. Sad! We could have passed an idle hour or so rolling pennies down chutes, knocking off coconuts, or trying to win a goldfish by playing hoopla. Few cafes were open. Cinemas were shut – it was the Sabbath. We found a tearoom eventually, but because of rationing, fare was sparse, the choice restricted. We took our time placing an order, it was warmer inside.

"I'm sorry, Paul," said Joan, spreading margarine on a hard scone. "It hasn't been an idyllic honeymoon and it's all my fault. I hope it's not an omen. Perhaps we should have listened to people and waited."

"You don't really think that?" I said, taking her hand across the table. Her warm brown eyes had an unusually troubled look.

She smiled briefly, "The problem is, Paul, I love you too much. Is that wrong?"

"You know it isn't. Anyway, you're not to blame for this weekend.

Castle on a Cloud

It's just bad luck about the weather, bad luck about the digs. Oh! You mean your fault that I lost the Sunday paper in the lake?"

"You daft cracker. I didn't mean that," she laughed.

"I wonder how 'the lads' got on, though."

I gazed out of the cafe window. It was raining again. The paper shop across the road was locked up. Then something caught my eye. "Hi, Joan! Do you see the billboard inside that newsagent's door, they must have taken it in when they closed this morning – United's great win! Can you see it? Which United would that be do you think? It wouldn't be referring to Manchester United; not in Scarborough. It'll be Newcastle, Joan! United's great win! That's bucked me up no end!"

I wasn't bucked up for long.

"What about Scarborough's team? Aren't they called United?"

"No, love, it'll be Newcastle," I said confidently.

"Well, what about Leeds United? They're Yorkshire. Scarborough's in Yorkshire. United's great win? More likely Leeds. Yes, it'll be Leeds United, love."

"God! I forgot about them. Oh, what the heck! Never mind Newcastle, love."

What was I saying? Never mind United? What was this love thing doing to me?

I found out.

"Never mind that horrible boarding house, never mind the rain. The main thing is that we're together. That's what I've waited for – waited more than three years. First wishing that the war would end quickly, then that stupid posting to India put a spoke in it. What's two days in rainy Scarborough? We've got the rest of our lives together. Anyway look, Joan, is that the sun coming out? Let's go see this sunny Scarborough."

We wandered down the zig-zag path towards the Marine Drive, dodging miniature waterfalls. Miraculously, the sky was breaking, blue patches appearing.

"White fluffy clouds, Paul!"

"Aye, they're cumulus. Look at that one with the sun shining on it. Wouldn't it be nice if we go and sit on it and bask in the sun?"

Joan took my hand, "You're a romantic, Paul; I've told you that before, haven't I? I love you for it. I get scared about the future sometimes, though."

"Why, love?"

"We might find it was OK courting, but different being married. Particularly as we won't have a place of our own. That worries me."

"We'll be together, love. We said that was the main thing."

"Just let's hope that our rooms in Low Fell will be OK. I know I agreed we'd get married just as soon as possible, but I did hope and dream that we would have our own little place, Paul. With a proper front door."

"Would you settle for a castle on that cloud?"

She squeezed my hand. "With you? Oh, yes."

3

LOW FELLITES

Her dream? I knew of her dream. I had it in writing; she had described her vision of wedded bliss in one of her letters to me in Meerut.

Now let's get this straight. Ah, yes! This was it: to have our own modest house – preferably with a garden – a garden with a willow tree. (She was a sucker for willow trees.) It would be a home that would echo to the pitter-patter of tiny feet. At that point in the letter, she went a bit overboard. I mean to say; nobody in our street owned a car, but, *she* reckoned we might own a little car one day. Perhaps a second-hand Ford, she'd said. (Something even better if we won Littlewoods Pools.) Littlewoods Pools! I knew we'd have to work at this dream, but the first part wasn't impossible – her mam and dad lived in a house with a garden (albeit a council house, and a garden minus a willow tree); her brother and sister had both heard the pitter-patter of tiny feet. But the second part? Well, she told of a posh cousin who had been the owner of a Jowett. So there'd been a car in the family, Paul. Why not us?

But what sort of car? An old jalopy, that's what. She told how Cousin Jack's pride had been dented one day in the hot summer of 1939. It was on the way to Filey that the Jowett had chugged to a stop near the top of Whitwell Hill. Young Joan, together with his other passengers, had to push the car over the summit. So it *was* just a banger, and he *was* her posh cousin, *and* the son of a banker! Some hope for us.

Anyway, those were her targets, those were her plans. I couldn't fault them (except for the car scheme), but for the present, even a 'little place' would remain out of reach.

We could achieve this, I thought. Let the Grand Panjandrum work yet more magic. How? Well this Panjandrum fellow hadn't got down to the nuts and bolts of the operation, but just give him time. Rome wasn't built in a day. It would come, it would come.

A little place, though. God! How I'd tried to rent a 'little place' for the two of us, but the housing shortage, legacy of the war years, had put a damper on such wild hopes. Nothing, but nothing, to let – only property to buy. Our local estate agent had been very positive about house purchase, until he discovered that our joint Post Office Account totalled £34.11s.9d and I was earning just four pounds ten a week. At that point, he rose to his feet, shook hands, and gave me some advice. The gist of his message was simple; come back when you've saved up properly.

What about a council house? Hmm, a snag there. The waiting list league table for such a gem was weighted towards families. A couple already with a house, whether a slum or not, could beget lots of kids, and lots of kids = lots of council house points. But a couple with no house whatsoever meant that having kids was undesirable, if not impossible. No kids = measly points. That seemed like a vicious circle to me. Nevertheless, we registered – couple No. 1757.

With that dilemma, there was only one thing for two star-crossed lovers to do – make the best of it. We weren't going to wait forever to get married – with me in Gateshead and Joan in York. No way, despite the voices of doom.

What was the best of it? Furnished rooms.

So here we were; in discussion with our elderly landlord and landlady – the Davidsons.

'A spacious sitting room and a snug attic bedroom', the advert had read, 'thirty shillings a week'. The rooms were in a large terraced house in Castle Street, Low Fell, Gateshead.

We were sat, the four of us, at their old dining table in their big kitchen/scullery, a table covered with what had once been brightly coloured oilcloth.

We had paired off, landlords on one side of the table, tenants the other. I got the feeling that our hostess was setting down rules of engagement. Almost like a battle plan.

"We haven't rented our rooms out before. Funnily enough, Mr Potts, we'd just put our advert in the Chronicle the night you called. You seemed well-spoken, you worked in an office, you hadn't a family, so

Castle on a Cloud

that was that. We couldn't do with children and we didn't want a rough couple you see, did we Mr D? Not at our age." She sniffed, eyeing us over the top of her pince-nez.

"Our son, Evelyn, got married to a lovely girl some five years ago; it was five years, Robert?"

"Yes, dear."

"Since then we've been living quietly on our own."

You stuck-up so-and-so, I thought. Let's get this briefing over. I wanted to relax. I looked around. Opposite the table was an archaic fireside range, then a well-scrubbed bench and sink, a gas cooker, and in one corner, a coal boiler. The warmth spreading from it was making me sleepy. We'd been awake quite a bit last night. I sensed they spent a lot of time in here; no doubt dozing in their wooden armchairs.

Mr Davidson hadn't said much yet, just that 'Yes, dear'. He hadn't had much chance, but his wife's whiny voice continued. "You'll understand that we don't want a lot of noise, blaring wirelesses and so forth."

Joan fidgeted in her chair. I thought I'd better ease the tension. "Mmm, we haven't got a radio at the moment."

"We'll be getting one," Joan cut in. "But we're not deaf, so that should be alright."

I fingered the table covering. In its prime it had been adorned with oranges and lemons; now, the oranges were lemons, and the lemons were imperceptible. Interesting.

But Ma Davidson hadn't finished. "Yes. Oh, and do be careful with the furniture. Some of our best pieces are in your room. Much of it from Fenwick's, Newcastle, you know."

I was becoming fascinated by her mean lips. I had read about mean lips; probably I had seen some, but not as mean as these.

Joan rubbed her nose. A rare mannerism of hers. I had learned to duck beneath the parapet at the sight.

"We won't kick it around," I said, seeking to lighten the air. "Will we, Joan?"

"My mother's got some valuable furniture and I've never kicked that, Mrs Davidson," said Joan, forcing a laugh.

I was pleased to see Joan had stopped rubbing her nose. But valuable furniture? This was news to me. I'd have to check out her mam's house next time we were in York.

Mr Davidson chuckled. His face crinkled into a nervous smile, his shock of white hair contrasting with his ruddy countenance. "You might hurt your toe if you did, love."

His wife's face didn't crinkle, except around that prissy mouth. "Be that as it may. I've put a notice on your door giving the times you can use the kitchen and all about the clothes washing arrangements. Just a couple of other points. There's a brick at each side of your fireplace to save coal, don't disturb them, and do be careful with the bath water – they say five inches maximum – this Attlee Government. 'Save fuel', you know."

Had we to agree to these terms? We had to for now. They had the house, they had the rooms. But was that it? What about breathing?

That seemed to have been given the thumbs up, because apparently she'd finished her diatribe. Just ending with, "Anyway, you'll want to get settled. I *hope* we'll get on."

Mr Davidson butted in bravely then, "I'm sure we will, they seem a nice couple, Mary."

"I told you she was a shrew, Paul," said Joan, closing our room door. "I knew from our first meeting. She'd better not interfere with us."

"No, Joan. We seem to be unlucky with landladies. Never mind, love, in here we can forget about her."

It wasn't all depression; the fire was laid ready to light, it just needed a match to kindle it into flame. There was a scuttleful of coal in the hearth. I was sure old Mr Davidson's hand was in this welcome.

"We haven't got a light, Joan. Are you going to ask Ma Davidson for one?"

"*I'm* not going; you go."

"Tell you what," I said, bottling out of another chit-chat with our landlady. "We need stuff at the shops, let's both go down the road."

"You know what that means?"

"No, what does it mean?"

"Your mind was wandering during her chat, pet. Did you miss the rule about using the back door? Every time we go out we'll have to go through the kitchen and they seem to live in there."

"It's their guardroom, Joan. I get the feeling that she'll happily sit there all day, monitoring our comings and goings."

Daylight was fading as we walked down to the Low Fell shops on the main road. From time immemorial, or from 'when Adam was a lad', as

Castle on a Cloud

Mam used to say, the 'Fell' had been *the* high class suburb of Gateshead. The shops were smart, and the shoppers snooty. Down Gateshead High Street there were very few 'la-di-da' folk around and any toffee-noses in the shops would stand out a mile. It was different on the 'Fell'; people said things like: 'I'm toddling down to the baker's', and 'Thank you, my good man'. On the High Street it was 'Aa'm gannin' doon t' the breed shop' and 'Ta, hinney'.

I'd explained this phenomenon to Joan at the time we had arranged to rent the rooms in Low Fell. (York didn't seem to have this clear-cut geographical division between the bourgeoisie and the hoi polloi.) At the risk of boring her, I gave her a brief résumé of the situation. "You see, Joan," I added, "we're 'Low Fellites' now."

In Dodds', 'High Class Meat Purveyors', we were the only customers; Monday was a quiet day for butchers. A young fellow stopped raking the sawdust-covered floor to attend to us. From his ultra short back-and-sides haircut, I guessed that he had been recently demobbed.

Joan used half our weekly meat ration to obtain a skimpy slice of frying steak. The assistant wrapped it, handed it to Joan, then looked furtively over his shoulder and spoke in a hoarse whisper. "Wud ye like a cuple o' pieces o' calves' liver, pet?"

This cloak and dagger manner of his puzzled me. Liver wasn't on the ration, was it?

"Can a duck swim!" The look of delight on Joan's face was the best thing I'd seen all day. (Well, since I'd read about Newcastle's win in the morning's Daily Mail.)

She was still smiling when we entered Laws, the grocer's. I wasn't smiling when I saw the queue. Joan took a sheet of notepaper out of her shoulder-bag and perused a list. I was impressed.

"You've got a list! When did you write that?"

"Ah!" she laughed, "You've got an organised wife."

"Not when it comes to towels, soap and tea, I haven't."

"I'll never live it down, will I?" said Joan. Then looked around the shop. "My! There's a crowd in here for a Monday afternoon, though."

"I suppose we'll just have to wait, Joan. Or starve; we need the things."

The little woman in front with her Mrs Mopp headscarf turned round then. "It's aalways the seym heor, lass. There's aalways a queue at Laws's. The lasses heor hev got one speed, ye knaa. Hor with the gammy leg's the worrst though. A gammy leg and deed from the neck up, that's hor. Aa wisht Aa'd gone to Walta' Wilson's, noo."

Mrs Mopp was giving me the hump, belying as she was my 'toddling off' and 'my good man' concept of a Low Fellite. I had to put Joan straight.

"There's always an exception to prove the rule, love."

"Why aye, pet!" she laughed, cottoning on.

We shuffled forward; Joan gave me the shopping basket while she consulted her list. She ticked the necessaries – a sliced loaf, margarine, a packet of Brooke Bond tea, a bottle of milk, Shredded Wheat, a tin of Spam.

Just our luck – as we arrived at the front of the queue, 'Gammy Leg' was there, waiting to deal with us. She limped around the shelves at the back of the shop bringing the groceries to the counter one by one. Then followed 'the surrender of the ration coupons' ceremony. Finally she rang up our bill – 7/6½d. We got to the door, me, scratching my head, wondering how I got to be carrying the basket.

"Hold on, what about the matches?"

Joan laughed, "Ooh! They weren't on the list!"

"You cracker, that's what we came out for in the first place."

Joan had made a plate of Spam sandwiches.

"Can you go through and make a pot of tea, pet?"

She was talking in her wheedling, yet attractive, difficult-to-refuse voice.

Nevertheless, I tried. "Why me?"

"I want you to spy out the lie of the land in the kitchen, love. Don't forget the matches for the gas ring."

Hands full with kettle and teapot, I pushed the kitchen door open with my behind. No surprise – they were at the table.

"Sorry I couldn't knock; just want to boil the kettle."

"Go ahead," said Mister, "I'll find you a tray you can use for coming and going."

He rose stiffly from his wooden armchair. Ma stayed in hers, but cast aside the Evening Chronicle to peer over the top of her pince-nez. I could almost feel her eyes boring into my back as I filled the kettle and set it to boil.

At last she spoke. "I've just been looking at rooms to rent in the paper. There're only two vacancies in the whole of the North East. You could be here some time; that is if we don't have any hitches."

"We could stay with my mother, Mrs Davidson; she would be happy to have us anytime," I lied. "We wanted to be on our own, though."

"I'm sure things will work out fine, Mr Potts. Mary's just a bit worried, it being the first time we've let our rooms."

Joan locked the door behind me. "How did you get on?"

"OK," I said, carefully omitting to mention Ma Davidson's gimlet eyes, or her snide remark. "The gas cooker's new. Mister's lent me this tray."

"Oh! Don't forget, we've got to unpack those boxes I sent up from York, Paul. There's a tray in there. Then there's your stuff as well."

"We're not doing that tonight though, are we love?"

At last, we were settled in *our* room, the fire glowing cheerfully within its brick-lined confines. Joan was in one of the easy chairs, hands cupping her mug; I sat on the floor at her feet.

Joan looked around, "This precious Fenwick's furniture has seen better days."

"It's a bit the worse for wear. Not as bad as Graveyard's, though. Hi!" I added, "Where have you put the food?"

"I've used the cupboard near the window. It'll have to be our larder."

I looked up at her. "Well love, here we are. What do you think?"

She ruffled my hair and sighed, "This place will have to do for now, but it will never be a home."

"No, love," I said, squeezing her knee and trying to sound positive. "Don't worry; we'll get our own place before long."

Joan giggled when I lifted her up and stumbled over the threshold of our sloping-roofed attic bedroom on the third floor of the rambling old house. She kicked her legs in mock annoyance. "Put me down, you daft lad. You'll be giving yourself a hernia. I'm too heavy for your skinny legs."

"I'll give you skinny legs."

She gave me a saucy look. "Oh, that's a disappointment; I had something better than skinny legs in mind."

The room was surprisingly warm; the heat of the kitchen seemed to rise to the upper floors.

"This room's not too bad, perfect for dwarfs," I laughed. "I spy a chamber pot, Joan. You won't have to crouch round the bed and down to the lav on their floor in the middle of the night."

"I'm not sitting on a gazunda when you're around, I'd be too embarrassed."

"It'll be better than banging your head in the middle of the night. Joan. I'll shut my eyes and cover my ears."

"Hmm," was all she said. Then, "What I do like about the room, it does give the feeling of being ours. I suppose it's because we're on a separate floor from the Davidsons."

"Our little love nest?"

"No, pet," she gently disagreed, "it's our little retreat."

Joan had got it wrong, it was our love nest. For now.

The next morning, I was back at my desk at the old firm, Caledonian Connectors. Honeymoon over, one day's pay lost. I had to buckle down now and wait for June. Come June, my wage was to be six pounds ten – almost a fifty-per cent rise. Come June, I would take over from old, bald-pated, past his best Jackson. Come June, I would be the new Cashier/Pay Officer, despite my lack of formal diplomas and suchlike. At twenty-two! Pity Dad couldn't have seen the day.

Was it only nine years since Dad had died of TB? His long years of illness had left the family almost destitute, the only support a parsimonious Board of Guardians with their abhorrent Means Test. Mam had to make do with a meagre income and Dad's legacy – four hungry sons. Now, one of those sons had progressed from being a deprived elementary schoolboy, to office boy, and after a three-year spell in the Pay Corps would soon have this senior position. To cap it all – married to Joan Speed.

With those pleasant thoughts, I hummed a happy tune under my breath. ('Painting the Clouds with Sunshine' or some such jingle.) No matter that the workers would call me, 'Young Pottsy' or 'That bugger that waaks oot wa pay' – officially I was soon to be the 'Da de da de da Officer'. Joan would be loyally proud, Mam would be begrudgingly proud (not too happy that her clever lad had flown from the nest just when he'd be starting to earn a canny bit of money), and Joan's parents would be delighted for their daughter. My earnings would be close to that of her engine-driver dad. (That is, if you ignored his beloved overtime pay.)

Castle on a Cloud

I *thought* I had been humming a happy tune to myself, seemingly, I hadn't.

"Will you stop making that noise? It's bad enough trying to get these figures to balance without that racket. You're not in tune anyway."

It was Jackson. Not in tune. The old bachelor was no music lover.

We were sat on high stools at our two-seater desk. Jackson was wearing his old black suit again, the one with the shiny elbows and frayed cuffs. The points of his badly-ironed shirt collar were flying high. Head bent low, he was laboriously totting up the columns on the voluminous wages sheets and getting irate. *Time* he retired, thought I.

"Sorry, Mr Jackson. Why don't you let me have a go?" It was four months since my demob, four months back in the office, yet he'd never let me touch his blasted sheets. I was getting fed up with his secretive manner.

"Let *you* have a go?" Cocking his head on one side as far as his stiff neck would allow, he looked at me through rheumy eyes, "You haven't got my job yet, my lad; married man or not. If you think you can do any better, then dammit, here you are. Why does anyone want to get married anyway?"

The sheets skidded across the desk and landed in front of me. This was uncalled for, crabby mood or not. Still, he wasn't a bad old stick; I would make allowances for this lonely fellow. I might act just as funny when I was sixty four and three-quarters. I picked up the sheets, shuffled them into order, and set them down. Well, this is what I wanted – action – so let's get cracking.

I knew the format, didn't I just; I'd watched him long enough. So I set to work. If he couldn't balance, there must be mistakes; I found them – first sheet OK now. I looked up, Jackson frowned. "That's it," I said, "that's the first one. Do you want me to do any more?"

"You had luck there," he said grumpily. "Beginner's luck. Try the next sheet."

Same result, 'mental' was my middle name. (Arithmetic that is.)

"Right, me lad, you can carry on if you're so clever. There's nothing I can teach you apparently," he said dolefully. "I'll have to bring some library books in to read this next couple of months."

By the sound of it, I was going to do the job without the extra pay. I'd have to wait until his retirement day for that.

That evening, I told Joan my news.

"Well, of course you can do the job," was her comment. (Her faith in me seemed boundless.) She didn't like the bit about the pay though.

"How have *you* come on today?" I asked, as we sat down to our meal of fried steak and onions, with potatoes.

"Don't ask," she said, "that woman *is* a shrew. 'I'm not keen on the smell of fried onions in the kitchen,' she'd whinged. Pity about her, if I want to fry onions I will do. Mr Davidson said *he* liked the smell of them, anyway."

"Don't let it get you down, love. You just do as you want, we're paying her enough."

"It's not nice, though."

"This steak's nice, Joan," I said, trying to cheer her up.

Later, we got the tram to Mam's to see her and the family in their upstairs terraced flat near the park.

Mam put aside her library book and took off her reading glasses to welcome us. "Sorry I didn't get to the wedding, Joan, but you understand my reasons. I could never set foot in a Protestant church. Did everything go alright?"

"Oh, smashing. All my relations were there, it was a pity for Den, though. His side of the church looked sparse."

Dennis – Den, I was called at home, always had been for some reason, so Joan would call me that tonight.

"Well, Den's uncles and aunts are Catholics too, Joan."

"We managed without them, Mam. It's over and done with now. We're happily wed."

"Mmm."

With the exception of Cecil, the rest of the family were there this night. Stepfather, Rob, and brothers Don and young Stephen. Bus conductor, Don, plump Don, was unusually quiet, tired after working an extra half shift.

Mam asked about our rooms. "I told you, you should have waited until you could get your own place," she said, shaking her head when we told her of some of the snags. "She seems a right bossy boots."

I squeezed Joan's hand as we sat on the settee. She got the message and held her tongue. We'd got rather accustomed to Mam's 'I-told-you-so's.

Later, around ten o'clock we arrived back 'home'. Three quiet cheers,

Castle on a Cloud

the Davidsons were in bed. We crept softly through the kitchen; I switched on our room light.

Joan gave a shriek.

4

COLEOPTERANS!

"Shh, don't wake the house up."
Joan gazed at the floor; then covered her eyes in disgust. I looked down. "God!"
Black beetles swarmed over the carpet – fifty? More?

They triggered a memory of those beetles in our dingy flat down Askew Road, but I recalled that then, it was just an odd one sneaking around our brass fender. Now, it was an army. Their antennae waved sinisterly as the hideous creatures scurried into crannies and cracks in the skirting board. They slipped and slid on the polished wooden surrounds of the room, desperate to escape from the sudden light. Crunch! I trampled hard on some of the laggards, but soon, the horde had vanished.

Gone; but no doubt waiting to emerge again when darkness returned.

I repressed a shudder. Joan did more than shudder; she clutched me, sobbing, her head on my shoulder. I held her tight.

"Oh! Paul, they're horrible, horrible. I hate crawly things."

"There, love, there, love, they've gone now. They won't come out again with the light on."

"Do you think they'll be in the cupboard amongst our food, Paul? Oh God! Say no."

"I'll have a look."

Reluctantly, she let me go.

Crossing the room, I quickly opened the 'larder' door; I wanted to surprise any scavengers who might be active in the darkness of the cupboard. I saw none on the shelves, but glimpsed two on the floor.

They were wrestling with each other to be first to scrabble through a crack in a corner and gain entry to the blackness beyond.

"No, Joan, none; none at all." It was a necessary lie.

"Thank goodness for that. I thought they might be in the bread or the Shredded Wheat. Ugh!"

I took her in my arms again, she was shivering. "It's alright now, darling."

She whimpered. "Let's get out of here and upstairs. They're going to have to get rid of them. Surely that woman must have known about them. I can't stay here knowing that they'll be crawling around our room every night. I can't, I can't. I'm sorry, Paul."

Her tears came again. "They're grisly, dirty things and so many! So many! I hate them, I hate them!"

"I'll see about it in the morning, love. They'll have to do something. Whether they know about them or not. They'll have to. No one would stay here, when they found it plagued with blackclocks. Not for long, anyway. Don't worry Joan, don't worry." Don't worry! That's a good one. Move! Where? Where?

There was *nowhere* to move. Didn't I know that? Three days, just three days married. Images flooded my mind; a vision of a couple sharing tearful farewells at Newcastle Station as the girl boarded the York train; a picture of a young man standing on an empty platform; bereft and desolate.

No way, no way that could happen. Already, Joan was my life. My new life.

We slept but little, Joan clung to me most of the night. During my catnaps, one dream kept recurring. Beetles in military formation, a scorpion at the head of each column, were crawling up the stairs to our attic room. Resourcefully (from some magical spring or geyser?), I filled bucket after bucket of boiling water, hurling the contents over the swarming black ranks. In the dream, Ma Davidson followed the beetles upwards, and waving a witch's broomstick, shouted at me crazily for ruining her stair carpet. In her temper, she became entangled in the broom shank, tried to fly; failed; and fell to the bottom of the stairs amongst the black corpses. It was usually at that point that I woke up – a smile on my face – a smile that always disappeared in the face of reality.

Next morning, bleary-eyed, I went into the kitchen to boil the kettle.

Castle on a Cloud

Ma Davidson was absent. (Still in bed nursing a sore head?) Her husband was there, stirring his porridge on the gas cooker. Collarless, shirtsleeves rolled up, he was whistling softly, deep in concentration.

I wasted no time in pleasantries; I had to get this beetle problem sorted quickly. I had work to go to. He hadn't noticed me come in and jumped nervously when I spoke. "Mr Davidson, do you know we've cockroaches in our room?"

His wooden spoon dropped into the porridge. "Ouch," he shouted, as he rescued it from the hot goo. He looked bewildered, then anxious, as at last he grasped the import of my words.

"What? Oh no! You've got some beetles?"

"Some? We've got an army. Joan nearly had a fit when we came in last night and I put the light on. You could hardly see the floor for the ugly things."

"I didn't know they were any in your room. I honestly didn't."

Somehow, I believed him.

"We had a few in the kitchen last autumn," he said. "Let's think, let's think, I remember now. We got rid of them with this."

His knees creaked as he crouched down under the sink and rummaged about on a shelf stockpiled with cans and bottles. He emerged at last, unbending slowly, like a worn-out jack-in-the box. He waved a rusty tin in triumph.

"This is it, this powder did the trick," he panted. "You just sprinkle it around the skirting board."

I was dubious. How old was this miraculous stuff? He hovered beside me like a worried hen. I tried to read the fuzzy blurb. I could make out Formicidae (Ants), Coleopterans (Beetles), and Annihilate. 'Coleopterans'? I never knew that. 'Annihilate'? A beetle apocalypse? I would settle for that, though.

"I'll give it a try," I said, "but if it doesn't work you'll need to get the pest controller, Mr Davidson."

The old man pointed with his porridgey spoon at the canister.

"It looks old, but we bought it only last year. It was very effective, it should work again. No reason why not."

He sounded convincing. A hint of a smile, an anxious smile, played around his lips. Until...

He sniffed the air, and abruptly realised the significance of the spoon in his hand. "The porridge! Oh dear, it's burning."

With sluggish haste, he tottered across to the oven, took the smoky pan off the ring, and in dismay, eyed the contents. "Everything's happening this morning, just let me open this window, I'll have to get the smell out of the kitchen before Mary comes down. She's got a headache to start with. She'll have bigger one if she sniffs this."

The reek of burnt oats was his problem, black beetles were mine. I looked at my watch.

"Look, Mr Davidson, I'll try this powder, but if it doesn't work you'll need to get the pest man," I said. This diversion was wasting my time.

God! Now, he was fumbling with the upper sash of the window and mumbling. "What a morning, this has turned out to be. What a morning!"

I reached up and opened the dratted window. "The Council Rat Catcher you would want, Mr Davidson."

"Thanks, Mr Potts."

The cold morning air blasted into the room. His white hair, now wind-blown, gave him the look of a mad professor. "But what did you say? The vermin man? Dear me, not the vermin man. Between you and me Mr P, Mary wouldn't want somebody from the council knocking at the door."

There was a troubled look on his usually cheerful face. "No, Mary wouldn't like that. What with the beetles and the burnt pan, she'd be like a bear with a sore head for weeks. It's not good to upset her. Let's try the powder, Mr Potts. That would be best. A truck marked 'Rat Catcher' or some such thing outside our door! People would think we had rats." (His logic was admirable.) "It doesn't bear thinking about. Mary wouldn't like to be the talk of the street!" He shook his head morosely and turned his attention back to the burnt pan. "Oh no! We don't want that," he muttered, as his spoon scraped furiously.

A brief wave of compassion overcame me. "OK, OK, I'll try this stuff." Then I steeled myself. That vision of two lovers in the Central Station surfaced again. "If that doesn't work, you *will* contact the council, Mr Davidson?"

Hesitantly, he nodded. A nod would have to do for now.

Joan listened to my story as I sprinkled the powder. She was not impressed with the rusty can; that much was evident. Dubiety was etched on her countenance, but she agreed to see if it was effective when I told her of Mr Davidson's wifely worries. Joan seemed to have quickly developed a soft spot for the old man.

Castle on a Cloud

That night, we went to see 'The Jolson Story' at the Capitol. Hopefully, songs of the twenties and thirties, songs like 'Liza', 'Mammy', 'April Showers', 'sung' by a black-faced Larry Parkes, would dispel images of black beetles. A sound theory, but it didn't work. Not for me it didn't. Not for Joan, either. All through the show, her tense, unmoving, cold hand nestled in mine. Out into the night air, we stumbled. Slowly, we walked; slowly 'homeward'. In truth, neither of us was anxious to arrive.

The kitchen was empty. I turned the handle on the door to our room.
Joan was behind me. "You go in first."
In my head, I paraphrased that wartime Yankee Air Force song – 'Going in on a Wing and a Prayer'. I opened the door and switched on the light. There *were* beetles, fewer, though, and praise the Lord, those mostly lifeless. A few were on their backs, legs moving feebly. None were scurrying to hide.
"What's happened?" Joan asked, not daring to come in.
"They're nearly all dead. That rusty old can's worked. Here, have a quick look, then I'll clear them up."
Nervously, she poked her head around the door.
"Oh! That looks promising."
"I'll get rid of them, Joan; then I'll be up with a drink."
With distaste I swept the cadavers onto the coal shovel and tossed them on the dying embers of the fire. The sound of their shell-like bodies crackling – like Jumping Jacks on Guy Fawkes' Night – was deeply satisfying.

Joan downed the last of her second Babycham, "Finish up your pint, love, let's find out if those horrible things have gone. It looked hopeful last night."
We were in the Cannon Inn. It was my idea; "When we go back to our dark room, we should know for definite." A couple of drinks would help pass the time, too.

Joan bravely switched on the light and was first to enter our room. Babycham courage. I knew it was OK – she stood her ground. Then she laughed and turned to me.
"Just a couple of dead ones!"

In bed that night, Joan snuggled up, as in days of old. Well, it seemed like days of old.

"Thanks, love, for getting rid of those horrible things."

I pulled her close. "You'll sleep tonight, then?"

Her sigh was a sigh of relief. "Eventually, darling," she whispered and nuzzled even closer.

"What's the verdict, Mr Potts?" The old fellow looked anxious, his immediate future hung on my words. Was it to be tranquillity or turmoil? Was a rat catcher about to disturb the fragile calm of his existence?

I had been non-committal yesterday; he was hoping for good news today.

I gave him a thumbs-up sign, his face fairly beamed.

"Just a few dead ones last night."

"Oh, good! We won't have to call out the rat catcher then. *Or* tell Mary." He lowered his voice, "I hadn't told her about the beetles, or the burnt pan! (That pan came up like a new pin!) I won't bother her now. She doesn't have to know now! Hee, hee." He smiled happily, "What a weight off my mind, Mr Potts."

"All's well that ends well," I agreed munificently.

It was nice to see the old fellow looking so happy. He had much to endure. He saw more of his wife than we did.

"Tell you what," he went on. "I'm making a rabbit pie today; there'll be too much for the two of us, and Mary's not keen on leftovers. Would you and Mrs P like some for tea?"

"That's very kind of you, Mr Davidson, I know Joan likes rabbit pie, I'll tell her."

Crisis over, but this married life was no pushover. Bad enough for me, but worse for Joan. Joan was miles from familiar surroundings, from her old workmates, from friends, from her doting parents. Plus points for her? Just me and a rabbit pie, in that order of course. Oh, and calves' liver.

I had to see her through this dodgy period. Help her to settle.

Fortunately, Joan had something else to look forward to. Easter was approaching and we planned to spend the long weekend at her mam and dad's. For a few days she would escape the confines of that room in Castle Street and the harping presence of Mrs D.

Castle on a Cloud

But first, a visit to the Post Office was required – funds for railway fares necessary. My current salary didn't allow for extras.

In the event, though, it was unnecessary to raid our savings.

5

IT'S A LONG WAY TO THE CHIPPY

"**M**orning, Sandra. Morning, Mr Miller."
Me, smiling first thing on a Monday. Reason? Four days to Good Friday.

"Hi, Paul," replied our typist/boss's secretary/office goddess.

"Good morning, son," muttered smarmy, general factotum, Miller, as he ferreted through his box of time cards.

Miller carried a huge chip on his shoulder ever since the day he discovered that a young pipsqueak fresh out of the Army, in the guise of me, had leapfrogged over him and landed Jackson's job – that Cashier/Pay Officer post. I was doing him a favour. He would never have coped; arithmetic was not his strong point.

I looked around our small office – the furniture and fittings had survived since Victorian days. (With the exception of Sandra's new desk and her state of the art Remington typewriter with its two-coloured ribbon.) No sign yet of Jackson, or of office boy, Freddie. Jackson was winding down, whereas Freddie, no doubt forgetting to wind up his watch, had obviously slept in again.

"You seem happy, Paul." Sandra's eyelids fluttered in the style of Disney's Snow White. She took the cover off her typewriter, but didn't sit down; instead she sort of hovered. A surprise that, she always sat straight down – on a chilly morning. Plonked herself in front of the office gas fire. That's where her desk was – blocking the heat from the rest of us. Sandra would hog that fire all day. No wonder her legs were mottled and her chilblains itchy.

"You seem all of a flap, Sandra." I said, climbing up on my high stool.

"You would be, if you were in my shoes, Paul. Look!"

She came across to me and flaunted her left hand under my nose.

"What at? It seems an ordinary sort of hand to me."

"Don't be a tease. My engagement ring!" she simpered. "I've had a whirl of a weekend. Algernon proposed on Friday night and he bought the ring on Saturday afternoon. He's a fast worker."

Fast worker? Algernon? The Algy who called at the office most every night to escort her home? The Algy who was an under-manager at Lloyds Bank on the High Street and had 'marvellous prospects'? That paragon of high finance? Short, balding, weedy, Algernon? *Fast?*

What a couple they made; sixpennorth of copper, Algy, and tall, raven-haired, strikingly impressive (from a distance), Sandra.

"Ee, congratulations, Sandra."

"Not another marriage in the offing!"

It was Jackson, he'd just come through the door and was grumping already.

"Whit's happenin' here?" Mr Patterson, our craggy-faced Branch Manager, joined the gathering.

"Sandra's just telling us she's got engaged, Mr Patterson."

"Congratulations, Sandra. Isn't thet great, Jackson?"

The old fellow's face twisted into a lopsided, perfidious smirk.

The boss waved a letter at Jackson, "Can you come into my office, Norman? I want to discuss this, before you start. Och, and ye'd better come in too, Paul."

"Tek a seat, both of ye."

This looked important – weighty matters to be discussed in the boss's inner sanctum. I straightened my tie, buttoned up my double-breasted jacket, sat down, and leaned forward attentively. All in the manner of a Spencer Tracy or Henry Fonda starring in one of those boardroom dramas on the flicks.

"E've got some news from Glasgow Head Office, some guid, some bad." He indicated the letter now on his desk. "Y'ken that the staff hev' been getting two weeks' bonus at Christmas, aye; end the worr'kers one week? Weel, Aa've just received this official notice. In the light of the guid results the company's heving these days, the staff are to get two weeks' bonus at Easter, fower in the summer, and fower at Christmas. The worr'kers, the poor worr'kers," he laughed, "they'll git *one* week's bonus three times a year."

'Hurrah for the white collar brigade!' was my shameful thought. Me,

Castle on a Cloud

who, whilst on leave during the 1945 General Election campaign, had, many a midnight, used up countless packets of chalk scribbling 'Vote for Konni' and 'Up the Workers', on all the gable ends, coalhouse doors, and backyard walls round our way. This Konni fellow was the far left Labour Party candidate for Gateshead that year, and was now its Labour MP.

I'd had a fleeting acquaintance with this soothsayer who foresaw the vision of a classless society. I'd stood next to him one night after a hustings' meeting in the local school hall. We were in the boys' urinals at the time. "You should aim high, Mr Zilliacus," I had said, with the youthful boldness of a nineteen-year-old, in response to his friendly hello. "You deserve to get into the Cabinet."

That night, however, we aimed low; those urinals weren't meant for six-footers.

But, 'Hurrah for white-collar workers'? How far I had fallen from the idealistic wartime days, those days when a brave new world of equality for all was the dream.

"Were ye ganging to speak, Paul?" Patterson's bushy eyebrows queried.

The question brought me back to the present. I shook my head.

"I ken it's a short week, Pace week, sae ye've got to pull oot aw the stops. Dae ye think ye can manage it?"

Pace week? Pace week? Oh! Easter week. Could we manage it? Two weeks' extra pay? I could manage it; Jackson could please himself.

"Oh, I think so, Mr Patterson."

"It's not much warning," frowned the old man.

What's he moaning about, I thought, it'll be me that bears the brunt. He just sits there twiddling his thumbs these days.

He was determined to have his say, though. "Pay day's going to be Thursday instead of Friday this week as it is, Mr Patterson. I don't know whether we can do it. Besides, I'm going to miss out on this summer bonus you're talking about. I'll be retired before it's paid."

"Och, daen't worry aboot the summer, Norman. A'll see thet ye get ye bonus." The Scotsman's smile was all craggy brow and jutting chin.

"We'll do it," I said.

"A'll let ye' get on then," said Patterson.

Jackson was still grumbling when we climbed onto our stools.

We made the Thursday deadline for the big pay out. Joan's face was beaming when I came in that night. She was still smiling when we caught the tram to the station, a smile that stayed with her on the train to York. A smile that had been missing too much lately. Much too much.

The front door to her parents' neat council house in Burton Lane was unlocked. We entered quietly.
"I bet your mam's in the kitchen."
She was. "My God! I didn't hear ye cum in!"
She smiled and wiped her hands on the ubiquitous apron that protected her ample dress. No disciple of fashion, her dark hair was, as always, straight. 'No bobby pins fur me. Straight hair fur a straight woman; Aa caall a spade a spade,' she would say.
Her daughter received a wrestler's hug, "How are ye lass? Ye look well, Aa must say."
It was my turn next, I braced myself.
"Aa hope ye lookin' after my lass, Paul luv."
"Of course he is, Mam."
"A've just bin mekin' a couple of fruit cakes, they're in the oven, Joan. Tha can tek them back with thee, Aa knows from your letters it's hard for thee to bake in that kitchen."
"*I* could have made some this weekend, Mam; there was no need for you to bother."
"Nay, lass, tha's on holiday. How's her ladyship in Low Fell, luv?"
"No better for asking, she's a nasty woman, Mam, she wants our money, but she doesn't want any bother."
"She sounds a right harpy. Niver mind, luv, ye'll get a place soon."
"Is dad at work?"
"Aye, but he'll be in in awhile. He's doin' a bit of overtime, just for a change."
She chuckled at her joke. "Aa'll get 'im to pop round and get sum fish and chips when he cums in."
"No, he'll be tired, Mam, we'll go, won't we, Paul?"
"Mmm." I, too, was feeling bushed. Figures were still buzzing around in my brain, I just wanted to flop down and relax after putting £1,395, give or take a penny or a tanner into a hundred and sixty three packets (times two). But "Mmm," seemed to mean yes.
"Alright, luv, if ye go now your dad shud be in by the time ye get 'em. Tek that ten bob note off the mantelpiece."

Castle on a Cloud

In the fish shop, Joan spotted Liza at the front of the queue. Her sister; short, plumpish Liza. She lived just around the corner from the chippy.

Liza, wearing a headscarf tied under her chin, turned, startled, when Joan poked her in the back. "Well I never! Joan! Have ye just cum down?"

I pondered, and not for the first time; why did Joan's family have Yorkshire accents, and yet Joan had a mere trace?

"Aa'm just gettin' sum chips for the bairns," said Liza, after more hugs had been exchanged. "Patrick was in a good mood. He gave me a pownd before he went out on the booze. Aa'm rollin' in it toneet, Aa'm havin' an 'addock."

"Are you trying to hide that bruise on your face, Liza?"

Liza pushed her scarf back, touched her cheek, and winced. "Oh that! That's nothin', Joan."

"Has Patrick between hitting you again? I thought he'd stopped. Why don't you leave him?"

I glanced around, wondering whether fellow queuers were agog to hear more about this domestic crisis. But gladly, in the general bustle no one seemed to have overheard.

"He has stopped, Joan." Gingerly she fingered her cheekbone again. "That were a cuple of weeks ago. Befower that he'd gone munths. He's awlreet now. He says he's turned over a new leaf. Aa cudn't leave him, he's me 'usband after all."

"You're a fool, Liza, he'll never change, will he Paul?"

"I don't think so, Liza. One of these days he'll be doing you serious damage."

Liza laughed and shook her head. "Anyroad, I'd better tek these chips home fur the bairns befower they go cold. See yers both tomorrow then. I'll bring the kids arownd."

By the time we returned with our hot, newspaper-wrapped suppers, Joan's dad was in, and had washed his friendly, smoke-grimed face. Although he was bald, he knew how far to wash – just as far as the crease on his forehead – the crease made by his railway cap.

I was dying to tuck in, but first more embraces for Joan. So much hugging was going on. Was it really only a few weeks since she'd left home?

My, I'd come a long way for those fish and chips. They were smashing, the first I'd had for months. We had chickened out of taking any into our rooms in Low Fell. We had this gut feeling that Ma Davidson would have sniffed disparagingly at the smell. We'd had enough of her sniffing ways. As for strolling along on a night in the main street of Low Fell eating out of a newspaper, Joan thought that would be infra-dig. Well, words to that effect. There were standards to maintain on the 'Fell'.

Now, as we sat at the table, her dad produced four bottles of John Smith's Magnet Ale and four tumblers.

"None for me, George," said her mam, "I wud like some tha knows, but it gives me an 'eadache."

"Aa know, lass." He smiled in full agreement, and poured out three foaming glasses of beer, putting his bonus bottle to one side.

He took a sup of ale and wiped froth off his upper lip. "Listen, lass, Aa'm bringin' the two o'clock express up to Newcastle in a fortneet's time, de ye think ye can get to the Central Station abowt fower o'clock say, on the Friday? Aa shud have summat ready in the garden by then. Aa cud bring a bag of veg up for thee."

Her mam chimed in then. "If ye doin' that, George, Aa cud mek a stek and kidney pie. Ye cud tek that as well. Aa'm sure Ned the butcher will give us a bit of beef off the ration, he owes me a favour or two."

"What sort of favours were they, Ida?"

"Not what yor thinkin', ye daft hayporth," she laughed. "Do ye mind that time Aa luked after his bairns when he and his missus had to go to Leeds for that funeral?"

"But mother, why should you bake a pie. You've enough on your plate."

"Aa doan't mind puttin' a pie on *yor* plate, lass. Aa know it's difficult for thee."

"Anyroad, Joan," said her father, "Aa'll write and let ye know for definite."

"OK, Dad."

We were soon in bed that night, in Joan's old room.

"Aa hope ye find Joan's owld bed cumfurtable, Paul. We're goin' te give it to thee's when tha gets a place," her mam had said.

I knew all about Joan's bed. Tonight would be the third time for me. It had already passed the test.

Good Friday was just like, well, Good Friday I suppose. No shops open, little or no sport, certainly no horse-racing. A black day for the Speed family; the Speed brothers were all devotees of the 'Sport of Kings'. Pubs? Just Sunday hours. Radio? Pretty serious stuff. Not only that, it was raining.

Then in the afternoon, Liza came round with her kids. "This is ye Uncle Paul," said Liza. "Ye've seen him befower but he weren't ye uncle then."

"Hello, Uncle Paul," said cheeky-faced eight-year-old David.

"Hello, Uncle Paul," said six-year-old blondie, Belinda.

Uncle Paul? Was I really an uncle? I didn't feel old enough. I don't think I was dour enough either. Not like the species of uncle I recalled.

"Grammaa, can we go in the front room to laik?" asked David.

"Of course ye can, ducks. There's more room in there. Tek ye shoes off though, if ye goin' to run abowt."

"Are ye cumin' in the room, Uncle Paul?" said Belinda, her little hand grabbing mine.

I couldn't refuse, not those bright blue eyes.

"We do cartwheels, Uncle Paul," said David.

"Can you do handstands, though?" I asked.

"Show us, Uncle," shouted Belinda. "Show us!"

I hadn't bargained for this, but surely, performing handstands was like riding a bike. A skill once acquired, never forgotten. I kicked off my shoes, only to hear David and Belinda cry in unison: "Ye've got a tattie in ye sock, Uncle Paul!"

I looked down. There was a hole in the heel of one of my socks displaying white skin. A bit like a peeled potato? I suppose so.

"Never mind the tattie," I laughed. "Just watch this."

Watch this they did. My first attempt at a handstand ended in my collapsing in a whirl of limbs, accompanied by uncalled for laughter. It *was* like riding a bike though; I was soon demonstrating my prowess against the room door.

During our courting days, Joan and I done a few things in the front room, usually on the sofa, but never handstands. No, none that I can remember. Except in a metaphorical sense.

David and Belinda responded to my expert tuition with a pleasing aptitude, so I thought we'd progress to standing on our heads. I was soon giving a phenomenal demonstration of this dying art.

"Count to a hundred, kids."

"Count to a hundred?" said David. "The blood'll cum out of ye nose!"

"Don't worry you two, I can do it," I said boldly.

My confidence evaporated when we hit a snag. The kids had difficulty in getting much past thirty without slowing the whole count down to a snail's pace. That snarled things up a bit; my feet began to feel empty. What fouled things up even more – the door suddenly burst open sending me crashing to the floor. I landed in an ungainly heap, eyes closed, red-faced and inert, as Joan stepped over my crumpled body.

"What on earth are you doing?" she cried.

I opened my eyes, "I think I've broken my neck, love."

She crouched down anxiously. "No, Paul, say you haven't!"

"You fell for it, you fell for it." I laughed, pulling her down and giving her a bear hug.

David and Belinda burst out laughing. "We've been doin' handstands, Auntie Joan," chuckled Belinda. "Uncle Paul showed us."

"Do ye know Uncle Paul's got a tattie in 'is sock?" that was stool-pigeon, David.

"Is he showing me up again? I told him not to wear that pair until I'd darned them. I'll give him tatties," she said, pretending to strangle me.

"Come on, Joan," I laughed, "we want *you* to do a handstand."

"Cum on, Aunty Joan," the kids shouted.

Joan put on a stern face. "I'm not doing a handstand for love nor money; you're not seeing *my* knickers!"

David and Belinda burst into stitches of laughter.

Until Belinda became pensive.

"I wish ye were my dad, Uncle Paul," she said wistfully. "Ye would be a proper dad."

"I can't be your dad, can I, Belinda? I'm married to Aunty Joan."

"If ye married Mam, you could be."

I looked at Joan; her eyes were brimming, moved as she was by Belinda's pitiful plea. "No, Belinda," I said softly, "I think being your uncle is better." (Better for me anyway, I thought. Joan or Liza? No contest!) "Why do you want me to be your dad, anyway?"

David spoke up. "Because our dad's allus showtin' and because 'ee hits our mam. When Aa grow up, Aa'm goin' te stop him. Could *you* stop him, Uncle Paul?"

"I'd have to think about that, David."

Castle on a Cloud

Joan butted in. "Your mam, says he doesn't hit her now."
"Well he'd better not," said David, grimly. "He'd better not."
The handstand game wasn't quite the same after that.

Following the somnolence of Good Friday came the stimulation of Saturday. We went into the city and looked around the shops, most of them had skimpy displays of their wares; post-war austerity still evident.
    Linking arms, we edged through the crowds in the quaint, picturesque Shambles. As we jostled, Joan squeezed my arm, "I've made two important decisions, Paul." She gave a laugh. "With your approval, of course."
    "And pray, what are those, madam?"
    "Well, first, I think we should get a radio. I know you'll say that bang goes our hope of putting money into our account. I know that. In fact we'll have to draw money out in the short term."
    "I'm darn sure we will, but I thought we were trying to save for a deposit on a house. We'll be waiting for ever."
    "No, Paul, we won't; you see I'm going to get a job as soon as I can. I've decided."
    "Oh, *you've* decided. Hold on, aren't I suppose to keep you in the style to which you're accustomed?"
    "That's a bit old-fashioned, love. These are the 1940s! If we want to move on we've got to get some money behind us. Besides, I don't want to be stuck in the next room to Ma Davidson every day."
    "Do you think you'll get a decent job? You'll be thinking of one in an office, I suppose?"
    "That's the idea, Paul. I *should* get one; I've got that good reference from Major Dixon in the Pay Office."
    "That one you keep showing me?" I laughed. She gave me a dig. "Don't be horrid. Anyway, what about the radio idea?"
    "You're on! I'll be able to listen to the Test Matches this summer when the Aussies play. Plus there'll be the Olympic Games' commentaries."
    "Trust you to think of that!"
    On we walked, hand in hand. We turned into crowded Stonegate. Joan stopped, gasped and pointed. "Look!"
    At first, I thought she was indicating the pub sign – 'Ye Olde Starre Inne', but then I realised that her attention had been drawn to a man in

a natty tweed sports jacket, emerging unsteadily from an alleyway. He seemed vaguely familiar.

"It's Patrick; he'll have been drinking again!"

Patrick! I'd never met this Patrick, he hadn't come to our wedding, but I remembered Joan showing me photographs of his marriage to Liza.

"This is fate, Paul. I'm going to bone him about the way he treats Liza. Come on."

"Hang on, Joan. You can't do that. It's not our business."

Joan thought it was. She brushed away my restraining hand and threaded her way forward.

"Joan," I shouted, "Come back."

She paid no heed. She'd made up her mind. I could do nothing but follow her.

Patrick had stopped to light a cigarette and turned when Joan spoke.

"Joan! How are you?" he said.

I detected a trace of Irish brogue. His dark eyes were piercing, his frame burlier than on those old photos.

"I'm alright," she said, stiffly.

I hovered behind her.

"Is this, Paul?" he said, offering his hand. "How-do." His handshake was a cruncher.

I offered a silent prayer to the deity: 'Please, don't let Joan cause any trouble, I don't want blood all over my best coat'.

The deity wasn't listening.

"Patrick, I want you to stop."

"Stop what?"

"Stop hitting Liza."

He twisted his upper lip into a sneer, displaying smoke-stained teeth which marred his dark good looks. "Has she been complaining? I hope not for her sake."

"No, she hasn't, but your own bairns are worried. You've got to stop." Joan's face was turning a deep red.

'Don't overdo it, Joan,' I said to myself. 'You've made your point.'

Too late. The big fellow shoved his head into her face. "What I do with Liza is my business. Don't interfere, Joan, or it'll be the worse for you."

That was it. That was it. Seconds out!

Sometimes, I do stupid things; this was one of those times. I pushed Joan to one side. I hadn't been so wound-up since the day I'd had that

Castle on a Cloud

bust-up in the Pay Office cellar with Jack Thoms. That was over Joan, too. There had been no bloodshed then, I hoped history would repeat itself.

"Patrick, get this," I said. His breath reeked of stale beer. "The only one it will be the worse for will be you. You have a loyal wife, a wife you don't deserve, so don't harm her, *or* those lovely kids. And don't ever threaten Joan."

Was this me talking? Here was me telling Joan not to bone him! I had a feeling it was me that had gone too far.

He swayed a little as if ready to swing a punch.

The punch didn't come; instead, he inhaled on his cigarette and blew a cloud of smoke into my face. Not nice, but better than a right hook. Perhaps it was only women he hit. "Aw, leave me be, the bloody pair of you," he muttered, then turned and walked unsteadily away. Soon he had disappeared into the throng of shoppers.

Joan grabbed my arm as we watched him go.

There was an unusual thumping in my chest. "I don't know whether that's done any good, Joan." I said.

I felt her tremble. Unless that quivering was me. "Whoo!" she gulped. "I don't know what came over me. Seeing him, I just felt I had to say something, though. Thanks, for standing up for me, Paul."

I laughed with relief. "That's what I'm here for, you little firebrand."

"Don't say anything to Dad, love. He thinks interfering only makes matters worse."

Her dad had a rare Saturday off. He was at the kitchen table, studying the Daily Herald's racing page as we came in. He looked over the top of his horn-rimmed glasses.

"Aa'm goin' to have a bet, do thee two want one? Here have a look at t'runners. Aa'm backin' Templegate's double; he gives them both a guid chance."

"A bet sounds a good idea, Dad. We'll have one, Paul, eh? We might win a few pounds. Perhaps enough for that wireless."

I was always game for a bit of a flutter, so we studied the form. At least I studied the form, Joan, looking over my shoulder, just said, "I'll back these two of Walter Nightingale's, I've always liked him."

I wasn't aware that she knew the fellow, but I was too busy weighing up the pros and cons of the runners in two likely handicaps – the three o'clock at Haydock Park and the four o'clock at Newcastle – to worry at that precise moment about who she knew or didn't know.

Time flew by; my mind was still in a quandary when Joan interrupted my deliberations. "Come on, Paul, have you finished? Dad'll have to place these bets on the way to the match."

I'd forgotten about the match. York City were at home and we three were going.

"Why are we going so early?"

"Dad says we can go in the bookies. He says he'll show you the set-up."

"What do you mean set-up? It'll just be a bookie in the scullery of a house in some back lane, won't it?"

Apparently not, it wasn't like it was in Gateshead. First of all, there were no back lanes on this council estate, and secondly the operation was not carried out in a scullery, but in the premises of what had once been a shop. Joan's dad told me a bit of its history as we walked along Burton Lane. "It used to be owld Dummler's, the pork butcher. Hans Adolf Dummler, his name. He was interned during the war. When he cem back to York to re-open his shop 'ee had no chance. 'Ee tried to mek a go of it, but Wrights had all the custom for pork pies and the like, be then."

We entered the premises where Frankfurter sausages, Black Forest Ham, poloney, hot pease pudding and other delicacies of that ilk had once held sway. Now it was where Ups and Downs, Round Robins, Shift Doubles, and Any to Comes reigned supreme.

The whole operation was a revelation to me. In Gateshead the heinous profession of street bookie – cash bookie, was cloaked in secrecy. Every effort was made by these men in cloth caps and rolled up shirtsleeves to hide their nefarious goings-on from the law. To be caught meant an appearance in court and a criminal record. Here in York, the operation evidently carried on under the very noses of the constabulary. A blacked out window was the only concession to concealment. However, with a tannoy system blaring out all the results and the latest odds into the street, it must have been obvious, even to a PC Plod, what institution lurked behind the window. Unless of course, PC Plod was deaf.

What an enlightened city York was, or was there a hint of police bribery and corruption in this arrangement?

Castle on a Cloud

I turned to Joan's dad as we entered. "Has there ever been a police raid on this place?"

"Well, it's bin two years opened and Aa've niver seen a bobby down here yet, Paul. Not durin' racin' hours, anyroad."

I shook my head in wonderment.

Joan was tentatively hovering at the door; then she saw one of her uncles. Jack was a younger edition of her father – except he hadn't lost all his hair yet.

"There's Uncle Jack, I thought we'd find him in here." Inside the premises, there were a score or so of men and a couple of middle-aged women in smart hats. (Had Royal Ascot come to Burton Lane?) It was a scene of intense cerebral activity. Copies of the Sporting Life and Sporting Man were pinned around the walls. The Easter race meetings had got under way, and punters, still full of optimism, were studying the form, scribbling bets, or hurrying up to the counter manned by three lasses.

Jack was one of those engaged in the appraisal of recent equine history. He turned round as Joan said hello. "Why, hello, Joan, how's married life? Hello, Paul, is George with ye'?"

"He's up at the counter with our bets."

"Oh aye, Aa see him. Ye've missed the foist race. Fairy Feet won it at six to one."

He carried his own Daily Herald. Already, the racing page was looking a bit tattered. He pointed to the name of a horse – Swift Flight. "Look at that, Aa marked it this mornin' when Aa was studyin' them in the lav. Aa was in there a while ye see, Aa had a bit of a gippy tummy tha knows. Aa think it was that ale at the Corner House last night. 'Arry Ford don't keep it like t'last landlord. Anyroads, when Aa cem out of the lav, Aa said to ye Aunt Francis, 'Aa fancy Swift Flight. 'Arry Wragg's the jockey.' The 'Ead Waiter' they call him, tha knows. He waits t't'last minute to pounce."

"So, did you back it?" I asked.

"Don't tell us you backed something else!" Joan laughed.

"Well, Aa was just goin' up to the counter when that bloody Ned Simpson said he had a gud tip for one of Captain Elsey's. So Aa backed that one instead. Aa wouldn't care, Aa put ye Aunt Francis's two bob on it as well. She'll give me blue murder. Unless Aa can find some winners, that is. Ye haven't got a gud thing, Paul?"

I hadn't. 'Good Things' and Paul Potts were not very well acquainted.

The Third Division North football match was a goalless draw in front of a few thousand spectators. The drink we had that night in the Corner House with Joan's dad, was an improvement. Harry Ford's beer tasted alright to me. A couple of pints drowned the sorrow of our losing bets.

Sunday was big dinner day in the Speed's establishment. One o'clock prompt, roast beef, Yorkshire pudding and all the trimmings. That plateful was followed by rice pudding. Joan had the skin, she loved the skin. So later, it was a very lethargic walk over the city walls to visit her brother Philip and his wife and little girl. After our huge meal, it was an effort to do justice to their cream cakes, apple tart, and meat paste sandwiches. Tea over, Joan dandled little blonde infant, Clare, on her knee. Joan looked made for the part, I thought. But not yet; first, we had to get our own place and a bit of money behind us and thus escape the constriction of Ma Davidson and her rooms.

Joan was quiet on the train back to Newcastle, I sensed a wistful mood. That weekend in York must have been a bright window in her short married life. She loved me; of that I was sure, but she was homesick, too. I knew the answer. To be in our own house where she could busy herself making it into a home. Easier said than done.

6

TERROR ON THE TERRACES

Meantime, a job would help. And a top football match. Joan was a football fan. She could now see some of the best on our very doorstep. Perhaps that might help to ease her despondency. The big contest at St James Park. Virtual promotion to the top division was just a win away.

Long overdue promotion for United.

That was the considered view of their diehard supporters.

'W' desorv to be with the Gunners, the Spurs, and that Manchester lot. Aa blaym them gadgees on the board ye knaa,' was the type of comment to be heard. 'End es for that Sunnerland doon the road, Aa divvent knaa' why they shud be in the Furst Division. There's nee way they shud be above wor lads,' they would add.

United were hoping to put that unhappy situation to rights. This Saturday they were entertaining fellow promotion candidates, Sheffield Wednesday. Winner takes all.

Joan had followed football for years, going to matches on a Saturday with her dad whenever he could tear himself away from driving his beloved 'Pacifics'. The downside for the poor lassie was having just York City to support. York City, denizens of the lower reaches of the Football League. This trip to St James' Park was going to be the highlight of her football life.

We boarded the tram to Newcastle, a tram which was soon jam-packed, clanging past scheduled stops, leaving desperate would-be passengers stranded. At the Central Station fans pushed and shoved to get off the tram and join the thousands of other supporters excitedly converging on the stadium. We joined a huge queue for the cheap

'Popular' side, and even with an hour to go to kick-off, our progress to the turnstiles was snail-like. It was all too slow for Joan.

Again and again, she checked her watch.

"I hope we'll get in," she would say.

"We'll get in alright," I would reassure her

I was right, but only just. At the entrance I plonked down two bob for the pair of us. Clank, clank. We were in.

Joan's smile was like the first day of spring.

"Well, bugger-a-hell man. Ye cannot dee that."

I turned to see a burly fellow, well over six feet tall, frantically trying to push the turnstile open.

"Sorry, mate. Orders. The gates are closed."

But *we* were in. We danced up the steps at the back of the steep spectator terraces.

"Get nearer the front if you can, Joan," I said. "It's less crowded than here at the top."

Behind us, I saw gatecrashers (the burly fellow was one of them), scaling the boundary wall in their eagerness to see the crucial encounter. The few stewards seemed powerless to stop them. We squirmed our way downward, Joan was leading and that fact helped our passage. The good-natured crowd, mostly Geordies, but yet with a tidy number of Tykes, gave due deference to a girl – particularly a pretty girl.

"This will have to do, Paul, I don't think we can get any further." The havens in front of the few safety barriers were already occupied but at least it was possible to stand with relative ease.

But not for long. United kicked off, and a portent of what was to come quickly became manifest. To the roar of the crowd, came pressure from the top of the terraces, as eager fans, deprived of a view, forced their way into the heaving mass. A wave of spectators moved downwards, and despite bracing ourselves against the tide of bodies, we were jostled lower.

Comparative comfort returned as the teams engaged in a ding-dong struggle. The idol of Tyneside, J.E.T. Milburn, 'Wor Jackie', came close to an opening goal with a flashing run and a shot that brought a roar from the crowd. A roar that was silenced a minute later though, when tragedy – Wednesday scored.

"That was a lucky goal," said Joan (honorary Geordie now), "Haway, the Magpies!"

'Haway, the Magpies?' My, she was a quick learner

Castle on a Cloud

"Nay, lass, that were a champiun goal. Cum on, the Owls!"

Joan looked down disdainfully on the little rat-faced fellow with his red-and-white scarf; she'd quickly decided that he was no authority on the quality or otherwise of goals. To me, his accent sounded suspect – was he an undercover Sunderland supporter? The strips of Wednesday and the Rokerites *were* similar.

The crowd was quiet now; Geordies nervous, as Sheffield pressed again. To our relief 'we' countered as Stobbart crashed in the equaliser. Joan's cry of joy was stifled as we were engulfed in another wave of ecstatic fans. It was all we could do to keep ourselves upright as people stumbled around us, and again we were pushed nearer the pitch.

The confusion lessened for a while; now it was just the crowd shouting for more goals.

"If Newcastle score again, watch out, Joan. It could be pandemonium."

My words were no sooner uttered, when United captain, Joe Harvey, urging his team forward, got his head to a cross and the ball almost broke the net. Two-one to Newcastle!

Our elation swiftly turned into alarm. For this time, it wasn't a mere surge, this time more of an avalanche of bodies. An English language newspaper headline I'd read during my time in India flashed across my mind. I could see the message now; 'DISASTER AT BOLTON, BARRIER COLLAPSE, 33 FANS DEAD'.

We were pushed, bundled and carried downwards in the wake of frenzied spectators all trying desperately not to fall, not to be trampled by those behind. People were spilling over the low wall onto the pitch surrounds.

Joan stumbled and lost her balance; desperately, I tried to reach her, but was brushed aside like jetsam on a stormy sea. Gratefully, I watched as a big chap sporting a boxer's nose, grabbed her and swung her over the wall to safety. It was the burly fellow – the one who had been locked out. Well, bugger a hell, I thought, thank God for gatecrashers.

Hastily, I vaulted the wall and scrambled beside her. Behind us, on the terraces, people who had been knocked to the ground were scrabbling to their feet. Police and stewards were trying to hold a line to enable ambulance men to stretcher off the fallen.

A semblance of calm descended as the referee blew for half-time. At last, there was some respite from the mayhem.

"Are you alright, love?" I asked. "Are you hurt? Do you want to get out of here?"

Yorkshire grit and tenacity surfaced then. "No, I'm OK. I think I've twisted my ankle, but I want to see the finish. Mind, I'm not going back in there at any price!"

She turned to thank her rescuer, but he was not to be seen.

During the interval, stewards and policeman shepherded our group of bewildered spectators along to the Leazes End. This part too was crowded, but nowhere nearly as bad as our original spot. The ten minute break gave us some respite.

"Well, we're winning, anyway," laughed Joan. "Let's keep our fingers crossed."

The second half was easier, we could concentrate on the football as Newcastle grimly hung on to their lead. Then disaster struck, Marriot equalised for the visitors. A draw wasn't good enough for Newcastle.

"Come on, United," shouted a man next to me. He was wearing a black and white scarf, a cloth cap, and a worried look. "Divvent let this lot spoil it." Turning to me, he cried, "Cum on, son, shout for the lads. Yor lass is maykin' more noise than yee."

It was an observation that I couldn't dispute. I only hoped she wasn't going to harm that dulcet voice of hers.

Three minutes to go. Exultation – Frank Houghton, the Irish halfback, bundled the ball into the Wednesday goal. United back on top.

Could we keep them out? We did more than that; Houghton, again put the ball in the net and in the process crashed into a goalpost. He was holding his arm in agony, but our agony was over – surely Newcastle were set for promotion now?

Ambulance men were again in action as they rushed onto the field of play to carry off the hero of the hour. It seemed that Frank had broken his arm. 'An injury sustained in a just cause', was the considered view of the perceptive supporters around us.

"He's a bloody hero," my new-found friend asserted.

That was another sentiment with which I fully concurred.

We were down to ten men now, but soon the final whistle blew. I hugged Joan, Joan hugged me – the chap on the other side of Joan also embraced her. Why, I don't know – he was wearing a red and white scarf. I would have clonked him, but he was bigger than me.

It was later that night, reading the 'Football Final', that I discovered that the official attendance was over sixty-four thousand. Plus the rest, I thought, remembering those hordes of gatecrashers. There had been some injuries in the crowd, the paper said, but miraculously, none serious. Thankfully, it was not another tragedy like the Bolton affair.

Still, we had seen football history in the making and the euphoria of that victory lasted a good hour. Dispelled only when we returned to Castle Street and the grouchy face of our landlady.

7

TITTLE TO HER!

"It's like life in the trenches," said Joan one morning, returning from a dawn raid into the kitchen to boil the kettle. "This time I've got back unscathed – nobody there."

There was a sparkle in her voice – she was meeting her dad in the afternoon.

"The old man's harmless, Joan," I said, spreading marmalade on a slice of Hunter's best white. No toast these days – no morning fire now that Joan had started part-time work.

"Yes, but *she's* not. She's a sniper. I've got to dodge the bullets every day."

"Sticks and stones, Joan."

I envied Joan today. I could have gone with her to the Central Station if it had been the weekend. This was the second time her Dad had arranged a delivery of what he called 'vittles'. Why had he chosen a Friday again?

I could have gone, if it had been a Saturday. Instead, sitting on my tall stool in the office, mundanely stuffing banknotes and coins into pay-packets, I could only imagine: Driver George Speed, bringing his engine to a halt at Platform Nine, the platform reserved for the London Express. Joan, waiting, guessing (no doubt wrongly) where the locomotive would come to a halt. Joan, scampering along to the front of the train. Her Dad alighting. No hugs, not with him in grimy overalls and her in her best sky blue coat. He'd hand her the bags of goodies. An eager chat. Her Dad climbing back onto the footplate. A wave of goodbye.

Their chat must have been a long one. When I caught the crowded peak hour tramcar for Low Fell that night, who should be sitting halfway up the car in a gangway seat? Our evening meal was going to be late.

I squeezed past standing passengers, grabbed a strap as the tramcar swayed, and tapped her on the shoulder. "Caught you!"

She looked up and smiled. "Oh! I am a lucky girl. A big strong man to carry these two bags up the bank."

The little old lady sitting next to her eyed me up and down, looked at the bags, and seemed puzzled.

'Big strong man' did seem to be stretching it a bit, but Joan had a funny idea that she could twist me around her little finger. Most always she was right.

The kitchen in Castle Street had its usual occupants. A carping voice greeted us.

"Well, miss, you seem to have done well there! You've got more than veg from your father's garden. Some people are lucky! Nothing black market, I hope?" Then; "My! What's that peeping out of the bag? It looks like a rabbit."

(It didn't just look like a rabbit, it *was* a bloody rabbit, you stupid woman.) Joan had told me on the tram that she would suggest that Mr Davidson could skin it and make one of his tasty pies for us all to share.

"The rabbit's for Paul's mother, Mrs Davidson."

I was quick to surmise that there had been a change in the pie plan. The bunny was only in transit.

"Oh, that's a pity," said Mr Davidson. "I could have cooked it for you."

We closed the door to our room.

"Why did you say that, Joan? Mam getting the rabbit? *We* were going to have that rabbit, weren't we?"

I wasn't expecting her response – she flung her best coat across the room and burst into tears. "I know, I know. It's that woman," she sobbed, "She's spoilt my nice day. She's nosey, she's hateful. I'm sick of her snide remarks. Black Market! Lucky! I'm fed up with this place. I wish we were out of here."

I dropped the bags on the floor and tried to pull her to me, but she pushed me away.

"Don't come near me!" she howled. "I hate these rooms."

Castle on a Cloud

"Ssh!, love, don't let her hear you. Don't give her the satisfaction."

"I don't care," she wailed, "she'll start her catty remarks again tomorrow when I warm up the steak and kidney pie." She wiped tears away with the back of her hand. "Why didn't you say something? Why didn't you tell her to mind her own business?"

"Look, Joan, that wouldn't do any good, would it? She would only be more nasty. We've got to live here until we find other rooms. We've had no luck on that score. The two places we *have* looked at have been hopeless."

Those tears came again, "I'm going upstairs and I'm not coming down again tonight. Don't you follow me or she *will* be gloating, I'm sure she likes to upset us."

To hell with Ma Davidson! I'd been blind to the effect on Joan of that woman's behaviour. Every mealtime a trial. Every washday a test.
Should I go up and try to console her? I decided, no. Hopefully she would calm down; perhaps come downstairs again. Damn that old woman, she's a harridan.

I picked up her coat, straightened it out and hung it in the cupboard. I slung my jacket on a hook and closed the door. Mooching around now, I kicked the fireside stool. "Ouch!" It hurt. Then I spied the two brown-paper carrier bags that Joan had collected from her dad. I carried them to the table and turned out the contents.

The rabbit flopped onto the polished surface – the rabbit that had caused the crisis in the first place. "You're on a charge, you stupid rabbit," I muttered, "I accuse you of upsetting the applecart and causing all this trouble. I find you guilty on all counts. Have you anything to say in your defence?"

There was no answer, although I fancied his ears pricked up a bit.

There, next to the rabbit, was the steak and kidney pie, still in its oven dish. The crust reminded me of a face – a hint of a smiling mouth and perky eyes. "Who are you grinning at? *You'll* cause trouble tomorrow." Despite its stupid smirk though, it looked appetizing and for the first time tonight I felt hungry. Was I light-headed, is that why I was talking nonsense?

I surveyed the rest of the goodies. There was a cabbage, a turnip, two Wright's pork pies, sausages, scones, half a pound of lard, sugar. Were nefarious activities afoot in Burton Lane, York?

I decided that it was no good moping. My stomach was empty; I would have some toast, then I would make Joan a sandwich. I could take it up later. Unless she surprised me by coming downstairs in the next hour or so.

I picked up our toasting fork. OUR TOASTING FORK! A recent investment. Even that had elicited a comment from the Davidson woman. "I hope you're not going to set the house on fire, burning toast!" she'd said, when she espied it poking out of Joan's shopping basket. She missed nothing, that witch.

I spread some of my favourite Shippam's Bloater Paste on the toast. Tonight it seemed tasteless. Then I made Joan's sandwiches.

I put all the goodies away in our makeshift larder, all except a pork pie. I would take that, and the sandwiches, up to Joan. With a bit of luck, I might get a piece of succulent pie.

I switched on the radio. Another investment! A new Bush model. Well, nearly new, just shop-soiled – ten per cent off; almost a pound saved! We'd bought it from Carruthers' Electricals, the previous Saturday. In its 'Bush Radio' box (retrieved from the back of the shop), I'd carried it through that dreaded kitchen. *She* was there as usual. "Oh! You've got a radio I see, let's hope it isn't noisy," she'd said. "My! You young folk! I was forty-eight before *we* got a wireless. You want for nothing, these days!"

Only a place of our own, away from your whiny voice, I'd thought.

The sound of a dance band came from the set. Joe Loss, I think. Whoever it was, they were playing 'In The Mood'. *I* certainly wasn't in the mood for shuffling around on a dance floor.

I tuned in to the Home Service. The BBC News had just started; trouble in the Middle East again. "The Palestinian Jews have proclaimed the state of Israel." Appropriately, the serious voice of Bruce Belfrage was imparting the bad news tonight. "Syria, Jordan, Lebanon and Egypt are preparing to attack the fledgling state." Oh, great! More war. "Reports continue to arrive of Russia's increasing hold over the countries of Eastern Europe."

No good news anywhere, not even in sport. The Australian cricket team led by Don Bradman had walloped another county. Was it to be the England team for the chop next? I switched off. I was agitated enough without this surfeit of gloomy news. I turned out the light and tiptoed quietly up the stairs. The fifth stair creaked, I'd forgotten about the fifth stair. "Drat."

Castle on a Cloud

The kitchen door opened, the light from the room was like a searchlight. I was caught in the beam. (Like a startled rabbit, ha-ha.)
"I thought I heard a noise! Having an early night?"
"Yes, we're both tired. You old bat." The 'old bat' bit was *sort* of sotto voce.

I was now halfway up to the first floor landing, surprised that she hadn't made a remark about the mercy food parcel under my arm. Was she slipping? Her eagle eyes must have missed that.

Upstairs, the bedroom was in darkness, except for the gleam of a street light through the curtains. I could just discern Joan in bed, with her back turned to me. There was an indefinable tenseness in her posture; I sensed she was still awake.

I undressed and got into bed. I put an arm around her, but she pushed it away.
"Let me give you a cuddle, love," I whispered. "Come on. Come on, love."
"No, get away." Those harrowing sobs started again.
"Come on, Joan. Please."
I tried again to hug her, again I was rebuffed.
"Leave me alone. Leave me be," she whimpered.
What happened next was stupid.
"Right," I said, "If that's the way you want it. If you don't want me, I might as well sleep on the floor. Goodnight."
With a swish and a flourish I jumped out of bed, caught my knee on the bed frame and landed with a thud on the rug. I bit my tongue to stifle a cry of pain.
'Checkmate!' I thought, 'I'm the wronged one now.' I curled up on the rug and rubbed my knee. I could feel a bruise. An uncomfortable night beckoned.
Joan's next move was a surprise. "Two can play at that game." she sobbed, rolling out of the other side of the bed with a thud.
Things were going from bad to worse. She was being pig-headed. This wasn't in the plot.
I lay for what seemed an age, distressed by her crying, but angry, too. She had spurned me, when my heart ached to console her.
As I contemplated the situation, my ire began to subside. Not completely, not at first, but as the cold began to penetrate I decided a

reassessment was called for. Like, what in Hell's name were we doing on the floor? Above our heads was a snug bed.

We had a stand-off – no argument about that. Had I acted rationally jumping out of bed in the first place? The answer was a resounding no. For one thing, if I'd stayed in bed I wouldn't have this sore knee. Could I have simply turned my back? Yes! But hang on though. Why did another supposedly intelligent member of the human race behave like a lemming and blindly copy me? Eh? Eh?

One thing for sure; this was checkmate no longer – more like stalemate.

Joan would be having regrets now. I was chilly, but Joan, would be more so – with just a flimsy nightie on. But that was no consolation to me.

Why didn't she pull a cover off the bed? Was she too proud, or too stubborn? If she'd done that, I too could have grabbed a blanket.

Mind, she did have that thick rug beneath her. Not like this hard, supposedly Persian thing under me, telling me I had bony hips. I wish I'd never been conned into buying it at that bazaar stall in Meerut.

Let's get this sorted, Paul. Let's go back to the beginning.

What was the cause of this farce?

Our landlady's bitchy conduct, that was for sure.

Was that a reason for Joan to blame me?

Well, maybe. But perhaps we should share the blame.

Could I have done more?

Like what? Like what?

I wasn't getting very far. Whatever, this scenario was idiotic.

Poor, unhappy Joan, I must comfort her if she would let me. But how?

I had an idea. Contact her under the bed! I stretched my hand as far as I could, and began searching. Bad start! I nearly knocked the chamber pot over. It sloshed. Evidently, she'd been too upset to stop off at the toilet on her way upstairs. I pushed it to one side and tried again. It was then I realised that I couldn't reach her by scrabbling with my hand under the bed, she was too far away. I didn't relish the alternative of jumping over the bedstead, especially with my sore knee. It would be my luck to bump my head on the low ceiling. Then again, she might rebuff me and what would happen to my fragile dignity if I was spurned for the second time? At best I would have to return to the Persian rug.

No thanks to me, there was a solution. Joan must have heard me

Castle on a Cloud

fumbling about and had worked it out. The width of a double bed is more than the length of an arm even with a hand upon the end. What was the answer? Two arms! Clever lass!

My heart almost leapt out of my ribs when her hand found mine. Joan had long, shapely hands, but never before had I fully realised how soft, how delicate, the touch of her fingers could be. How could hands be so eloquent? How could fingers speak so clearly of love?

For long moments not a word was said.

At last; "Joan," I murmured, "I love you." My voice sounded strangely resonant.

"I know you do, darling," she whispered, "I'm sorry for saying those things." There was melody, even in her whisper.

"What a how-de-do," I said.

"What a pretty mess." She laughed tearfully, squeezing my hand again.

"Is this a Gilbert and Sullivan comic opera?" I asked.

"They always have happy endings, Paul. It must be."

"What are we doing on the floor, Joan?"

"Because we're stupid. Holding hands is nice though, don't you think?"

"It is, isn't it?" I said. "We'll have to stop meeting like this, all the same. People would think we're barmy. Not only that, it's cold."

Reluctantly, our fingers separated and we got to our feet.

"Can I cuddle you now?"

She lay on the bed and held out her arms in answer. "Will you forgive me for being so nasty, Paul? I'm sorry I was mean, I shouldn't take it out on you."

I kissed her tear-stained eyes and then found her lips. Soon, not only hands, but every facet of our beings became involved in breathless reconciliation. Minds, bodies, souls.

Later, we sat up in bed, languid and content.

"You know what, Joan?" I said, still panting a little. "I don't mind you getting upset with me every night if that's how it ends up!"

She smiled, "It was nice, wasn't it?"

"It was blooming marvellous."

"I'd better put my nightie on, I suppose."

"No, darling, not yet, just stay as you are. Do you want something to eat? You must be starving."

"There's one thing I'm not starving for, but I wouldn't mind a bite to eat, Paul. Doesn't this loving lark make you hungry? But don't go downstairs just for me."

"I don't have to, I brought you a sandwich. Plus a Wright's pie."

"You're a lovely lad, a thoughtful lad. I'm sorry I got upset. I'm not going to let Ma Davidson get me down again. Now I've got this job at the Royal Insurance we'll be able to save for a mortgage and get out of here."

In the street-lamp glow she looked herself again. Incredibly, more stunning than ever.

She held out a sandwich, the movement causing a delightful ripple. "Would you like a nibble?"

"I would that!"

"A sandwich I mean."

That night heralded a turning point in our attitude to our landlady. "Tittle to her in future," said Joan, and over the next weeks, Joan did seem to 'tittle'. With some success. The part-time job with the Royal Insurance Company helped; she spent less time trapped in our room. Their branch office was near the Low Fell tram terminus. The only other occupant was Mr Witherstone, her boss, and he spent much of his time out of the office monitoring his agents.

Mr Witherstone was a dapper, thin little man. A bachelor. He wore a uniform on his travels; a bowler hat, a navy pin-stripe suit, a black overcoat and carried a black umbrella, the latter always at the ready.

Witherstone re-introduced us to the theatre going we'd enjoyed during our courting days in York. Joan's boss had an arrangement with the Newcastle Theatre Royal, whereby he displayed playbills in his office window in exchange for complimentary tickets. He often invited us to accompany him to the theatre, and afterwards, to a drink in the nearby Shakespeare Inn – a quick drink before 'last orders' were called.

We enjoyed those nights; the show, then rubbing shoulders at the bar with some of the actors from the performance. Michael Hordern, Nigel Patrick, Joan Hickson, even Gertrude Lawrence (inevitably in a Noel Coward play), were just some of the names we could bandy about now. Martyn Green, the doyen of Doyly Carte Operas, was in the pub one night. He'd been playing Robin Oakapple in Ruddigore – the first staging of the comic opera since the destruction of its scenery in the London blitz.

Castle on a Cloud

One night in that pub, I picked up Patrick MacNee's umbrella, thinking it was Witherstone's, only to feel the thespian lay a firm hand on my arm. "I think that's mine, son," he said.

Hastily I put it down, but 'son'? He wasn't much more than twenty-five himself.

With a little embellishment, this hobnobbing with well known actors enabled me to trump brother Don's oft-repeated anecdotes of his claims to fame. 'Claims to fame' in his vocabulary meant brief encounters with celebrities away from their usual background.

Every other Tuesday night at Mam's (those weeks when Don was on early shift), he would regale, again and again, any chance listeners (too often Joan and I), with the minutiae of these 'episodes'. He interspersed his narratives with recollections from his bumper fund of wartime adventures. *His* celebrities were usually people who had been on his bus. Why bigshots would be travelling on buses at all puzzled me, particularly buses to destinations like Consett Ironworks, Dipton Colliery, or Team Valley Industrial Estate.

Well, apparently, VIPs as famous (?) as Tommy Callender, the Gateshead centre-half, Hughie Gallacher, of Newcastle United and Scotland, now down on his luck, even Ron Lundy.

"Who's Ron Lundy?" I was once foolish enough to ask.

"You know, the opening batsmen. He got fifty-three for North Durham in the Tyneside League in that match last year."

"Oh, aye," I would yawn. "That's real fame, I must say! But not to be compared to Michael Hordern, is it?"

"Who's Michael Hordern?" he would ask and then embark for the umpteenth time on a saga, such as his exploits in Holland with a Bofors gun, or fraternising with Fräuleins in conquered Germany.

Perhaps I never did trump his stories – too busy thinking of his next tale, he never listened to mine.

8

A LUMMOCK FROM LANCASHIRE

"Do you think there'll be a war, Paul?" Joan looked up from her hand of cards. We were sat at the table playing crib and listening to the BBC News telling us of the crisis in Europe.

Summer 1948 – only the third full summer of peace, my first English summer for three years, yet once again, war clouds were gathering. Russia had cut off land links to US, British, and French forces occupying West Berlin, a city which was now just an enclave within Russian dominated East Germany. Joseph Stalin seemed hell-bent on forcing the withdrawal of Western troops from the old German capital. 'Uncle Joe', as Stalin was affectionately nicknamed during World War II, had changed from hero to villain in a few short years. The Allies had responded to the blockade with a massive American-led airlift to supply the city. Any action from Russia to block the air corridor would threaten the fragile post-war peace. Did Stalin's Russia now possess the atomic bomb? The spectre of a score of Hiroshimas threatened.

"Fifteen-two, fifteen-four, fifteen-six and six is twelve. That's it, Joan. Game to me."

"You lucky devil, you always get the cards." She punched me in mock annoyance. "What about this war though? You haven't said what *you* think."

"No, Joan, I don't think we'll have a war," I said rubbing my arm. "It's just Russia and America sabre-rattling. Joan shivered. "Gosh, I hope not. But it's a worry."

"We can't do much about it, can we?" I asked, shuffling the cards. "Do you want another game, love?"

"No thanks. Not against you with your luck tonight!"

"It's not luck, it's skill. A bit like Henry Cotton winning the Open the other day."

"Our cricketers haven't much skill then. They're getting walloped by Bradman's lot."

"That's because there're too many Yorkshiremen in the England team, love," I chided. "Your county's not even going to win the championship this year, Glamorgan look the winners to me."

"Well, that's OK if they do. I've got Welsh blood in me. So there!"

She took my hand, "Paul," I sensed a change of mood.

"What, love?"

"It's less than two weeks to our summer holiday."

"Ah-ha?"

"We've definitely decided to stay at home that week?"

"That's what we agreed – stick my bonus in the bank towards a deposit on a house."

"I've been thinking, Paul."

"That's bad news."

"No, don't laugh. What if there was a war? You could be called up again and we won't have had a proper holiday together. We could have a *real* honeymoon. The first was a bit of a disaster, wasn't it?"

Honeymoon? I was getting interested. Then I frowned. "You mean go back to Scarborough?"

"No, I was thinking of Blackpool. We just have time to get booked. How about it?"

I walked to the half-open window and gazed out. The Davidsons' tiny back garden plot looked bedraggled, a rusty looking rosebush, a lupin, its tired flowers turning to seed pods. Dusk was stealing in. A couple of fat-bodied moths fluttered against the glass. Any moment, they would be inside the room. I pushed the window shut; Joan hated moths, especially the fat-bodied variety. I pondered; at first wondering whether moths or black beetles were top of her hate list, and then whether we should go on this holiday. For a minute I delayed my verdicts.

"Bang would go the bonus, Joan."

"Not all of it, love."

I sat down in my easy chair. I knew when I was beaten. "OK, Joan, if that's what you want, I agree."

The whirlwind was unexpected. Suddenly I was in the eye of a cyclone, I found Joan on my lap, hugging and kissing.

Castle on a Cloud

"Hold on," I laughed, "we've got to find a place. That could be difficult at short notice."

"Not really, I've picked a likely boarding house from the adverts in tonight's Chronicle. Vacancies they say."

"You crafty little devil, is that why you let me beat you at crib? To soften me up? I chuckled. "I hope it's not a Mrs Appleyard's, though."

"Me too! Anyway, this could be your first real holiday, Paul, couldn't it?"

True, apart from hill leave in India.

Joan's childhood had been affluent when compared to mine. Her family, boosted by their concessional rail travel perk had always spent a week at the seaside (until war intervened). Blackpool, apparently, was her favoured childhood resort.

That was the Speed side of the holiday coin; it had invariably come down heads. The Potts coin always landed tails. Annual holidays for we kids from 'Asky Road' would be a day out on the electric train to Whitley Bay (the high spot a tuppenny ride on the Cocks and Horses in the Spanish City); or a trip to South Shields on the branch line train. I could still recall travelling in those tatty old carriages, with the small tank engine chuffing us to the seaside. A couple of such jaunts laden with buckets and spades, sandwiches, and a bottle of water, would augment occasional outings to the local park. Even those seaside trips ceased when Dad was forced to give up work.

Blackpool though! Hurrah! Seven days without the sight of Ma Davidson peering over her pince-nez every time we passed through her kitchen sanctum. Her pince-nez! They irked me more and more each day. When I had first met her she was wearing a conventional pair of spectacles. If I'd known then that her pretentious pince-nez were at the optician's being repaired I would have thought twice about renting her rooms, desperate as we were. I'd detested those kinds of specs ever since infant class. Strict Miss Marble, squinting over hers, still haunted my dreams. Miss Marble of the hard right hand, a hand with which most of her pupils made painful acquaintance. She too had had a prissy mouth.

But Blackpool in August! It had to be better than a miserable Scarborough in March. OK, we were trying to save, but we needed a break. Anyway, four weeks bonus at my new salary with old Jackson now gone would still leave a little over to put into the Post Office.

So, one sunny Saturday morning, with cases bulging, we caught the tram into Newcastle and there boarded our long-distance coach. We'd agreed that a road journey was the thing; the fare was cheaper than the train. Plus, I had suggested to Joan that the journey would be more scenic.

Well, we saw the sights alright, Ripon's cathedral and Harrogate's splendid avenues, they were OK. But then, it was Leeds and Bradford (you couldn't see the join), with hordes of white faces scurrying up and down the main streets. Halifax, Burnley, Blackburn, Preston, followed in a dreary procession, broken only by a brief touch of Pennine greenery. We saw more old mill chimneys, more power station smokestacks, more roadworks, more level crossings, more traffic lights, than we'd ever seen before.

"Do you know, love, they have Autobahns in Germany and Autostradas in Italy? Straight as a die they are, two lanes each way. No traffic lights either," I said, at one lengthy hold-up.

"We'll never get things like that in this country. We're too hard up. Don't forget, we won the war."

I laughed. "It might happen!"

'Tower View' was our guest house; it was just behind the sea front. It looked spick and span. The door was open so we rang the bell and entered the lobby. I wondered what kind of landlady would pop up.

A tiny, chubby-faced, red-cheeked, cheery looking woman of about forty appeared. Could this be a landlady? It was.

"'Ello," she smiled, "Aa'm Gladys Ramsbottom, tha mun be the Potts! Ah was abaht to give you up. 'Asto had a rotten journey?"

"Sorry we're late, Mrs Ramsbottom. The traffic was busy all the way," Joan said, easily translating the dialect. "Call me Gladys," she said. "Tha'd better cum in. Aa'll show thee tha room. Then cum down an' ull give thas a cup o'tea, you mun be clemmin'. Just ring the bell here when theer's ready."

This was more like it, I thought, as we dumped our suitcases and gazed out of our room window at Blackpool Tower. It was almost like being in Paris. Even the language was foreign to me, although there was more than a dash of 'Yorksheer' in it. Joan could be my interpreter.

"I'll just smarten myself up, Paul, before we go downstairs. I look a mess."

She didn't look a mess to me, but then she never did, except perhaps when she had her rollers in. Even then she was a pretty mess.

The bedroom was as bright as the exterior; cheerful flowered curtains

Castle on a Cloud

and bedspread, there were even a couple of wooden easy chairs; plus a washbasin – almost en-suite with the toilet and bathroom just across the landing.

Downstairs, Gladys ushered us into the dining room and beckoned us to a table. "'Igh tea is at six thirty. This'll be tha table. Az asked 'Arry to bring a tray in. 'Arry's me 'ubby."

Harry, broad-framed Harry, must have been six-foot-six in the plimsolls he was wearing. Gladys was about five-foot-two in her high heels.

"'Arry, meet Mr and Mrs Potts," she said, looking up to him as though to a skyscraper. Then turned to us. "What's your foist names, luvs?"

"Paul and Joan,"

"Paul an' Joan, 'Arry. Remember!"

The big fellow put the tray on the table. He seemed a shy, gentle man, but his handshake was firm. "Aa'm suited to meet thees," he said diffidently, looking down at his pumps.

"We'll leave thas to it and see thees in a while, then," said Gladys. "Come on, you big lummock."

"What's a big lummock, Joan?" I asked after they had left the room.

"Well, I suppose a gormless cracker would fit the bill, but in this case I think it's a term of endearment," she said, as she passed me a cup of tea. There was a plateful of scones on the tray.

"It's very good of her," Joan said, "not many landladies would bother to do this."

"I know two that wouldn't anyway, love," I said, attacking another scone.

First impressions were spot on. To unworldly me, the modest boarding house could have been the Ritz. Joan was a little more blasé, having twice had post-war holidays in Devon with girl friend Helen. Nonetheless, she agreed that Tower View was very pleasant.

"Only very pleasant?" I queried.

"This is the very best, darling," she said, "you're here with me."

I couldn't argue with that.

"They do offer a good menu," Joan said, on the third day. "How do they do it?"

"I don't know love. Eggs every morning, chicken last night. Chicken! Plenty of veg. I have a theory, though. Listen to this."

The other guests had departed; we were lingering over our last cup of tea. The maid must have been on a day off; Gladys and Harry were clearing the tables.

"Have you finished, luvs?" asked our landlady, coming across to us.

"Yes thanks, Gladys," said Joan.

"Gladys, does Harry have a smallholding or something?" I asked.

"Whativor makes tha think that?"

"Well, I saw him getting off the tram this morning with two big baskets before the shops would be open."

"By, you're a sharp lad, Paul; he does have a patch with chicken shed unall – on Sent Anne's Road."

"So that's where you get your eggs from, Gladys," said Joan.

"'Arry, cum 'ere, luv."

The big chap was clearing dishes away on a nearby table. He lumbered across. "What, Gladys?"

"Paul knows, tha know, "'Arry."

"Knows what, luv?"

"Don't gawp, 'Arry." She gave him a wink and nudged him in the ribs, or as near the ribs as she could reach. "'Ee knows where tha gets your eggs!"

"Oh, does he? It were supposed to be a secret, Gladys. 'Ow does he know?"

"Ee seed thee with the baskets."

"Oh 'ee's a sharp un, that Paul. He mun be abaht afore breakfest, Gladys."

I wasn't abaht before breakfast. I had seen him carrying his produce when I had looked out of our bedroom window. A walk before breakfast? That was anathema to me. Even getting up for breakfast was a struggle when Joan was in nuzzling mode.

He gave me a brief, shy glance, then looked down at his wife. "'Ee'll know abaht chickens unall, then?"

"Corse he'll know abaht chickens you stone jug, that's where you get tha eggs from."

"Nay, lass. Aa mean when we has chicken dinners, luv."

This was almost like a music hall act.

"I bet you grow vegetables as well, Harry," I said egging him on.

"Ee says tha grows greens as well, 'Arry."

Castle on a Cloud

"Aa knows what he said, Aa 'eared him, Gladys."

"'Arry's grown greens sin' 'Dig for Victory' days, but 'ee kept ut secret, 'ee didn't want 'Itler to find out."

"Doan't be daft, Gladys. It were Charlie Dean. Aa didn't want him to know. He's a reet cadger."

"You do very well, Harry. Eggs, chickens, veg. I'll keep it hush hush, though."

"Oh, ta, Paul," He lumbered off with a trayful of crockery and Gladys in his wake.

"What do you think of that for a bit of detective work?"

"Clever clogs," Joan laughed. "I don't believe he thinks you'll keep his secret."

I think he trusted me though. For the rest of the week he took every opportunity to give me a playful nudge and his screwing up one side of his face version of a wink. "Paul, you're a sharp un!" he would say.

The days (and the nights) sped by swiftly – walks along the prom, hand in hand, paddling in the sea, me with my grey flannels rolled up to my skinny knees, Joan with her skirt tucked into her knickers. Sticks of rock; picking winkles out of their shells with a pin; visits to Feldman's Theatre of Varieties; the Tower Ballroom with Reginald Dixon on the Wurlitzer; Yates Wine Lodge; a comfortable bed.

A comfortable bed! A bed made for a couple on an early second honeymoon. What a wonderful week it was. Ardour tempered with affection, desire coupled with love.

Our last night, we visited the Tower Circus. I'd never seen a circus. My dad had told me, when I was little, of the great Barnum and Bailey's Grand Circus, with the stupendous Big Top. Of the elephants, the lions, the clowns. Thus, I looked forward to this circus night, albeit, a circus lacking a Big Top. Joan, too, was eager to rekindle memories of childhood visits.

We enjoyed the show. Well, who couldn't enjoy Schumann's Norwegian Fjord Horses, jugglers, Les Troi Pierre Alizes on the trapeze? Who couldn't thrill to Vojtech Trubka and his Seven Tigers? Who couldn't laugh with the famous Cairoli's Clowns complete with custard pies in 'Charlie's Birthday Party'? Certainly not the kids who formed a significant part of the audience. Certainly not two young second-honeymooners sitting amidst those kids.

To add to the excitement we had a Communityland sing-song

during the interval with Jack Morgan and the Tower Circus Orchestra. Gems such as 'How does a hen know the size of an egg-cup when she lays her eggs?' and 'Ten Green Bottles', had everyone in fine voice, Joan and me included. We had gone to the show determined to enjoy our last night, we'd paid 3/6d each for the best seats and 6d for the programme, so enjoy it we would.

Later, we wandered along the North Promenade. The sun was sinking ever closer to a clear horizon. Above, cirrocumulus clouds were capturing the fading sunbeams, producing magnificent bands of red and golden hues. We watched, arms around each other, admiring the ever-changing patterns, the varying shades, as the golden orb touched the sea and appeared slowly to sink beneath the waves. Saddened we were, as we realised our holiday was almost over; Low Fell beckoned.

"Do you know something, Joan?" I said pointing. "The sun will be setting in Ireland there in the west now. I was just thinking that my mam's parents came over this sea and settled in Gateshead, perhaps fifty years ago."

Joan, not to be outdone, pointed southwards over the water. "Wales is over there. My grandfather travelled from Wales to settle in York."

"It's amazing," I laughed. "All this to-ing and fro-ing, how did we ever meet?"

"I've told you before, Paul, it was destiny."

I pulled her to me and kissed her, she flung her arms around my neck showing a warmth that told me of her love.

Next morning, we said our farewells to Gladys and Harry.

"'Ere's a present for tha, Paul," said the huge fellow, handing over a brown-paper bag. "A've wrapped them up for tha so they won't brek. They're eggs tha knows. Three weeks ration, theer."

"Thanks very much, Harry."

"And thank you too, Gladys," said Joan, "we've enjoyed our stay."

The last we saw of them as we stood at the corner was a picture of Harry lifting Gladys up to wave to us as though she was a schoolgirl. She kicked her little legs in mock fury, but both were hooting with laughter.

9

THE STRANGE AFFAIR OF THE MYSTERIOUS BOX

The Berlin land blockade continued and the airlift carried on. It was almost routine now. The tension had eased.
Plus Christmas was coming. This was to be our first Christmas together. After four months back in that Low Fell house haunted by Ma Davidson, Blackpool was now but a memory. Our savings were growing, but only slowly. A mortgage still beyond our grasp.

"We've received some spiffing news this morning."
Blast! It was our landlady, halting our dash through the kitchen. She waved a letter.
I had mumbled a "Cheerio" – we were off to see Newcastle play Arsenal.
"Mr Davidson and I have an invitation from our son in Royal Tunbridge Wells. He wants us to spend Christmas with him and his family."
Joan was almost out of the door. She stopped in her tracks, turned, and retraced her steps. "You'll be going then?" she asked.
I swear her breath was bated.
"Yes, we couldn't refuse. We must see his fine new house. I've never told you much about our son, Evelyn, have I? He and his wife have a lovely son, Roderick. Evelyn works in the City, gets the commuter train up to London, you know."
Never told us much about Evelyn? We were sick of hearing about her wonder boy lately. But this was interesting. Carry on, Ma.

"They usually come up to Gateshead at this time of the year, but they want us to see their big detached residence. They've just moved in and have room for us now."

"We're dying to see our little grandson again, he's four you know," said Mr Davidson.

"When are you going down?" I asked.

"Well, we're going on the twenty-second and all being well, coming back on New Year's Day." Ma cooed, "Aren't we, Grandaddy?"

Whenever she launched into simpering mode, I felt queasy. But, hang on! They would be away about ten days! Had the sun come out, or was it Joan's beaming smile that suddenly lit up the room?

"There'll be no need to worry about your house whilst you're away," Joan said. "There was something I was going to ask you, though. Will it be OK for my Mam and Dad to visit?"

"They're coming up at Christmas?"

"Well, I was waiting to find out whether Dad would be off work during the holiday. I've just heard from them to say they can probably make it."

"It'll be fine if they want to come. We'll just charge five shillings a night for one of the spare bedrooms," she said magnanimously. "That's providing you can launder the bedclothes afterwards, won't we, Robert?"

Robert turned to Joan. "Is that fair enough?" he said, almost apologetically.

"Well, I'm sure my mam would have left something for your trouble in any case."

Was that Joan's hackles I could sense rising dangerously? I looked at my watch. Let's vamoose, I thought; vamoose whilst the going's good. "We'd better be off, Joan, or we'll miss the start."

Walking down the road to the tram stop, Joan was still seething. "I'm hopping! The old Scroogess, fancy charging for a Christmas visit. It's a wonder she didn't tell us that there's no room at the inn!"

"Think on, lass, though," I laughed, "we're going to have ten days without her. Mind, you had me worried for a minute. I thought you were going to give three cheers when she said they wouldn't be back until New Year!"

Joan laughed, "Did I look pleased?"

Castle on a Cloud

And so it came about, that in the year of Our Lord, 1948, the Yuletide celebrations began early in one house in the 'Fell'. There, the first day of Christmas was decreed to be the twenty-second of December. It was on the morning of that day that the departure of an old couple caused joy in the hearts of a young man and his wife. I didn't see the manner of their going, I was at my office desk, but hurried home that night eager to hear confirmation from Joan, that they had indeed gone.

I expected my darling to be in a carefree, joyous mood, but when I greeted her in the kitchen, it was with a perturbed, offhand manner that she accepted a kiss. I'd heard of hearts dropping like a stone, I could believe it to be true; because, for an instant, I felt that was happening to mine.

"What's the matter, love, don't tell me they haven't gone? Ma Davidson is upstairs ill? The old man's had a stroke?"

She gave a feeble smile. "No, they've left alright. They should be nearly there by now."

I smiled, breathed again, and walked across to the boiler to warm my hands.

"Good. So what's happened? You look worried,"

"Well, just minutes after they'd gone, just as I was about to leave for work, there was a knock on the front door."

"So?"

"It took me ages to open the blooming thing; we'd never opened that door, had we? It's always been tradesman's entrance for us. Anyway, when I did unlock it, there was a National Coal Board van outside and a man standing on the step asking me to sign for a delivery."

"What was it? Was it coal?"

"No, it's a big cardboard box. You know Mr Davidson was a big noise with one of the private coal companies before the war? Well, I think he must still get a Christmas present every year. I've left it in the hall anyway. It's heavy."

"There's no problem, is there? We'll just leave it until they return."

"But there's a stumbling block, Paul. The label on the parcel reads 'Fresh Produce – Open Immediately'. What can it be and what are we going to do?"

"Well first, love, let's have a look at it."

There it was, on the lino-covered floor near the front door – a bulky parcel alright. I bent down and lifted one corner. "Blooming heck, you're right it's heavy. It must weigh nearly two stones. I can see now why you didn't bring it through. We'll have to open it though. It might be something that goes off quick."

"Like a bomb?"

"Don't be daft, you know what I mean. Fetch the scissors, love." I knelt down, cut through the string around the box, and, with a struggle, opened it. Inside I found corrugated brown paper and tearing that aside, even more protection; this time greaseproof paper. I delved in; my hands touched something cold and soft. Ugh! I looked down at pale skin.

"You know what I think it is!" said Joan, awestruck. "It's a turkey!"

"A turkey? Golly! I think you're right, Joan. It's a blooming big turkey!" I stood up, stepped back, looked at Joan, then back at the box.

Joan seemed as flummoxed as me. "What are we going to do with it?"

"I know what I'm going to do, right now, Joan. I'm going to have some tea first. That's if you've got some ready. I'm starving. A man can't solve this one on an empty stomach."

We sat in their warm kitchen. Why not? We had the freedom of the house. It was ours for ten glorious days.

"What are the alternatives, Paul?"

I pushed my plate away. "Well, we could just eat it, bury the remains in their little garden plot," I said, half in jest. "Just pretend it never came."

"You must be kidding; be serious, Paul. I've signed for it."

That put paid to that idea. "I'll tell you what, Joan. This fabulous Evelyn, the city gent, he must be on the phone. I could go to the booth on the corner and speak to Ma. They'll have got there by now, won't they? Did she leave his number?"

"No, I've got his address, but he's not on the phone. She said they're waiting to have it installed."

"So what do we do? We can't eat it, it's not ours. A letter would be no good; it probably wouldn't reach them until after Christmas. One thing I'm not doing is humping it down to the NCB offices on the Trading Estate. Can you see me going to the receptionist, dumping the box on the desk and breathlessly asking if I can see the man in charge of the turkeys? She would think I was bananas!"

"She wouldn't be far wrong!"

"Wait though, Joan! I've had a brainwave. We'll send a telegram to Royal Tunbridge Wells!"

"You can't tonight; the post office'll be shut."

Castle on a Cloud

"The main post office in Newcastle isn't. I think it's open until ten o'clock. I'll have to go across."

On the tram, there were only three passengers.

"It's quiet toneet, Aa think people are saving the'selves for Christmas," the lanky conductor said, as he selected a threepenny ticket and punched it with a ding on his machine.

I didn't tell him that Christmas had already begun in our house; a Christmas complete with a turkey and minus a Scrooge. Instead, I mentally composed my message. So at the post office all I had to do was write it:

'DEAD TURKEY ARRIVED UNEXPECTEDLY TODAY STOP A WHOPPA STOP WHAT SHALL WE DO WITH IT STOP P POTTS STOP'

I didn't hang around; I caught the same tram back to Low Fell. The lanky conductor didn't recognise me.

"It's quiet toneet. Aa think people are saving the'selves for Christmas," he said as he punched my ticket. I still didn't enlighten him about *our* Christmas. I just sat back contentedly. That telegram will explain the situation to the Davidsons; at last we're getting somewhere. Hopefully, there would be a reply; perhaps tonight.

"What did you put in the telegram?" asked Joan.

With a smile of satisfaction, I tossed my coat on the back of Ma Davidson's armchair and told her, word for word. Surprisingly, her response was to laugh. "You barmpot. There was no need to put 'dead', there was no need to put 'unexpectedly', and why put 'whoppa'?" she chuckled.

"I don't agree," I said, huffily, "it was all true. For a start off it might have been a stray live turkey escaped from some farm. I was just clarifying the situation."

A loud rat-a-tat at the front door interrupted our erudite discourse. We both scrambled to answer the knock. Joan beat me to it, nimbly stepping over the turkey. Over her shoulder, I spied a fresh-faced telegraph boy. With one hand he steadied his bike, his other hand held a missive.

"Telegram for P. Potts," he piped.

"That's me." I reached over Joan and tore open the envelope.

'EAT IT STOP MR DAVIDSON STOP'

That was all it said. Mr Davidson had always been a man of few words. He had no option.

"There's no reply," I said to the boy, whilst graciously allowing Joan to read the message. We wandered back into the kitchen.

"Eat it!" said Joan, flopping down into Ma's armchair. "You've got to cook it first. I've never cooked a chicken, never mind a turkey! My God! Not only that, Mam's bringing a goose. She told me in her letter that she was getting it tomorrow."

"We'll have to stop her. The turkey should be enough for the four of us don't you think?"

"It'll be enough for an army, but how *can* we stop her?" Then she smiled, mischievously. "Oh yes, *I* know!"

I groaned. "Don't tell me! Don't tell me!" I said, struggling back into my topcoat.

"Wait, I'll come with you this time, love. Don't panic I'll pay my thruppence. You keep your pocket money."

That tram of mine must have had a long stop at the Low Fell terminus. It was the same conductor. He was just as lanky. "It's quiet toneet. Aa think people are saving the'selves for Christmas," he said as he punched two tickets this time (two dings). I still didn't tell him that Christmas had come early for us, turkey and all. Plus a goose, if we couldn't cancel its flight. Instead, I listened to Joan, struggling to compose our telegram.

"Leave it to me, love," I said at last, "I'm an expert on telegrams."

"OK. You'd better make it clear to Mam."

'DONT PANIC MAM STOP NOBODYS DEAD STOP EXCEPT THE TURKEY THAT TURNED UP AT THE FRONT DOOR TODAY STOP DONT GET THE GOOSE OR YOURS IS COOKED STOP JOAN STOP'

I was quite proud of that telegram, a pride that was undiminished, even though, after having read my draft as we walked back to the tram stop, Joan laughingly belaboured me with her handbag. In the kerfuffle we nearly missed the tram. "Your tram's quiet tonight," I said, to the omnipresent lanky conductor. "I think people are saving themselves for Christmas. Don't you?"

"It's funny ye should say that," the beanpole fellow said. "I was just expressin' the saym sentiments to a guy earlier toneet. Funnily enough, 'e looked a bit like ye an' aall, but 'e wus on his own, so it couldn't have been ye could it?"

"Hardly likely," I said, "but you don't know a conductor called Don Potts who works on the Northern, by any chance?"

"Na, Aa divvent, w'doan't hev much to dee with the busmen. Why div ye ask?"

"He reminds me a bit of you, with his interesting talk, except he's not tall, more dumpy in fact."

I was glad to get to bed that night, I felt I had been travelling on trams for yonks. I still had the energy to get my revenge on Joan, however, grabbing her just as she was about to pull her shorty nightie over her head. "Get off," she screamed in mock distress. "Help, help! There's a madman attacking me!"

"I'll teach you to biff me with your handbag," I laughed.

"Help! Mrs Davidson, help!"

"There's no help for you, you devil, in this empty house. Nobody to hear your screams," I said, as I found her ticklish zones.

Her shouts dissolved first into infectious laughter as we collapsed on the bed, and then into murmurs of endearment as we fell into a loving clinch. It was fun to be as boisterous as we wanted to be, it was great to know that no one could hear us.

By and by we lay quietly in each other's arms.

"I love you so much, Joan."

"I do too."

"You love you, too, do you?"

She laughed lazily, "I love you, you loony."

"You know what I'm going to do now, love?"

"Don't you think you've done enough?"

"Not yet, I haven't," I said, jumping out of bed. "I'm going to open this attic window and shout to the street. Look up, folk, look up! See the luckiest man in the world. Not only has he has a lovely wife, but he has a beautiful turkey for Christmas!"

"Shush, don't be potty, Pottsy," she laughed, "you'll be had up if you stand at the window like that!" She sat up and held out her arms, "Come back to bed."

I took one look; that was enough. "I think that could be a better idea, love," I said, leaping into her embrace.

We snuggled up again. "You're crazy, Paul, you must know that. But do you know what I think of you?"

My lips closed on hers. I never found the answer that night, not in so many words, anyway.

"Well, 'ullo, luv, how are thee? Merry Christmas."

Christmas Eve; Joan's mam and dad were at the front door. *She* gave me a hug, we men just shook hands.

"Merry Christmas," I said, as Joan appeared behind me. "Don't trip over the box," I added.

Their greetings were renewed fourfold with their daughter. "Hang your coats up and come through to the kitchen where it's warm," Joan said. "We'll show you your room in a bit."

"By, it's cowld outside," said Mr Speed. "It's luvly in here, lass, though."

"Yes, it's warm in this kitchen, but not so hot in our room. We're living in here most of the time when they're away."

"Ye do right, luv," said her mum, "but what's all this about a turkey, lass? That young telegram lad gave your fether and me a right turn, Aa thowt summat had happened. Until Aa read the fust words – 'Don't panic.'"

"You got the telegram in time, Mam, then? You didn't get the goose?"

"No, Aa went down to the butchers in the Shambles and towld 'im the story. He was awlreet. Aa didn't want to oopset him tha sees. We might need a goose next year and they're 'ard to get. Besides, 'ee keeps the best. Where's this turkey then?"

"In that box you nearly fell over near the front door," I said. "We thought that it's about the coldest place in the house so we left it there."

"It's ginormous, Mam. I think we'll have to do it in this old cooking range here. I'm sure it won't go in their gas oven. I thought *you* might roast it. I remember you cooking on the old range in our kitchen in Burton Lane."

"Eh, lass, thee thought Aa might cook it did thee?" she laughed. "Aa've nivver cooked a turkey befower. They're a damn sight bigger than a goose, tha knows!"

"This one is," I laughed.

"Paul got a cookbook out of the library yesterday; that might help." said Joan.

"Oh, did he? Aa've got a better idea, luv, Paul could cook it!"

Castle on a Cloud

"Doan't look so worried lad, Ida's only kiddin'," said her dad. "Let's have a look at this turkey."

With a struggle, I carried the box in, laid it on the wooden bench and unwrapped it.

"My gawd!" said Joan's mam. She stepped back almost as though it *was* an unexploded bomb. There was reverence in her voice, she did like good food. It *was* an impressive sight, now that it was lying in all its naked glory. "By gum. Yon boid must weigh twenty pounds; don't ye think so, George?"

"If turkeys went in for boxin' it would be an 'eavyweight alright. We should manage to get a dinner out of it, anyroad."

"This one will tek a few hours to cook, George."

"Well," I said, "we thought it must weigh twenty pounds at least. We looked in the butcher's window yesterday; he had twelve pounders hardly half this size. Didn't he, Joan?"

"He did, Mam. We reckon it could take five or six hours to roast. That's according to the book. Anyway, you must be hungry, Mam. Seeing as we'll be eating turkey for the rest of our days, I've made some salmon and cucumber sandwiches. Paul's got some bottles of Newcastle Brown and a bottle of whisky, Dad. That's as well as a bottle of port, Mam, and some lemonade."

Joan's dad smiled. "That sounds alright to me, Paul. Aa've brought a bottle of rum. Oh, Joan, doan't forget Aa've brought thee sprouts, a couple o'tunnips and a few parsnips from the garden; as well as some tatties. Aa said Aa would, luv."

"*Aa'd* better not have too much to drink, Joan, not like your dad, not until we've sorted out how to cook that boid. Mind, Aa do like a port and lemon."

"How's everybody in York, Mam?"

"Philip popped in at the weekend. They're fine. Clare was with 'im. She's a lovely bairn."

"What about Liza?"

"Oh, we see a lot of her with David and Belinda."

"She's never away, Joan, always short of a bob," said her dad.

"Aye, George, but she seems 'appier these days. Patrick seems to 'ave turned over a new leaf. Touch wood."

Joan said nothing, just smiled.

Yes, Christmas Eve. The Christmas Eve, I discovered that tinned salmon and brown ale were not complementary. The beer tasted finer, however, after the sandwiches were out of the way. Joan's dad was of the same mind judging by the way he delayed his first swig until after he had finished eating. It was with a familiar gesture that he wiped the froth off his upper lip. "Aa've got a couple of cigars, Paul. Aa luv a cigar at Christmas, tha knows. 'Ere have one."

I didn't smoke, so had misgivings about this big fat cigar. Nevertheless, I lit up, sat back, and was soon puffing merrily. The pervasive aroma of cigar tobacco produced a Christmassy atmosphere in that austere kitchen. Too much so for Joan. She looked troubled. "I hope that smell doesn't linger too long. I wouldn't like Mrs Davidson sniffing it when she comes back."

I laughed, "Surely, it won't last a week?"

"Nay lass, don't fret," her dad added, a happy smile on his face. Then to me. "By, this is a champion drink, lad." He took another sup, "Are we goin' to the match in the mornin' to see Gateshead?"

I looked at the turkey, then I looked at Joan, then I looked at her mam. I stubbed out my cigar (I was feeling a bit woozy, anyhow), and tried to look as though it wasn't my idea, this football thing.

"By you've kept that quiet, George," laughed Joan's mam, "You're goin' to' tittle off to the football, are thee?"

"Let them go, Mam. We can cope without them."

"Nay, lass, Aa'll see to the dinner. Thee get theeself away as well. Ye like football. Aa'll manage the turkey. No boid's goain' to get the better of Ida Speed."

I wasn't too sure, though. Could she handle it alone?

Joan and I did our bit for the morrow; we found we could prepare the veg and have a drink at one and the same time. After a few glasses of Newcastle Brown, however, I got to thinking about this Christmas dinner. Could we risk leaving the whole turkey operation in the hands of one person, capable as she might be?

"As I've been peeling these spuds, I've been thinking," I said.

I leaned forward in true Churchillian manner aiming to imitate that great leader. Pluckily, in the search for authenticity, I relit my cigar. I puffed it into life, cleared my throat, screwed up my face, and hunched my shoulders. Joan looked at me as though I was not quite right.

"In the grave, nay, desperate crisis we find ourselves in tonight, we must never surrender. We must face the challenge of the Turkey with heads held high. I propose we have a council of WAAAR."

Castle on a Cloud

"What on earth are you talking about? You're drunk!" said Joan, merrily.

"Don't you like my Winston Churchill act?"

"Oh! That's who it was supposed to be?"

"Don't be nasty," I laughed, "Seriously, Joan, I think we should check our plans for the bird. We can't leave everything to your mam. It's not fair," I said, before having another sup of Newcastle Brown.

"Aa think we should bung it in the oven about eight o'clock. It should be ready by the time we've been to the match and 'ad a quick pint at the Cannon befower they close," said her dad.

"Don't be daft George, and what's this about a pint?" laughed her mam, downing her second glass of port and lemon. "Aa'll tell you what though, Joan, has your landlady got a roastin' tin?"

"It won't be big enough, Mam."

"Have you got two roastin' tins, then, luv?" Her dad was getting a trifle hilarious.

"That's not so gormless, Joan. Have you got two with a bakin' tray underneath?"

"I think so, but what about the muslin to cover its breast, though?"

"It's not goin' to a fancy dress ball, is it?!! A'll tell thee summat for nothin', lass, Aa didn't bring any muslin. What does the boid want muslin for, anyroad?"

"Well, the book says you cover it with muslin soaked with melted butter, Mam."

"Aa've nivver done that with the goose, luv."

"But a goose is more fatty than a turkey, Mam. Mind, we'll be using up our butter ration, but it's all in a good cause." Joan turned to me. "I've just had a brilliant thought, Paul. Your Airtex vests are sort of meshy, a bit like muslin; we could use one of those!"

"Oh great," I said, "You think my vests are good for any old thing."

"Oh ho!" laughed her dad, "a turkey in a vest! What about Paul's underpants? The boid would be more decent then."

"Ah doan't know about Paul bein' tipsy, George, Aa think the brown ale's too strong for thee, as well!"

I came downstairs with my spare vest, that vest would never be the same again, I knew it. We'd have to get another one in the January sales. Not only that – dry bread for a week. By now, I was wishing I hadn't started this 'council of war' thing. I could hear the tinkling of glasses and the sounds of laughter from Ma Davidson's kitchen. A 'council of war'? The meeting had got out of hand. It didn't sound like a war council to me, mind it didn't sound like a temperance convention either. Then I heard Joan's dad in an inebriated, yet pleasant, baritone voice, burst into one of his First World War songs.

"Belgium put the kybosh on the Kaiser,
Britain took a stick and made him sore
When we enter Germanee
Knock the Kaiser it will be...."

What would the Davidsons think if they suddenly arrived on the doorstep tonight and heard all this strange jollity in their usually quiet kitchen? In my somewhat squiffy state, I had a daft idea. I'll knock on the front door – that'll give them a big laugh.

A blast of icy air greeted me as I opened the door. That knocker made a big bang. Three big bangs. The noise gave *me* a scare and I was expecting it. I closed the door quickly.

The singing stopped.

"What's that?" I heard Joan shout, followed by a yell and the sound of breaking glass from the kitchen. "It's not them. God, say it's not them! No! No! Where's Paul?"

I hadn't expected this reaction, It seemed that *I'd* put the kybosh on the party. I made for the staircase to escape from the scene, thinking they might think Christmas carol singers were in the street. I wasn't quick enough.

Opening the kitchen door, Joan saw me at the foot of the stairs. "Who is it?" she cried.

I laughed diffidently. "Just a joke, Joan. Just a bit of fun."

"Don't say *you* knocked on the door. You frightened the life out of us. I thought it was them come back early!" She sounded a smidgen upset.

Why did everything seem to go downbeat, just because of a knock on the front door?

I walked into the kitchen. "It was just a prank," I said, to all and sundry.

"Aye," said her Mam.

"Aye," said her Dad, on his hands and knees, busily wiping the floor with his hankie and collecting the remains of his broken tumbler.

"A joke, just a joke."

Nobody laughed.

Castle on a Cloud

Later, in bed. "That was a silly thing to do, Paul. My heart's still pounding. I haven't forgiven you yet."
"You will by morning, love, won't you? It's Christmas Day."
"I might, I might."

She did of course. It was an upbeat sort of day all round. Knocks on doors forgotten. Yes, upbeat, just as you would expect a Christmas Day to be. Gateshead won, the turkey was cooked to perfection, and we sat down just in time to listen to the King's Speech on the wireless.
"He don't sound well," said Joan's mam.
"Aa'll tell thee what," said her dad, "Aa bet his grandson's not listenin'."
"Well he won't be you daft 'ayporth, he's only weeks owld. Fancy, the little bairn'll be Charles the thoid one day. Aa'll tell *thee* wot, Aa won't be around to see it!"
It *had* been upbeat.

There *was* a bit of turkey left. I reckoned we could have some for sandwiches later, some at midday on Boxing Day, a whack for my mam, and plenty still left over. Forget about the Christmas of the turkey, it was going to be the week of the turkey.

On Boxing Day afternoon, the four of us went across to Newcastle, her mam and dad were catching the train for home. Her dad was on duty early the next morning. We stood on draughty platform nine. Joan's parents had been quiet on the tram, but now her Mam spoke, "Listen, your dad and me were talkin' in bed this mornin'. Your dad says we could loan thees the money for the deposit on a place of your own. We've got a bob or two in the Co-op bank tha knows. You could pay it back without interest."

"That's very kind of you both," I said, I turned to Joan, "What do you think? Personally I wouldn't like to borrow money unless we could clear it pretty quickly. The snag is we would have the mortgage payments every month."

"Well, I don't know, Paul. I would love our own place, I hate our rooms, but I wouldn't like a big debt, I don't know."

"Well, luv," said her Dad, "think about it and let us know. Aa could let you have a hundred, a bit more even and there wouldn't be any hurry to pay us back. Aa know tha both would as soon as you could."

"Anyway, thanks, Dad, we *will* think about it."

10

POSH NO LONGER

We thought about it. Too right we did. We discussed it on the tram going back to Low Fell. We talked about it going down to my Mam's on that Boxing Day night. (We went bearing post-Christmas gifts – a couple of pounds of turkey breast and a big fat leg.) We were still mulling it over when we got back home, still considering the pros and cons in bed.

I was chary. "Par for the course!" was Joan's comment.

"But look, Joan. In another twelve months or so, if you're still working, we'll probably have saved up enough ourselves. We had a bit to start with, didn't we?"

"Yes, I know, but don't forget we'll need some furniture. I know Mam's giving us that gateleg table, my bed, chairs, other bits and pieces, but we'll need a three piece suite of some sort, even if its second-hand. Then there're curtains, rugs."

"I'm looking forward to having a new vest as well, pet," I laughed.

"Be serious for once, Paul. Anyway, we'd better get some sleep, goodnight," she said, turning her back on me.

This loan thing was undoubtedly to the forefront of her mind.

In truth, for weeks, the subject was never far from my thoughts either, particularly after the return of the Davidsons from Kent.

One miserable snowy day in February, a day when Ma had harped on about slush on the doormat, Joan closed our room door. "Well, aren't you getting sick of her nagging ways? Don't you think we should take the money?"

"It's OK saying that, but what if you should have a baby? How long would your dad have to wait for us to repay his hard-earned savings?"

"They're for his retirement, Paul, that's over ten years away, there'd be no panic. Besides, I'd better not have a baby, loan or no loan, not until we *do* have our own place. God! A baby here in rooms!" she cried. "But that wouldn't happen, she'd throw us out. You know what she said about families."

"Calm down, pet. We'll work something out."

Joan tried to work something out. She was forever pondering the issue. Most Saturday evenings, whilst supposedly listening to Saturday Night Theatre on the Home Service, she'd be at the table perusing our savings book and engaging in mythical calculations. Every now and then she'd shake her head, frown, and bite her pencil. Meanwhile, flopped in an armchair, reading, or just listening if the play was any good, I'd pretend not to notice her wistful planning. It was difficult; sensing her there figuring out the possibilities, my firm resolve not to be saddled with such a huge debt became distinctly wobbly.

Then came the 15th March – just five days before our first wedding anniversary. That was the date for sure; it was the day that clothes rationing ended. We were on our way home that night, having seen Humphrey Bogart in 'The Treasure of the Sierra Madre'. What a film! That was our considered verdict. The line uttered in rasping broken English by the scruffy-looking, walrus-moustachioed Mexican bandit masquerading as a 'Federale' lawman, was the high spot for me: "You ask us where are our badges, gringo? Show you our badges? We don't need no stinking badges."

I repeated the line betwixt chortles walking up the hill. Joan's laughter ceased after my fifth performance. "You're getting as bad as Don at repeating yourself."

"Thanks very much." I said huffily. Surely I wasn't really that bad?

I changed the subject. "You'll be going out shopping tomorrow afternoon, Joan?"

"Why do you say that?"

"You'll be having a clothes spree?"

"If I could afford to," she said ruefully, "but a house is more important just now."

It was a spur of the moment thing – I stopped under the light of a street lamp and pulled her close. "Joan, love."

"Yes?" those limpid brown eyes look puzzled.

"Joan, let's do it. We'll take your Dad's offer of a loan, eh?"

Her pounce was unexpected but pleasant; I never tired of her kisses

Castle on a Cloud

or her cool cheek brushing mine. "Oh, Paul! What's made you change your mind, darling?"

I was a 'darling' with knobs on now. "I want you to be happy, love. Mind, we must pay it back as soon as we can – two years at the most. We'll have to be extra careful, we mustn't have a baby."

As we walked, she hugged my arm. Chirpy was the word for her now. "No, that would be disastrous; I'd have to give up work. You know, Paul, we rely on your willpower too much though. You know, when we haven't a 'thingy'. The trouble is that those packs of three soon go when you're around."

"Well, you can't blame me, you're just so irresistible, Joan." I laughed. "The trouble is, those things become expensive."

"I wonder if you can buy them wholesale?"

"Now you're being daft. You mean find out if you can buy a gross at a time?"

"Well, if you could, they would last you a month or two," she chuckled. "Mind, it's a pity we can't recycle them!"

"I'll work on it!" I laughed.

"You haven't got a prototype to experiment with!"

"I could have in an hour or so," I suggested, as we reached the Davidsons' back door.

She clocked me with her handbag, but it made no difference – if I'd wanted the necessary artefact for experimental purposes, it was soon to hand.

Now that we'd made the decision about the loan, we looked around, assessing our price range. We would have to settle for a pair of flats – that way we could have the rent from the second flat to help. Gateshead had many streets of paired terraced flats – an upstairs and a downstairs – each with its own front door. Plus most had a separate backyard. The streets dated from Victorian and Edwardian times; some were now slums, but others were well kept and considered 'ever so respectable'. The snag was that in the post-war world of house shortages, even properties for sale were soon snapped up with people often willing to pay more than the asking price. Whether the adverts appeared in the Newcastle Evening Chronicle or were displayed in the windows of local estate agents, the results were the same – 'Sorry, you're too late'.

Then we had a stroke of luck – old Witherstone, Joan's boss, came up trumps. It was the day that Joan had been given time off to check on a property, but had returned to the office disappointed after another unsuccessful mission.

"Listen, Joan," he'd said, "I know a fellow in Pattinson Estate Agents; I'll ask him to look out for something."

So it came about that one day in the Wimbledon fortnight of 1949 (the Wimbledon when pictures of Gorgeous Gussie Moran's lace-trimmed panties were plastered in the newspapers), we were inspecting a downstairs flat in Dover Road, a middle market area. Not as swanky as Low Fell, but not as crummy as Askew Road. The price of £650 was within our hastily revised budget. Better still, the twenty-five shillings a week rent from Mrs Dawson who lived with her husband and little girl in the upper flat, would help to pay the mortgage.

"What do you think of the street?" I asked as I opened the front door.

"It looks quiet enough. Except for the bus stop outside."

"There's only one bus an hour along here, Joan. It's not a main road." I held up the house key. "This could be the passport to our own place, Joan."

"Don't speak too soon, love."

We entered the short passage; there was a door on our left. Joan opened it. "This must be the front bedroom – with a fireplace too. It's quite bright and roomy and they've left the curtains."

We explored further, the living room, the second bedroom, both looking into the backyard; and then the kitchenette. "The scullery's small," I said.

Joan laughed, "Get up to date, love. We don't call it a scullery any more. It's small because part has been converted into the bathroom, *and* with a gas water heater. Look!"

"I wondered where the bathroom was going to be," I said. "The lav must be in the yard – an outside netty still, love!"

"We can't have everything, Paul. I think we should get straight back to Pattinson's and take it. It's no good humming and hawing."

I could sense an undertone of poignancy in her voice.

"Right, love, let's do that then."

She looked surprised, I wasn't usually so dynamic.

We wasted no time that day; our offer was accepted and then a visit to the Abbey National confirmed our mortgage. Could it be just a matter of weeks before we were moving in? Would there be a snag?

Witherstone had recommended a solicitor – Conker and Son, Grey

Castle on a Cloud

Street, Newcastle. He believed it was an old-fashioned firm, but his brother had used them a few years before for conveyancing and everything had gone smoothly then.

So one hot sunny Wednesday afternoon, me in my best suit, wanting to take my tie off and open my shirt collar; Joan wishing she wasn't wearing her smart but warm, light-blue jacket over her blouse and skirt, we ventured into the famous street. The heat reflecting off the classical Georgian buildings was overpowering, but we had an appointment, an appointment requiring sober dress.

The broad street was enhanced at the upper end by the splendid Theatre Royal and the imposing Grey's Monument. Grey's Monument – the tall column which was a memorial to the Prime Minister who carried both the 1832 Reform Bill and the act abolishing slavery through Parliament.

We wandered down the parade. Most of the premises were occupied by building societies, banks, financial institutions, law offices. Conker and Son were near the foot of the street on the way to the Quayside.

"Here we are," Joan said. The brass plate was well worn, the name now faint, the location, 'FIRST FLOOR', even fainter. It was cooler inside. We climbed the stairs. On the landing was a glass door, the top panel was marked ' ONKE   S N'.

Joan was quicker than me on the uptake. "This is it."

I knocked and opened the door. We entered through a narrow, dimly lit passageway, squeezing past the mountains of files that lined each wall. Files that threatened to tumble down on top of us. They'd been there some time I guessed – so yellow and dusty were they. Dubiously, I looked at Joan, Joan looked at me. Had we boobed with our choice of solicitor?

A strident cry of "Hello!" pierced the air. It was too late now to cut and run. At the end of the short hallway was a small office, its door open. A grey-haired, bespectacled lady reminding me of a dizzy Margaret Rutherford looked up from her desk and gave a bright smile of welcome. "Come in, come in," she twittered, "You'll be Mr and Mrs Potts? Nice to see you, always nice to see a client, we don't get many these days you know."

I was fascinated by her chin; it was going sixteen to the dozen, almost like a ventriloquist's dummy. "The impatient folk today want whipper-snapper solicitors, not gentleman of the old school." She sighed, "Alas! Those days have gone, gone beyond recall." I felt a small twang on one of my heart-strings as she creaked to her feet. "Anyway, sir, follow me. Young Mr Conker has been expecting you."

She ushered us into a larger office with more dusty files piled on the floor and the furniture. An ancient, white-haired fellow sat behind the huge desk. Framed by mounds of papers, he peered at us over thick pebble-like glasses. Could this possibly be young Mr Conker? Whether or not, *his* days of whippersnappery were over.

He struggled to his feet and stretched out a shaky gnarled hand. His frame was skeleton-like, his face gaunt; his jacket hung loosely off his narrow shoulders.

"Aah! Mr and Mrs Potts, at last!" Were we the personalities of the week, or was it of the year in the Conker chambers? Everyone so glad to see us?

"Miss Tavistock will have told you," he wheezed, "I'm Conker the younger. I'm the last of the Conkers! No more you know. Yes, yes – Conker the elder conked out many years ago." He gave a whinnying laugh. "Sit down, sit down," he beckoned. "Just move those documents onto the floor."

We cleared the chairs and brushed our hands free of dust.

"Excuse all the papers; I'm going to have a clear out in due course. In due course," he muttered as he fumbled in his jacket pockets. "Ah! here's my pen. Now the file, the file."

There was a file on his blotting pad, a file in mint condition. Reading it upside down I could make out 'Dover Road'. I waited.

He leaned forward, his head only a few inches from the desk. I thought he was going to drop off to sleep. "Ah! Of course! Here it is, here it is," he croaked. "The whole thing seems to be quite straightforward; I'll need a bit of information, a few formalities you know, a signature or two, that sort of thing. Then I'll process things. Get things moving, eh? Get things moving, that's what you want. Then I'll see you again."

Bumblingly, he explained the complexities of conveyancing. Title deeds, searches, fees, surveyors, stamp duty, restrictive covenants. I couldn't follow it all. Yes, yes, all well and good I thought, but when will we get the keys? When will we gain entrance? It didn't seem straightforward, not the way the old fellow was telling it.

But gain entrance? My mind wandered for a moment. Let's just move forward in time. What do I do on the day we get the key? If we ever get

Castle on a Cloud

the key. What do I do when I open the door? Carry Joan over the threshold? Probably not; a belated gesture indeed. Certainly not, if there's a queue at the bus stop.

My attention came back to the present to find Conker had completed his talk-in. All we had to do now was to sign on a few dotted lines. It was then that he must somehow have perceived our two anxious faces, even through those pebble lenses. "It seems complicated, but not to worry, it will all come right, it will all come right," he said.

Grimly gripping his desk for support, he got to his feet. I felt the coldness of his fingers as we shook hands, a strange coldness on this sweltering day. "I'll be in touch, Mr and Mrs Potts. Very soon I hope."

We left that queer, antediluvian office and hit the oven that was Grey Street. Perspiring, I pulled off my tie and opened my shirt collar to give some relief from the heat; but that move didn't stop me sweating over doddery Conker the younger. Could he finalise things before he expired? Would he lose the Dover Road folder? My qualms increased when I remembered seeing a meerschaum pipe and a box of Swan Vestas on his desk. Would his trembling hand accidentally drop a lighted match on the tinder-like files? God! The contents of the office would make a giant bonfire.

On the tram back to Gateshead, Joan also expressed her misgivings. It didn't help when I mentioned the pipe; she hadn't noticed that – or the matches. My big mouth!

No need to worry! Oh we of little faith! Three cheers for Conker the younger and a cry of Hosannah for Witherstone. The conveyancing went through without a hitch and in good time too.

There only remained the pleasant task of notifying our landlady. We had a fight over that. "I'll do it, Joan."

"No you won't Paul, I want the pleasure."

"Alright, we'll both tell her."

"Mrs Davidson, we want to give you a fortnight's notice that we'll be leaving," said Joan.

"A fortnight we'd agreed," I added brightly.

We were coming through their kitchen late one Saturday afternoon in the middle of September. We'd had a grand day. For starters, we'd bought a second-hand three piece Rexine-covered suite *and* an old wardrobe for delivery to Dover Road on the big moving-in day. Then to crown it all we'd gone to see United play Manchester City. Four goals to two for the Magpies! George Robledo, the Chilean born forward was the star. Newly signed George was already Joan's favourite, even ahead of Jackie Milburn. Not only did he have a Yorkshire mother, but she declared that he had the sexiest brown legs she had ever clapped eyes on. This sort of talk would have upset me on any other day, (how could she cast Jackie to the scrapheap, and was she not happy with my fine limbs?), but Newcastle's glorious win and the thought of reclining on our very own bargain sofa eased my hurt.

"You've got a snip there!" the man in the loud check jacket had said as we stood in the 'Superior Used Furniture Emporium' on Coatsworth Road. "You've caught me on a good day. Twenty pounds for the fine suite and look – just a fiver for the wardrobe – cheap at twice the price! The suite's almost new, hardly been sat on," he added, as he counted out our cash – ten one pound notes and three big rare white crisp fivers. (The kind that looked like handwritten promissory notes signed personally by the Chief Cashier of the Bank of England himself.) We'd put *them* away from my summer bonus; not in the Post Office – but in a biscuit tin. Better than figures in a bank book. When the mood took me I would open the tin, take those notes out, and admire them. I was sorry to see them go, even in exchange for seventy-five per cent of a fine three-piece suite that had accommodated very few bums.

Yes, it had been a good day for us so far and our enjoyment was continuing. Ma's pince-nez dropped off her nose, Mr Davidson, mouth open, looked over the top of his Evening Chronicle. "What do you mean, leaving?" said the witch. "You're not giving us much notice – two weeks!"

"That's what we'd agreed," I said, adopting a studied, Cary Grant kind of nonchalance that I'd been practising for this very scene.

"Two weeks, either way," added Joan.

"You must have known earlier. I suppose you think you've got better rooms, young lady," Ma said petulantly.

"Oh no! Not rooms. We've got our own place in Dover Road."

"Oh! That's good for you," said Mr Davidson.

Ma Davidson gave him an icy look – he would suffer for that remark. "Dover Road! That's not Low Fell, though. Not quite the same, is it."

"It's not as posh as Low Fell, but nevertheless, they seem decent people down there, Mrs Davidson. Even if they don't put on airs."

Castle on a Cloud

For a moment I thought Joan was going to stick her tongue out and say, 'So there!' But she didn't.

I wandered from room to room. We had more or less got settled into our flat a couple of hours earlier – our bits of furniture sorted into place. Joan was cooking the Saturday tea – fried egg, bacon and mushrooms, with fried bread and tomato sauce. Afterwards, we'd have the big cream cake I had collected from the bakery just around the corner. After all, it was a sort of celebration tea.

"What on earth are you doing, love? You seem to be pottering about," she said, as I poked my nose into the kitchen for a sniff of the forthcoming meal.

"Just surveying, just surveying, Joan. Just counting our rooms, admiring the views from the windows, that sort of thing. Looking around our estate, if you like."

"Will you ever stop being a daft cracker? Even you can't think that the vistas from our windows are envied by lesser mortals. At the front you're looking at a lamp-post and the houses opposite, at the back you're looking at the coalhouse and the lav."

"Yes, but it's our coalhouse and our netty, don't forget."

"After we've paid the mortgage, they are, Paul!"

She brought the plates to the table, took off her pinny and pulled up a chair. "Ah, that's better, a sit down at last. We've had a hard day, Paul. At least we've got the curtains at the windows and the bed put up. We've just got to make it, then we can relax. It'll be lovely having our own place."

"Our own place, yes. Did I ever tell you that I'm the Grand Panjandrum? Don called me that when I was a kid," I said, spreading Heinz Tomato Sauce on my fried bread.

"You've kept that dark," she said, as though she knew what I was talking about; but then curiosity got the better of her. "What the devil is a Grand Panjandrum, anyway?"

"Oh! just someone who achieves marvellous things, such as marrying someone like you, except there's no one like you; getting our own house and having nice kids. Have I never told you before?"

"Hang on, I agree the first bit about marvellous me," she said dipping a piece of bread into a runny egg, "But we've only a flat, and we haven't got children. You're only a Lesser Panjandrum, if that," she laughed.

"I'm working on it, I'm working on it."
"You'd better not be working on children yet."
"No," I laughed, "but you don't mind me rehearsing?"
Joan put her hand on mine, her eyes were shining. "I never mind that, Paul, you know that."
I jumped up. "Let's make the bed, love; then I'll wash the dishes whilst you have a bath. Don't empty the water and I'll hop in after you're finished."
"I'm pleased you said after I'm done!"
"Well, I haven't checked the bath for size yet, love. I don't want us to get stuck."
"Well, don't get your tape measure out tonight," she laughed.
Happily washing the dishes and listening to Joan next door splashing, I burst into song. "I've built a stairway to Paradise, doodle-do-do do-do-do." Then I heard Joan join me in counterpoint from the bath – the girl had hidden talents! Even after knowing her for five years she kept surprising me.
She startled me once more when she dashed out of the bathroom almost knocking a plate out of my hand and swept past wrapped in a skimpy towel. "I forgot my nightie," she laughed, as she disappeared into the bedroom.
"Don't bother about that," I shouted after her.
"Ha, ha!" came her cry.
We went to bed early that night; we'd had a tiring day. Not too tiring mind.
Afterwards, we sat up pleasantly fatigued.
"You know, love," I yawned. "I've been worrying about you."
"Whatever for?"
"I was thinking you might be upset that you've left posh Low Fell for down-to-earth Dover Road."
She laughed, "I don't think so love. I know what my mam would say about some of the supposedly posh Low Fellites – they're all fur coat and no knickers!"
"You didn't tell me that before, Joan. Would that apply to that bonny young woman that used to smile at me? The one who wore the imitation mink coat? You know, the one who lived opposite the Davidsons?"
Fortunately, the only thing she found to hand was a pillow, not as menacing as a handbag.

11

OIL AND WATER

As winter approached, we were engrossed in the novelty of setting up house. Bit by bit, we gathered the paraphernalia generally considered essential in any respectable family home. In Joan's eyes, these were such things as a dressing table, a chest of drawers, a Ewbank Carpet sweeper, a kitchen cabinet, a gas boiler *and* a dolly peg (for possing the washing) – second-hand all of them. Those things were OK I suppose, but in my eyes, a record-player, a scarcely thumbed Oxford Abridged Dictionary, a 1934 Pears Cyclopedia in mint condition, and an atlas of the world circa 1938 with British Empire territory indicated in bright red on almost every page, were equally important in a cultured, well-rounded household.

I had struck a bargain for the record-player at our favourite 'Used Furniture Emporium' and the canny man in the check suit had thrown in a box of '78' records for free. What an impact those wax discs had on my musical education. Vocal gems from the 'Vagabond King', a Regal Zonophone record of music from 'Yankee Doodle Dandy' with *the* Reginald Dixon on the organ, a Parlophone recording of 'Der Frohliche Wanderer' (that meant Happy Wanderer, it said so on the label). The latter was sung in German by the Obernkirchen Children's Choir. Not only that – if I ever got tired of this foreign air I could melt the disc down and make it into a plant pot.

Then there were the tomes, the tomes I had bought at a veritable cornucopia of a second-hand bookstall in Newcastle's Grainger Indoor Market one lucky Saturday. It was a doubly lucky day – we had gone browsing into the market after having seen United win at St James' Park. Making a bee-line for the shop, I had left Joan queuing at one of the fruit and veg stalls – late Saturday afternoon was half-price time, the greengrocer's trying to flog off overripe stock before the weekend shutdown. Joan did OK; a carrier-bag full of mushrooms, tomatoes, apples and a cauli, all for 1/6d; better than my old books, she averred. That was surprising, she didn't often talk rubbish.

We had continued to acquire other useful bits and bobs – Mam, in a bout of magnanimity, gave us her old Acme wringer. (Don and I half carried, half dragged that mangle along cobbly back lanes to our flat.) Joan's mam chipped in with pots and pans. The highlight for Joan was the day her mam's old treadle sewing machine arrived – courtesy of old Dick Ramsbottom. Dick, a neighbour of her parents in York, mosied about the North, driving a Bedford van and delivering bits and pieces, here and there, now and then. To do Mrs Speed a favour, he made a detour from Sunderland to drop off the Singer. Petrol rationing seemed no problem to old Dick.

With Christmas coming, Joan now decreed that house decorating was to be the name of the game; in my view nothing more than a necessary chore, but from her peculiar feminine perspective, almost a pleasure.

One Saturday morning, we were in the midst of near chaos, when there was a knock on the front door. I was standing on a chair whitewashing the kitchen ceiling and beginning to look like a snowman, Joan was up the ladders in the living room hanging wallpaper. I had convinced Joan that she had the talent to be wallpaperer-in-chief, she had all the skills and finesse required for the job. Joan wasn't sure whether that was good or bad.

I pretended not to hear the rat-tat-tat; I was hoping Joan would go to see who it was.

The knock came again, this time louder. "Who's that?" I shouted nearly falling off the chair.

"Damn!" came a cry from the living room, "I've cut this piece too short." Then a muttering and a pause, before: "There's only one way to find out!" I quickly figured that meant me getting down from the chair and going to the door. It also meant discarding my headgear – a whitewashed-splattered handkerchief knotted at the corners.

"Why me?" I muttered.

Joan frowned, and descended the ladders. In some frustration, she scratched her head thus displacing her Mrs Mopp headscarf. The scarf, now sitting jauntily on one side, made her look crazily attractive. Her pleasure in decorating, however, seemed to have faded. "These walls are skew-whiff. I've got enough on my plate without answering the door to every Tom, Dick and Harry."

So it was me opening the door, it was me that was knocked for six by the sight of the tall blonde fellow standing there. Brother Cecil; Cec who I'd thought was at the other end of the country, twenty-year-old, pleasant-mannered Cec. In civvies.

"Hello! I thought you were in those Oxford barracks. Have you been demobbed?"

He laughed, "Not yet. Next year I think. I'm on leave."

"Come in, Cec, nice to see you. Watch out for Joan, though, she's in a bit of a mood."

"I heard that, you cheeky devil! I'm nothing of the kind," Joan said, putting down her scissors and smiling.

My, how her disposition could change! She had a soft spot for Cec – her favourite brother-in-law. "Have you been demobbed?" she said looking at his old raincoat and grey flannels.

"No, I got a surprise leave. Demob? Next year, I hope." We seemed to be going around in circles.

"Mam said you two were decorating, I thought you might want a hand. That's why I've got my old civvies on. I've put a bit of weight on with all the food and exercise at camp, this old clobber is beginning to split at the seams. I'll have to by some new stuff when I'm discharged, I won't be so lucky as you, Den – getting a demob suit."

"Well, you weren't in the war, my bonny lad. But talking about help, you can whitewash the passage ceiling. (What was that saying about a gift horse?) "That's if you can reach standing on a chair. Joan's hogging the ladders."

"*You* can have them Den, if you want to do the papering." She had lapsed without effort into 'Den' mode.

"No, love, you're paperhanger extraordinaire."

"Oh, I'll manage on a chair," Cecil said, taking off his coat and rolling his sleeves up. "Lead me to the whitewash."

"Here, Cec," I said magnanimously, pouring some of my whitewash into an old bucket, "Have the big brush, I'll make do with the little one." I turned to Joan. "It'll take me longer with this mind, Joan, you'll make allowances?"

The morning passed by swiftly – thanks to my 'new' record-player. Talk about 'Music While You Work'! Things became quite raucous when I played the Yankee Doodle record. The cacophony of two James

Cagneys and a Joan Leslie was a fearsome sound and things went further downhill when the needle got stuck in a groove. Over there! Over there! Over there! Over there!

Joan switched the machine off. "That's enough of that, you're not concentrating, Den. You've missed a bit."

"Where, Joan?"

"Over there!" she laughed, dodging my attempt to give her a white nose.

"Hey, Joan, look at the time! It's time to lay down our brushes; we'll be late for the match."

"What do you think, Cecil?" said Joan, "Should I make a sandwich?"

"Seems like a good idea to me, I've finished this ceiling, anyway." Good old sensible Cecil and such a canny lad into the bargain. He could come and whitewash our house any time.

But Cecil was only home for three days. "Back to Oxford on Monday," he'd said, "and I don't work on a Sunday." So bang went that plan. It was a blow, but we managed to complete the refurbishment a couple of weeks before Christmas, thus achieving Joan's deadline.

That red-letter day, we cleaned our brushes and picked all the sticky bits of wallpaper off our footwear for the last time. Joan wandered from room to room – she had a proud self-satisfied look about her, I suppose it was the sort of smirk that Michelangelo would have had when he finally put his tall ladder away in the Cistine Chapel. I didn't inspect our handiwork – I just flopped on the settee waiting for her to finish her appraisal. At last she dropped onto the sofa beside me. "Paul, love."

Oh ho, I thought, what's coming now?

"Shall we ask Mam and Dad to come up from York for Christmas?"

"So you can show off your decorating talent? We'll have to get a hold of a bed for the spare room."

"Well, we need one in any case. We should get one at our furniture shop. Your Christmas bonus will easily cover it."

"True." Upheaval over, I was in an expansive mood.

"We could ask your Mam and the family on Christmas night, Dad's never seen them and Mam only that once when she came up to Gateshead to look for a house for us, remember?"

"I remember." Would I ever forget? Mam wasn't at her most hospitable that day – she was anti-everything that would mean her

Castle on a Cloud

beloved Dennis leaving home. I hadn't told Joan of the uneasy tension that developed – her mam obviously had also played it down.

"Do you think that's a good idea?"

"Well, it's Christmas, love, and your Mam's never been here yet, although we've asked her."

"OK, Joan," I said, fingers crossed.

Christmas night, we heard the front door opening followed by an 'Oo hoo!' and the wiping of feet on the doormat. I jumped up nervously, "Here they are!"

Things had gone well up to now on this Yuletide holiday. Joan's parents had arrived on the morning of Christmas Eve – just in time for three football fans to get to the match and see Newcastle beat Wolverhampton Wanderers two-nil, thanks to an Ernie Taylor shot and a Christmas-box own goal gifted by the Wolves. Then we'd had a good night (no mysterious knocks at the front door); and today, a nice Christmas dinner, even without the presence of a giant turkey. Instead, we'd made inroads into a succulent vestless goose from The Shambles.

However, that was then, this was now – the meeting of the in-laws – uncharted territory.

"All the best everybody, come in, come in."

Mam, Rob, Don and Stephen entered the living room; Joan's Dad jumped up as I made the introductions.

"Reet glad to meet you, Agnes. A Merry Christmas."

"George, isn't it?" said Mam, a shade superciliously, offering her rouged cheek. Into her fifties, she could still look smart.

"How are you, Rob?" said Joan's mam from the settee.

"Very canny, Ida. Divvent get up, you look cushy there." Her Mam didn't try – once she was down she was down.

"'Ello, Don.'Ow are ye lad?"

"Fine, Mr Speed," said Don, shaking hands firmly. "You're not driving a Pacific today then? *I* used to work in the railway sheds you know."

"Aye, ye told me that at t'wedding, lad. But Aa'm beggared if Aa'm driving an engine today. And you're Stephen, the quiet one?"

"I am, man, I am that," said brother Stephen, giving a nervous giggle and quickly melting into the background. He was becoming more nervous and withdrawn every day. We had seen a marked deterioration on our last visit to Mam's.

Joan bustled around serving drinks as people found seats. Rob an armchair, Joan's mam, dad and my mam squeezed on the settee, Don in the other armchair.

"Ta, Joan," said Rob, "Broon ale! This is me forst since befower Christmas dinner. A'v worked up a reet thorst."

"You've been asleep since dinner," laughed Mam. "Don's got some bottles in that carrier bag, Den," she added.

Well, things seemed to have started all right. Could it last? Only time would tell.

At first the conversation was of the weather, the food shortages, the power cuts — a happy consensus prevailed. Even politics caused only the merest hint of discordancy. Mother was a staunch Labourite, so too was Joan's dad. Her mam, usually so forthright and independent-minded, succumbed to the long held working class tradition — vote as your man votes. Vote Labour.

Rob, however, did add a note of cynicism to the discussion. "They're aall the saym, politicians, just lookin' to feather their nests. Aall of them, from Ramsay MacDonald to Winston Chorchill." Even this statement caused little dissent.

"Aye, they're all the same," said brother Don, now settled comfortably and puffing his pipe. "From Ramsay MacDonald to Winston."

At that point, Mam, supping her third rum and orange, slipped into a mawkish mode, "I wish Cecil had been home for Christmas," she said to one and all. "It's years since I had all my lads home together. Going to Midnight Mass together. Having Christmas dinner together. I'll never have them all at Christmas again now Den's a married man. I didn't want him to leave home, Ida, you know. I got such a shock when I found he wasn't getting married in a Catholic church."

"Hold on, lass," said Ida, "don't be daft. They mek a lovely couple, Agnes. They'll be happy together, Aa'm sure."

"I hope so, I hope so."

I could see Joan's face flushing. I butted in: "Mam, don't bring that Catholic thing up again, I know I've made a good choice."

"Oh! I've nothing against Joan, you know that. It was only the principle."

"Let's forget it then, Mam. How about a game?" I added, anxious to perk up the party. "Let's play housey-housey, I've got the tombola cards and counters here, penny a time, winner takes all. If I shout a number on your card, put a counter on it."

"Aye," said Joan's dad, "Let's have a game, Aa could do with sevenpence."

"Housey!" said Mam, "That's an intellectual pursuit I must say. I'd rather read a book. A Dickens or a Trollope. Do you read books, Ida?"

"Not much, Agnes."

"Herrumph."

"Come on, Mam," said Don coaxingly, through a cloud of blue smoke, "You can't read a book on Christmas night. Ee, I've never played housey since I was in the RAF Regiment. It was in Holland, there was a lull in the fighting at the time. I had some experiences in the war. I could tell you some stories, Mr Speed."

"Don't bother telling stories, Don," said Mam, her cheeks rosy and not just with the rouge. "If that's the choice, I'd rather play the silly game."

Housey was a not a howling success, the attention span of the assembled company was substandard. First game, Joan's dad won his sevenpence, second game he won again.

"I wanted thirty-three," announced Don.

"Thirty-three was out, Don," I said.

"Was it? I must have been thinking about that time in Holland," he laughed.

"Aa don't know what Aa wanted, Pawl," said Joan's mam, shifting in her seat. "Aa've knocked the counters all over me lap."

"I wanted twenty-seven," said Mam.

"Twenty-seven was out, Mam. You mustn't have heard."

"You're not shouting loud enough then, Den," she said testily.

"We'd better stop then. If I shout any louder Mrs Dawson upstairs will wonder what's going on."

"That's fine with me, let's stop." said Mam.

"Ney, Agnes," said Joan's dad, rattling a handful of coppers, "it's a grand game. What do you think, Rob?" he added. Rob's response was a snore. Patently, he'd never been in contention for the sevenpence.

"He's asleep," said Don, sagely.

It was then Joan got up, "I'll bring the sandwiches in." I looked at my watch – was it only that time? A bit early for supper surely? Although, OK, taking everything into account, perhaps Joan had made a wise move.

The sandwiches went down well. At first.

"This ham's nice, Joan," said Mam.

"Mam brought it up from York."

"Oh! A bit of under the counter, Ida, eh? I wish I could get my hands on this under the counter stuff."

Joan's mam took it in her stride. "Aa just know somebody, Agnes. It's not what you'd call under the counter as such."

"It's not right, though, really, is it Ida? Fair shares for all – that's my motto."

"If Aa can see to me bairns, it's alright, that's what Aa say."

Thankfully, it was then that Rob woke up with a start and pulled out his pocket watch. Stephen must have bumped into his chair – he'd been pacing about the room, eating sandwiches on his perambulations and talking to himself.

"Ee lass, is it that time? Shouldn't we be gannin' yem?"

"Don't you want a sandwich, Rob?" asked Joan.

"Don't worry about me, Joan. Should we be gannin', Agnes?"

"I suppose so, Rob," said Mam.

"Are you going already?" asked Joan, succeeding quite well in hiding a sigh of relief.

"We'd better," piped up Don, "I'm on early shift tomorrow. The buses never stop, Boxing Day or not, Joan. But I've enjoyed the night. We'll have to meet again, Mr Speed, and talk about trains."

"Aye, lad," said Joan's dad, standing up. "Good neet, Rob, and good neet, Agnes."

It seemed to me that a good neet was the one thing it hadn't been.

"Well?" said Joan as she hopped into bed.

I was winding up the alarm clock, checking the alarm, then realised I was off work on the morrow. "Well what?"

"What do you think?"

I caught on fast. "Oil and water love, just oil and water."

"Are *we* oil and water, then?"

"You know we aren't, Joan. We mix like coffee and cream, or milk and honey."

"I've seen cream stay on the top in coffee."

"Not when you blend it with care, love."

"Humph."

12

SKIPPING FOLLY

A Sunday morning in February – Christmas night was now but an uneasy half-forgotten memory. We were sitting up in bed, Joan was wearing a woolly bed jacket, me, a pullover on top of my pyjamas. Our portable electric fire wasn't throwing out much heat yet; it took ages to make an impression on the winter chill in the bedroom. I had collected the Sunday Sun from the front door and had made a pot of tea. Joan gratefully wrapped her hands around her warm cup as I scanned the front page of the local paper, a page full of comment on last week's General Election.

"They're still on about that five-seat Labour majority, Joan. They say there'll be another election sooner rather than later."

Joan, her eyes closed, made no response.

I turned to the back page to do some real reading and became engrossed in the report on the United game.

"Paul."

"Mm?" Jackie Milburn seemed to have had another good match.

"Paul."

"Yes, love?" I said, still preoccupied by the account of the ding-dong struggle.

"I'm worried Paul – I'm a week late."

"What?" I asked, failing at first to grasp the import of her words.

"Are you listening? I'm a week late."

"What! You're not!"

"I am but."

"Are you sure you haven't got the weeks mixed up?"

"Of course I'm sure," she snapped. "You should have noticed that I've been worried sick."

She gave a muted sob and supped a mouthful of tea.

I dumped the paper on the floor and put an arm around her. "OK, OK, love. Why didn't you tell me? Have you been late before?"

"Not really... No... I don't think so." She buried her face in my chest. "Oh, I don't know. I think once, but I wasn't bothered then." She looked up at me and smiled ruefully, "You see, in those days *you* weren't around. I keep hoping; I keep hoping it will come. We don't want a baby yet, just when we're getting a home together." She snuffled. "I don't want to have to give up work. Not until we've paid Mam and Dad off and got a little bit of money behind us."

"Do you think it's possible – a baby I mean?"

"I do think it's possible. We've been carefree at times."

"I've tried to be careful love – always. Perhaps you're just going to miss a month. Can that happen?"

"I don't know, I just don't know." The tears came then. I pulled her close trying to comfort her.

"Don't cry love, it might be just a hiccup, let's hope it'll come alright."

The days seem to pass quickly by. Every night I would come in from work, "How are you, love?" were always my first words, before giving her a hug.

"OK, unfortunately," she would reply ruefully.

Then one Sunday, she said, "In a few days it will be eight weeks. I'll be due again. Starting tomorrow, I'm going to do some skipping in the backyard to help it on."

I laughed, but then realised she was serious. "Do you think that's going to do any good? Surely if it's going to come it will. Besides, you haven't got a skipping rope," I joked weakly.

"I'm going to buy one. It won't do any harm to skip, will it? Anyway, I could do to lose a bit of fat."

I took her hand. "No, love, I don't suppose it'll do any harm. You don't want to lose too much weight, mind, I don't want you skinny."

She laughed, "Fine chance of that. But you agree?"

"They don't tell you *not* to exercise, do they, even if you think it is a baby?" I asked dubiously. Then on a lighter note; "What about the Dawsons? They'll think you're daft if they look out of their upstairs window and see you skipping and hear you shouting 'Salt, vinegar, mustard, PEPPER!"

Castle on a Cloud

"Where on earth did you get that one from? Was that another one of your weird back-lane games?"

"No, love, skipping was a cissy's game in our street, we lads wouldn't have heard the last of it if we'd been caught skipping. The lasses were always at it, though, when they weren't playing hopscotch. Prancing about skipping and shouting. When I was a kid, I got this idea that it must be unlucky to skip unless you sang the condiments. I'd go so far as to say I thought it was mandatory to sing them. Although I didn't know what mandatory meant in those days. Come to think of it I didn't know that salt, vinegar, mustard or pepper were called condiments either."

"What are you rambling on about? Anyway, I can shout what I like; all the Dawsons are out on a weekday afternoon."

"OK, love. I'll keep my fingers crossed, love."

It got to Wednesday – for three nights I'd asked the question. For three nights the same answer. "No signs, I'm afraid."

"It's a waste of time, isn't it?"

"Not really, I think I've lost a few pounds." It was gratifying to see her laugh, despite her concern.

Day four – Thursday. I came in the back way as usual, pushed open the kitchen door, expecting to see Joan, at the cooker. But there was no Joan in the kitchen, no hint of an appetising aroma, no sign of food.

Puzzled, I walked into the living room. "Joan," I called; then heard a plaintive voice.

Puzzled, I hurried through to the bedroom. Joan was spread-eagled on the bed; a blouse and petticoat her only covering, her face a pallid mask of pain. Skirt, stockings and shoes were strewn on the floor and beside them a bucket.

"Lord! What's the matter, love?"

"Oh! I'm glad you're here at last. Help me Paul, I feel awful. It's *come* alright. I feel drained. I feel I've lost something precious. What have I done? I wanted to phone you, but there was no way I could get to the box." She was shivering, I put my hand on her brow; it felt cold and clammy.

"It's freezing in here, why didn't you put the electric fire on, love?"

"It was all I could do to flop on the bed. Oh, Paul," she groaned, her icy hand feebly grasping mine. "I've been lying here for hours."

I switched on the fire. "You need the doctor, Joan."

Her voice was almost a whisper, "No, Paul, have a look in the pail –

he'll raise hell. I shouldn't have been so stupid, skipping like that. I had some bleeding yesterday. I didn't tell you. But this is much more than the usual. I feel dizzy, and the pain I've had. I'm scared. Perhaps it'll be alright in the morning though, mm?"

I peered into the bucket; there were blood-soaked pads, and God! A lot of gunge. "We're not waiting until morning, Joan, and don't be daft, he won't play hell." I squeezed her limp fingers. "Do you want me to help you into a nightie first?"

There were no more protests; she was too weak for that. She'd placed a towel under her; I changed it for a clean one.

Dr Bloom's surgery was five minutes away. What's more he lived on the premises. It was quicker to dash there, than go to the phone box. A youngish woman answered the door to my urgent ring.

"Mrs Bloom?"

"Yes?"

"I've just got home from work and found my wife very ill. She's lost a lot of blood. Can Doctor Bloom call?"

"Vait here in the porch, luckily, you've caught the doctor in, but first giff me your name and address."

I waited impatiently; it seemed a lifetime before the woman returned. "The doctor says to go home, Mr Potts, he'll be vith you very shortly."

He was; hurrying back, almost running; I had just reached our front door, when a big black Ford, a Zephyr, drew up. A far from old, yet bearded, dark-suited man, wearing a skull cap and carrying a black bag jumped out of the car and bounded up the front steps.

This doctor was new to me – a replacement for doddery old Manley – our 'panel' doctor from pre-NHS days. "Mr Potts?" the new man asked, putting his hand on my shoulder, "Don't look so vorried, ve'll sort this out." His manner was calm, positive, reassuring.

I led him into the bedroom.

"Now, my dear, what's all this?"

Joan gave him a wan smile. "I'm sorry for bringing you out, Doctor."

He picked up the bucket, "My, my! When did you hev your last period?"

"Eight weeks ago, doctor."

"Vell, my dear, looking at this and if I'm not very much mistaken and I'm sure I'm not, you hev had a miscarriage. Vhat is more you hev lost a lot of blood."

He felt her brow, then took her pulse. "You, Mr Potts, can you boil a kettle then I vill examine your vife."

As the kettle whistled, he came through to the kitchen. "Giff me ten minutes, Mr Potts," he said, taking the kettle and a basin.

Left on my own, I wandered around aimlessly. What had we done? Seeing Joan's ashen face had given me a scare. Dr Bloom had said she'd lost much blood. I'd heard vague stories of tragedies in similar circumstances. I sat down on the settee. Surely she'd recover, she had to, but what would be the aftermath? Would she be OK? We hadn't wanted a family yet, but not for this to happen.

"Mr Potts. Come through."

Joan looked so frail.

"Ve believe the bleeding has stopped. I'll leave these painkillers. I've told your vife she may need a transfusion if she looses much more blood. In which case she vould have to go to the hospital. Ve'll see what tomorrow morning brings. I'll be back again before surgery opens. The main thing is, don't vorry, either of you. Oh, and get rid of the contents of the bucket down your WC, Mr Potts."

"Will Joan be alright doctor?" I asked, as I escorted him to the front door.

"Ve'll get her through, and vithout any after effects I trust. Don't let her do anything silly again, eh?"

Returning to the room, I lit the coal fire which Joan had laid many moons ago, but which we'd never used. It needed the old trick of an upright shovel against the hearth and a double page of a newspaper to promote a draught, but soon the flames were leaping.

"Whoah, love, don't go up in flames," said Joan feebly, as the paper caught fire and the charred remains floated up the chimney.

Was that my puny burnt offering to the Gods?

"Go and get yourself something to eat, Paul."

"What about you?"

"I'll just have a cuppa, please."

Later, she dozed fitfully. I sat up in bed beside her trying to read a library book. With little success – the words just ran one into another. About ten o'clock she gingerly raised herself up. "Look, Paul, you've got to get some sleep. Why don't you go in the other room?"

"Don't be daft, love, I'm not leaving you this night. Do you want to use the pot before we try to settle down?"

"I suppose so, if I can get out of bed."

"Can I help you?"

"I'll try to manage, love. If you like, you can bring me a cup of cocoa."

By the time I'd made the drink she was back in bed. "That was an effort, Paul," she said breathlessly, "I didn't look in the potty. I was frightened what I might see. You have a look."

"Thanks very much," I said, taking the container across to the light. "Mm, it doesn't look too bad, love. Just a little pink."

"Let's keep our fingers crossed then. I'm sorry for giving you all this bother."

Her tears were not far away. I bent and gave her a kiss – her lips were cold. "Don't be barmy, Joan. It's you I'm sorry for."

We slept little that night. I was up at seven, hoping the doctor would soon be here. I hadn't to wait long; I hurried to answer his knock. He brushed past me with a 'Good morning' and entered the bedroom. "Give me a few minutes, Mr Potts."

I waited fearfully until at last he beckoned me in.

"The prospects are good now, the little help I've given, has vorked. I don't think a blood transfusion will be necessary. I'll come back after sunset tomorrow to make sure."

"That's good news, Paul." Joan looked a lot brighter. "Why did he say after sunset, though?"

"Well, love, the Sabbath ends at sunset on Saturday, you know."

"Oh! Of course, I am stupid."

"No, I'm stupid, letting you put yourself in danger. We both knew this was a possibility, didn't we?"

She squeezed my hand, her eyes brimming with tears. No answer was necessary.

13

AS WE LIKE IT

DRAMATIS PERSONAE:
PAUL POTTSIO, A citizen of Gateshead
JOAN, His wife
ACT I SCENE I – *A bedroom in Paul's house.*
DAY: New Year's Day, 1951
TIME: Twelve Noon

JOAN *(spread-eagled), asleep in bed, centre stage*
Enter PAUL (tousled hair and bleary-eyed) from kitchen, carrying a tray laden with a pot of tea and two cups
PAUL: Wake up, good mistress, Joan! *Through a dizzy haze (wondering what he was doing in this play)*
Exeunt PAUL. (He'd forgotten to put milk in the cups)
Pause
Re-enter PAUL. JOAN sits up, rubs her eyes as the shoulder strap of her nightgown slips down revealing a pleasing view, even when the viewer is suffering from a sore head. Still in theatrical mode, PAUL wonders how the Lord Chamberlain had passed this scene for public showing. JOAN pulls the lacy strap back over her shoulder. This might please the Lord Chamberlain but doesn't please PAUL
JOAN: *(still sleepy)* A cup of tea! A cup of tea!
PAUL puts tray on his wife's lap and clambers gingerly into a bed that seems to be lurching in heavy seas
PAUL: *(mumbling)* Thank God New Year's Eve comes but once a year. *(Then remembers to speak up so the back row can hear)* THANK GOD NEW YEAR'S EVE COMES BUT ONCE A YEAR!

JOAN: Ooh! Don't shout. *(Takes a gulp of tea)* That's better.
PAUL: *(Partakes of a mouthful of the nectar-like drink)* Aah!

It was then my head stopped spinning long enough for me to realise that this was not a play – never had been. Just a case of befuddlement – (a) At Christmas, Joan had bought me the complete plays of Shakespeare in one volume. "Just second-hand from the Grainger Market bookstall," she'd confessed. (b) I'd been reading the bard in bed every night since (except last night). (c) I was still dizzy from the New Year celebrations. Fragments such as: Scene, 'A room in Olivia's house', 'Olivia's Garden', 'Enter Sir Toby Belch', were floating around in my fragile head.

I sat up in bed adjusting to the real world.

Joan shielded her eyes as though the dim January light was blazing summer sunshine. She spoke softly as though she too was brittle, "Paul."

"What?"

She turned to me, trying to focus, squinting with the effort. "What was all this 'good mistress, Joan' talk? Have you got one?"

"Got what?"

"A mistress called Joan?"

"Don't be daft, but that's an idea. If I had, I could talk in my sleep and you wouldn't be any the wiser!"

She made to give me a swipe, but changed her mind. (Probably thinking her porcelain head would drop off with the effort.)

"Truth to tell, Joan, I was in a Shakespeare play, they talk like that you know."

"*You* talk barmy."

I took another mouthful of tea. "We drank too much last night at Mam's."

"Not only that, you lot sang too much, that's why I've got a headache. I don't know which of you hogged the floor the most."

"It was Don who sang too much – 'Begin the Beguine', not once, but twice! It's a song that goes on forever anyway. Then that 'tallyman' ditty, was it three times for that one – 'tally me banaaanas'? I bet Harry Belafonte was eating his heart out."

Joan laughed gingerly, "It takes a lot to put Don off; my yawning didn't stop him doing his Robert Mitchum impressions all through the night. It was a long night. Mind, you have no room to complain – you and Cecil. Flanagan and Allen, then some more Flanagan and Allen – talk about these new long-playing records."

Castle on a Cloud

"Well, we had to keep Mam happy. She likes the oldies."

Joan, eyes closed, took another sup of tea. "I'm glad that 1950 is over, Paul. I'll always remember it as the year of the miscarriage."

"Mm, I was scared stiff for you, love. You're alright now though, aren't you?"

"We'll find out when we try for a baby. It would break my heart if, because of my stupidity, we couldn't have one."

"When are we going to try? I can't wait until I can get close to you. Really, really close. Absolutely, ever-endingly, close."

Joan laughed, then winced, "Oo, my head." She squeezed my hand. "It won't be ever-ending. I know you're good, but even you are no miracle man!"

"But when?"

"Don't be impatient. You're like a kiddie waiting for Santa Claus."

"So when will Santa come?"

"Well, we should have Dad's loan paid off by the summer."

"Crikey! The summer! That's a long way away! I'll tell you what, Joan. Wouldn't it be romantic if we settled for our third wedding anniversary – the 20th March? With a bit of luck we could have a Christmas baby."

"Christmas!"

"Well, with a bit more luck we might take a month or two to succeed; it could be a spring baby, lots of time for closeness."

She snuggled up to me, almost purring. "I'll think about it."

"Gee thanks."

"Don't mention it."

Although not in a fit state to demonstrate as such, I was eager to discuss at length all the delights of baby-making, Joan, however, was musing again. "Half a century gone, love. Nineteen-fifty was a funny year all-round though, Paul. No sooner does that Berlin business die a death when, hey presto! we're involved in Korea. My cousin Dick's over there. What on earth we're doing in a place like Korea, I don't know. Our lads getting killed again."

"It's UNO supposedly, but it's mainly Americans. They're trying to put the world to rights. Behind it all, I think the Yanks are suspicious of China."

"They're always suspicious of somebody."

"There were some good things last year, though."

"Like what?"

"Like points rationing ending, like soap rationing ending, like the little princess."

"Anne? *She'll* get spoiled."

"Like in sport, then?"

"Like what in sport?"

"Like... Like... Like... Like Wales doing the rugby grand slam. (Three cheers for your Welsh blood.) Like football... Like... Oh no! Not like USA 1 England 0."

Joan, put her feet over the side of the bed and stretched indolently. Lazily, I caressed her creamy white shoulders. She wriggled sensuously. "Your hand's nice and warm. Why don't you just stroke my shoulders instead of prattling on with your facts? Facts, facts, facts."

There were more facts though; they were blazoned across the local papers that winter:

FA CUP THIRD ROUND SLAUGHTER. UNITED 4 BURNLEY 1.
NEWCASTLE 3 BOLTON 2. JACKIE TWO MORE!
UNITED THROUGH TO NEXT ROUND. WIN AWAY AT STOKE!
THROUGH TO SEMIS AT BRISTOL – ROVERS BEATEN 3 – 1.

Euphoria filled the hearts of two football fans in the Potts' household that spring, and euphoria overflowed on the morning of our wedding anniversary. So much so that I was late into the office. Fortunately, the boss didn't enquire why. Just as well; it was not for him to know. Some things are private. What happened that night after our celebratory fish and chips takeaway was not his affair either.

Those were blissful times. In a way, we followed the advice of the old proverb (paraphrased). 'If at first you're not sure you've succeeded, keep on trying.'

More bliss! Newcastle United were in the Cup Final, having disposed of Billy Wright's 'Wolves' in the semis. Blackpool were the only obstacle to the trophy now. The legendary Stanley Matthews was their star player. The nation would be willing them to success. All but the Geordies. All but the Geordies.

"I would love to go to Wembley, Paul."

"We can't Joan. We couldn't get a ticket for one thing."

Castle on a Cloud

"Why not?"

"There's only twelve thousand for Newcastle supporters. When the season-ticket holders have had their dollop, Joan, we wouldn't have a cat-in-hell's chance. Besides, could we afford it?"

"Pity we don't have a television set then."

"Don and Cec hope to see the game in Carruthers' electric shop on the Fell. I told you, didn't I? Don saw the notice in their window. 'Come And See the Match On Our Television Sets. Admission Free'. We could try to get in."

"There'll be crowds there, Paul. We'd be lucky to get through the door. We'll just have to listen to Raymond Glendenning on the wireless."

At least we lost little of the atmosphere of the pre-match Wembley build-up, as we listened to the band of the Coldstream Guards backed up by a choir of a hundred thousand voices. 'Abide with Me' had Joan in tears, 'Lilli Marlene' brought back memories of the two years I was in India, the two years I was parted from her – 'I knew she was waiting' said the song. The Geordie fans belting out 'Blaydon Races' steeled our resolve to shout the 'lads' to success. Would they hear us, though?

"Ee, it was great, Joan. This television thing takes some beating." Brother Don was pontificating, as he tamped Erinmore tobacco into his pipe. It was Tuesday night at Mam's.

"You got into the shop alright, then?"

"Well, we had to stand, Den," said Cecil. "It was crowded. I bet they sell a few televisions after that sales gimmick. Particularly when you think that if you had a television in the house you wouldn't be thirty or forty feet away. That's how far the tellies were from where we were standing. They had two of the big sixteen-inch sets tuned in, but even so a couple of guys had brought their binoculars."

"Newcastle don't win the cup every week though," laughed Joan. "You were lucky seeing it, mind. We'll have to be satisfied with the bit they'll show on Movietone News at the Coatsworth tomorrow. Did you get a good view, Don? You're not as tall as Cec."

Don frowned; he was still upset at being the short one of the family. "I missed one of the goals," he said, puffing his pipe into life.

"The best one," said Cec.

"Aye, I missed it. There was a bonny young lass next to me. She was complaining about this big burly fellow with a broken nose who'd pushed in and blocked our view."

"Well I never!" butted in Joan, "A fellow with a broken nose?"

"Aye, a broken nose he had. But this lass was canny, we laughed about not seeing the goal."

Cecil chuckled. "I had to explain to them how little Ernie Taylor had backheeled to Jackie who'd walloped it into the back of the net."

"I didn't see much more," said Don, "but I knew we'd won by then. Two up!"

"He was chatting to this girl after that."

"Did you make a date, Don?" Joan asked.

"No, but she gets the eighty-two bus. I'll look out for her next time I'm on that run."

"He's always looking out for girls, that's as far as it gets." This was Rob; he had just woken up from one of his naps.

Joan laughed. "You're twenty-nine, Don. It's about time you settled down."

Judging by Mam's face, I think Joan had said the wrong thing. A change of subject was called for.

"Where's Stephen, Mam?"

Mam laid down the book she'd picked up when the football chat was going on and wearily brushed away a stray lock of greying auburn hair. "He's out walking the streets with a queer lad he met in Saltwell Park. A little fellow about eighteen – he's called Ephraim. Funny name for a funny 'un. He seems a bossy boots, a martinet type, back straight as a ramrod, I think he has a poker up his jumper, but Stephen likes him. When you think though, Joan, Stephen's nearly fifteen now, yet there's no way he could get a job. He's more strange every day that passes, giggling and laughing about nothing at all. He's not with us some of the time. I'm worried sick about him these days."

"Are you going to take him to the doctor's again?"

"I think I'll have to. At least if he's declared unfit for work, he may get some sickness benefit or something."

I was becoming more and more convinced that Stephen was mentally ill. Was his malady linked to him being conceived when Dad was carrying the TB virus?

"The Festival of Britain, Paul. Let's go!"

"What?"

Castle on a Cloud

"You heard me." We were sitting on the sofa listening to the radio. 'Take it from here', with Jimmy Edwards, Dick Bentley and Joy Nichols had just ended. Joan knew I was in a good mood. The comedy half-hour had been well up to standard.

I'd heard her alright. Funnily enough, I'd been thinking about the Festival earlier that evening. Perhaps it was not all that funny, as Alvar Liddell, on the six o'clock news, had been reporting about the final preparations for the big opening.

So Joan had hatched a plan?

"When were you thinking of going?"

Joan sat up with a start. I'd surprised her by not immediately using my veto, even if it did usually end up worthless.

"Well, in August, of course, if it's possible, darling, when you're on holiday." I could almost taste the honey on her lips.

Ah! But I had a counter-plan. "It'll be busy in August, you won't get moved."

"Here we go – spoilsport again. That's the only time you can get time off – the factory holidays."

"Not so, my pretty lass." I laughed. "I think I could take three days off any week."

"You've kept that quiet. I thought you were indispensable!"

"Well, yes, I am." I said modestly. "But listen, will you? If I could get all the piecework bit of the wages done by Tuesday – I'd do that that by writing out the workers' pay-slips instead of typing them...."

"But, but..." Joan giggled, "Typing's faster than writing, that's the whole point!"

"I know, I know," I said tetchily, "but I've just started typing. I am aiming to produce a professional looking document. For modernisation purposes, Joan. For modernisation purposes. It's just that I'm not all that speedy yet. It's Sandra's old typewriter I'm using, it's not as smooth as these new ones."

"You mean *you're* slow. You're a scream Paul Dennis. You're going to *write* the pay-slips for quickness? Why don't you just get Sandra to type them?"

"Where's your logic, clever clogs? I'd have to write them out first, wouldn't I? Nobody else at Gateshead knows all the formulae. That's why I'm indispensable," I said smugly. "If I was sick, they'd have to send someone down from our Glasgow head office, particularly as I've heard that old Jackson is doting in his retirement."

"Nobody else knows the formulae! My, you're a smart one! Alright, alright," said Joan, brushing a laughter tear from her eye. "You've convinced me. So, say you've done all the piecework slips. What then? What about the rest?"

"I'm going to tell you, if you'll listen," I said, pretending to strangle her. Her white throat always attracted my hands, but I don't think she was ever worried.

Not this time anyway. She screeched with laughter. "Get off!"

"Well listen then, you vixen. Elsie, the new woman in the Works Office could put the wages up with help from the boss. She did wages in her last job. I think old Patterson would agree – he's trying to arrange cover in the holidays anyway – responsible people to look after the shop."

"Responsible people to look after the shop," Joan mimicked, "by, it's a good job you don't wear a hat these days, you'd never get it on!"

Her smile changed to a puzzled frown of suspicion. "Hang on, Paul Potts; you've got a bee in your bonnet about this Festival."

"Now would I have any such thing? But why don't we go in June?"

"You actually agree to go? You *have* got a bee in your bonnet!"

"No, no, not really. The Lord's Test is on in June, that's all."

"I rest my case," she laughed. "Mind, I would like to go to Lord's myself."

"Could we afford the trip, though?"

"There you go, there you go. We could get the overnight coach to London and stay in a bed and breakfast," said Joan warming to her plan. "We could see a show. 'Kiss Me Kate' is on at the Coliseum, with Bill Johnson and Patricia Morrison. Sid James is in it as well."

"Whoa, love, you're gettin' carried away. Who the devil is Sid James, anyway?

"He's in that new picture – 'The Lavender Hill Mob', with Alec Guinness. You've heard of *him*?"

"Oh, aye! I'm dying to see Sid James then."

What were the high spots of that June holiday? Let me see:
   The Dome of Discovery **
   The Skylon *
   Kiss Me Kate ***
   The Test Match ****
   The Coach Journeys???

Castle on a Cloud

Joan had already missed two periods *****

Ah! Those overnight coach journeys. Outward bound to London was a trial – little sleep – we wandered like zombies around the Festival grounds. Two days rest basking in the sun and watching England getting the better of South Africa restored most of our well-being, but we were dreading the Saturday return trip. That London to Newcastle ride was made in a coach which surely had history written on every component. The engine, the seats, the suspension, the tyres, even the brakes. Pre-war history.

It was at Stevenage, with the June daylight fading, that I asked the driver to stop. There, Joan was sick. At Grantham, she was sick, At Wetherby she was retching. Eight hours of unrelieved suffering for Joan, eight hours of worry and concern for me. Those hours were one long nightmare, a nightmare that continued into the early dawn of a midsummer sunrise. Was it travel sickness? Was it morning sickness? Or was it something worse?

Newcastle at last. A nearby taxi-rank – a taxi waiting in the stand. Soon we were home.

It was with relief that I planted our suitcase down. Joan had preceded me and with some haste disappeared out of the backdoor. I observed her from the living room window as she hurried up the backyard to the WC. She was holding a handkerchief to her mouth. Anxiously, I awaited her reappearance. At last, white-faced, she emerged and trailed forlornly into the house.

There was a look of fear in her eyes. "There's blood below, Paul!"

"No, love! Don't say that."

Her face looked drained of life. "I'm going to bed. You can get me a cup of tea."

"I'll do that; then I'll call on the doctor. It may be nothing, Joan."

She sobbed as she came into my arms. I hugged her, my lips brushing her hair, a pathetic attempt at consolation. She was shuddering as I led her to our bedroom; she flopped on the bed, her head burrowed in a pillow.

Mercifully, Doctor Bloom was in; Sunday, a day of rest for him perhaps, but otherwise just another day. Déja vu – again he followed me home and again he arrived without delay.

The doctor's call last year had been made in response to my concern for Joan. This time my worry was not only for Joan; but for her baby – our baby.

"Mr Potts," the doctor beckoned me into the bedroom. "You're vife has been telling me about the coach journey, a most unfortunate thing. But no lasting harm done this time. The good news is that your vife is still pregnant. She'll need to take care for a few days, nothing too exerting. You understand this time? Both of you?" His memory was remarkable. And his acumen.

He turned to Joan. "Come and see me on Vednesday morning, dear." Then he gave a brief smile, a rare smile. "And you, Mr Potts, you I'll see around what you call New Year."

I was slow to grasp his meaning. Lack of sleep I suppose.

That smile came again. "When I come to deliver your baby."

14

CUPS AND BOTTLES

"Tomorrow, Joan, I'm going to Boots."

She'd slept all through the day. She'd missed a lovely summer Sunday. A glorious day. Just the sort of day to push a spanking new pram, with a spanking new baby all the way to Saltwell Park. Just the sort of day in fact when a couple still in love could meander around the park lake with the quack-quacks quacking and an infant gurgling. But we didn't have a new pram; we didn't have a new baby. Not yet. Not a new baby as such, anyway.

The moment I'd found Joan awake, I'd taken her a sandwich and a cup of tea (Brooke Bond's new PG tips). Her cheeks had regained some of their normal rosy hue and her eyes a glint of that attractive sparkle I knew so well.

"Boots?" she said, with that little frown of a question mark on her forehead.

"For lots of cotton wool," I said, sitting on the side of the bed and holding her still cool hand.

"Cotton wool?"

"Uh uh. To wrap you up in."

She chuckled. "You daft brush. I'm not going to be mollycoddled. Give me a day or two and I'll race you around the block."

She didn't get to race me around the block. I didn't get to wrap her in cotton wool, either. Instead, she got her Singer machine rattling at sixteen to the dozen; not blouses or dresses now, but pram covers, cot coverlets, little smocky things, all white, and all just waiting for a final bit of appropriately coloured lace, ribbon, or embroidery. Her knitting needles were busily clicking too – transforming balls of wool into bootees, bonnets, socks and suchlike.

As the year slowly passed, the flat became a veritable cornucopia of baby's apparel; enough bootees for triplets, enough smocky things for quads, enough coverlets for a dormitory of cots.

On into the autumn. The autumn of a year when 'believe it or not' items appeared in the press with great regularity. 'Smoking can cause cancer' – that seemed far-fetched, but it was comforting to know that neither of us smoked. 'Over fifty thousand horses a year eaten in England'. There must be a multitude of families all over the land where people could say 'I could eat a horse' and mean it. The queerest story of all when you come to think of it was the General Election. Labour ousted by Winston Churchill. A Churchill who was now 77 years old! An old fogey. Mind, Labour had had their chance since the war and had made a bit of a pig's ear of it. One glaring example – it had taken them six years to end food rationing; six years of peace – six years of rationing. And some rationing was still with us.

No, Joan never did get to race me around the block. Any chance of that happening became even less likely as her bump became bigger. Sometimes, I would lie gently on her burgeoning belly in bed, listening for a heartbeat. One night, I thought I heard one. "I hear it, I hear it!"

Joan laughed, 'That's my tummy rumbling!"

She couldn't kid me – it was a heartbeat alright.

She didn't run round blocks, but nothing would dissuade her from going to see Newcastle United every other week. Even into the final weeks of the year.

"Don't go today, Joan. The birth is only weeks away. Those crowds, the crush. It's not safe," I would say.

I might as well have saved my breath for all the notice she took.

Mind you, nowadays, as a sop to my conscience, we stood in the less packed but pricey Centre Paddock. To pass through those turnstiles meant breaking into a ten-bob note.

"You're very magnanimous, love," she'd laugh.

"I can be profligate when the need arises, Joan," I would smugly say.

Nevertheless, it was money well spent. There in the paddock, the crowd seemed calmer; those around us giving due respect to her ever more conspicuous condition. Just 'one for instance' – those fans in the

Castle on a Cloud

paddock always allowed her to stand in front of a crash-barrier for protection.

It was at Christmas that she at last took my advice; or was it her mam and dad who persuaded her of the folly of her ways? Her parents had come to stay over the Yuletide; her Mam earmarked to cook the dinner, leaving her Dad to hover over Joan. (Burgeoning belly? Conspicuous condition? Hover over? Pull yourself together, Paul. You're getting carried away.) Her dad's other assignment was to accompany Cecil and me to the derby matches on Christmas Day and Boxing Day. Joan was most upset at missing the game at Sunderland, when she discovered that United had won four-one and her hero, Robledo scored two. She was in a huffy sort of mood that Christmas, a mood not improved when the return encounter ended in an exciting two-two draw.

"Look, Joan, there were nearly sixty four thousand at St James' Park, it would have been dangerous."

"Aye, lass. Paul's talkin' sense. It were a reet crush."

Newcastle were drawn at home on the first Saturday of the New Year. On that day they would commence their defence of the FA Cup.

On the eve of the match Joan was reading the Chronicle – news of the team and its prospects plastered over front page and back. "It's going to be a fine day tomorrow. I'm going to the match."

I was immersed in reading The Day of the Triffids, and finding comfort in the knowledge that we hadn't a garden. The book had been all the talk in the press and radio and at last I'd managed to borrow a copy from the library. That was why the import of her pronouncement hadn't penetrated into my mind's eye picture of hordes of deadly plants.

"I'm going to the match."

I heard her this time. Reluctantly, I put the book down, ready to argue her out of such a stupid idea. I didn't get the chance.

"You're not going to put me off, so don't try. I've got a plan."

"You have a plan?"

"Yes, we go in the Leazes End. We wait until kick-off to go up to the terraces, then we stand right up at the corner on the fringe of the crowd. We can come away before the final whistle. Honest, love, it'll be OK."

I considered this theory carefully. It seemed sound, providing she didn't go into premature labour. If that happened, I envisaged a headline in the 'Football Final' – 'Newcomer in United Boardroom!'

Joan's face, as she waited for my response, triggered off a long forgotten, pre-war memory of a little girl at a seaside peppermint-rock stall in Whitley Bay. The child was trying to pull her dad towards the counter, her warm brown eyes pleading. The way Joan's brown eyes were pleading now. I remembered wondering then, why a kid could make such a fuss about a stick of rock; me, I didn't like the stuff. Joan's pleading now, I could understand – it *was* Newcastle and it *was* the FA Cup.

I weighed up the pros and cons; the only way she wouldn't go was if I didn't go. That settled it. "Be it on your head, Joan. You've got it all worked out, haven't you? You realize though, that you may not be able to see all of the pitch? The main stand could block the view?"

"We'll *be* there though, Paul."

"Alright, alright. You've talked me into it as usual."

As we carefully ascended to the back of the terraces, my doubts surfaced again. I must be mad to let her do this, and her expecting a baby in a handful of hours' time.

Even more mad when Aston Villa went two up after a quarter of an hour. Foulkes pulled one back for Newcastle, but it was two-one until deep into the second-half.

Soon, a trickle of disappointed, pessimistic fans became a stream as they passed us on the way to the exits. "Bang gans the cup this yeor," "What a shower," "Aa divvent think Aa'll come back here in a hurry," were some of the comments we heard. One chap looked Joan up and down. "Your babby's ganna be grown up before we win the cup again, lass. We need a new team."

I turned to Joan, she looked tired. "*We'd* better go, love, before you get crushed in the rush."

"No, Paul, we can still draw," she said, her chin jutting stubbornly.

"We'll stay; then we'll wait at the side out of the way until it's quieter."

With our restricted view, we couldn't see Newcastle's right-wing play as they pressed towards the Gallowgate end. We didn't have to. Seven minutes to go and left-winger, Bobby Mitchell blasted in a twenty-five yard equalizer. Joan jumped up and down with glee.

"Stop it, Joan," I said anxiously.

Only for a minute did she stop, only until Mitchell scored again to

Castle on a Cloud

put United ahead. Then she calmed down, taking the last minute clincher by Robledo in her stride.

Now a happier crowd of more faithful supporters surged past us. Intermingled here and there I spied the shocked white faces and purple scarves of Villa fans.

The buzz of excitement was almost tangible. Newcastle were off on the road to Wembley again!

"Aa knew we'd do it," someone said. ""Haway the lads!" shouted another. Agony had turned to ecstasy in the twinkling of a goal or two.

But what of Joan! I turned to see her take a deep sigh and unsteadily lower herself onto the bare concrete of a terrace step.

"Here," I said, taking my topcoat off and folding it into a cushion. "Sit on this, Joan."

She took it gratefully.

"Are you alright?"

"I'm not sure, Paul. I think so. Just a little queasy. It must have been the excitement."

"You're a silly beggar. I told you not to come."

"I'll be fine," she said.

I hoped and prayed so.

Prayers are sometimes answered.

Three days later, just three days, Dr Bloom had delivered. Joan's contractions had started in the middle of the night. True to form she hadn't roused me – wanting me to get my sleep. At six o'clock I stirred to wakefulness – no longer could she silence gasps of pain. They warned me that things were happening. I sat up quickly.

"I'll go tell Dr Bloom."

"No wait a bit, Paul. It's early days yet. Let the doctor have his rest."

I let him have another half-hour, occupying myself by boiling the kettle, filling pans, checking spare bed sheets, finding towels, pacing up and down. These seem to be the sort of things to do. Every five minutes, I would pop my head round the bedroom door.

"Shall I go, now?"

"Wait a bit," she'd say.

Then, from the kitchen I heard a more intense cry. "Paul," she shouted, "you'd better fetch him. Yes, you'd better fetch him."

A couple of hours later and Dr Bloom had kept his promise to me. Joan told me afterwards, that the young midwife, who had arrived minutes after the doctor, was allowed only to observe the delivery. Now that Bloom had dashed off to his surgery, his task complete, the midwife, too, was getting ready to leave. "You can go in now, Mr Potts; your wife is ready to show off her baby. I've tidied her up."

I'd been wandering about impatiently, listening to howls and soothing words from the other room, and then a small, pitiful baby cry. I had wondered whether to burst in, but such an intervention would surely incur the wrath of the doctor – husbands keep out!

Joan had been impatient too. Anxious to show how clever she was. Pale, exhausted, but smiling, she was cradling a small bundle.

"What's that you've got there?" I asked, kissing her dry lips.

"It's what you call a baby, you daft lad."

"It's little," I said, awestruck. "It can't weigh much!"

"It might have weighed a little bit less."

"What do you mean?"

"If it had been a girl, you ninny."

To tell the truth, I didn't care – boy or girl – just as long as it was a baby. "So this is the little fellow that went to the match? What's he doing nuzzling around there? Doesn't he know that's my territory?"

"Don't fret, love, but you'll have to share things for a while."

I almost ran between my assignments that morning. First to Mam's to tell her the news. She slung her coat on. "I'll come straight down. A little boy! I know all about little boys, don't I just!"

I left her in a happy frame of mind as I turned off to the post office. Next target, a telegram to York. This time no 'don't panics!' This time to tell of a parcel much smaller than a turkey.

Arriving back home, Mam was beaming, sitting at the bedside, cradling her grandson and fussing over Joan. A sight for sore eyes. "What are you going to call him, Joan?"

"Well, Grandma. I can call you Grandma now?" she laughed. "I wanted to call him George, but Paul wanted to call him Jackie. You know Robledo and Milburn?"

"So what have you decided on?"

"Mark; don't ask me why. It was Paul's idea."

This was news to me. Mark was just one of half-dozen names we had finally bandied about. Mind, when I came to think about it, five of them were girls' names.

Joan's mam didn't waste much time – just five hours from receiving the telegram to her appearance in our front room to gather her grandson into her arms.

The little mite must already be wondering what this world was all about. Cradled by one giant being and then another, chucked under his tiny chin, huge fingers coaxing him to grip them with his tiny hand. Stupid beings. Get off! Now and again he would condescend to peer through tiny eyelids at big white blobs of faces. But the light! This wasn't the warm darkness that had been enfolding him for so long. He wanted to go back. He would give a cry, a pitiful cry of sorrow, only assuaged when his first warm human cradled him and his little mouth searched and found a soft fountain of nourishment.

Peace had descended, everyone had departed. Don, Cecil and Stephen had paid visits to their nephew. Poor, bewildered Stephen had been stunned by his minuteness. "What a little tiddler! It's not real, is it?" he giggled. "It's not the size of twopennorth a copper, man!"

"You were once that size," laughed Cecil, "and look at you now. You're getting fat."

"No, Cecil," said Stephen, looking puzzled. "I was never that little. I've always been this size, haven't I?"

Yes, visitors had departed, except Joan's mam; she was staying the week so that I could return to work. "Ye must be clammin', Paul. Aa'll get ye somethin'"

"Why don't you have a gorgy sandwich?" suggested Joan, "There's some Danish Blue in the kitchen cabinet."

With an effort, Joan's mam got up from her chair; she was putting on ever more weight. "Aa'll get it, Paul."

"Right, Gran," I laughed. At last I'd found a name for her. All these years, and I'd never addressed her much by any name – Mrs Speed in the early days perhaps?

'Gran' returned with a plateful of sandwiches and a cup of tea. I'd given Joan something to eat earlier, but hadn't realised how hungry I was. I took a bite, almost spat it out, but couldn't, not with Gran looking. Mustard! A combination of mustard and strong blue cheese. Was this some curious reward for helping to produce a grandson?

"Nice?"
"Uh uh," I spluttered, as I felt beads of sweat on my forehead.
"Right, Aa'll go and get meesen summat, then."
"What's wrong with you, Paul?" asked Joan, after her mam had left the room. She was still cradling her treasure. "You're looking feverish."
"God! So would you if you were eating these," I said opening a sandwich and displaying its contents.
"Oh! You poor thing," she laughed, "there must be a pot of mustard on there. Mustard and strong blue cheese! What's Mam been thinking about? Take it away from little Mark, the smell will poison him!"
"Your mam must be in a state of shock," I said, wrapping the sandwiches in a piece of newspaper. "I'll hide them under the bed for now. I hope she doesn't come up with any other funny ideas in the next few days."

"What's all this?" asked Joan "I thought we'd agreed on Mark?"
I had handed her the birth certificate. "Well, yes, Mark," I said, pointing. "Look, there, Mark."
"I can read. I can read. But what's this?"
"Oh, that. Well, Joan, when I got to the registry office, I got to thinking. Just one Christian name for the bairn didn't seem right. I've got two Christian names, your brother has two, so have my brothers. Perhaps we hadn't thought this thing through. Perhaps Mark should have two as well."
"Don hasn't two!"
"He has. I told you years ago, you must have forgotten, Joan. Don't you remember me telling you that he'd asked Mam years ago why he didn't have two names and she said he had – Donald Gary. He doesn't brag about it, mind."
"I'm not surprised – Gary! But this is a practical joke; this isn't the real certificate – Mark Jet Potts?"
"It is, love."
"But, Jet. Did you mean Jed?"
"No, love. J.E.T. Milburn. John Edward Thompson – Jet! Jackie!"
"My God! I'll crown you!"
I remembered thinking in that office when the registrar's clerk gave me a puzzled look, that perhaps Joan might be a bit upset. But not as bad as this. "It was a spur of the moment thing, love. We can probably get it changed if you don't like it."

Castle on a Cloud

"We can't get it changed now, you blockhead! Even if we said they'd made a mistake, that you'd meant Jed. That would be just as bad. We'll just have to keep it quiet. The poor bairn, Jet Potts! Jet Potts!"

The way Joan said the name it did sound bad. Yes, I'd grant her that now. But blockhead? That was nasty.

It took her a while to calm down – about three weeks – if my memory serves me right, but calm down, she did.

One good thing, the relationship between Joan and Mam improved after Mark's birth. By the time Mark was a couple of months old, Mam was entering fully into her new role as Grandma. Always willing to look after him so that we could have a night at the pictures – the Odeon or the Ritz. 'The Third Man', 'The African Queen', 'The Caine Mutiny' – there seemed to be a superabundance of great films to see. Afterwards, we'd call round at Mam's to collect Mark. She would have given him his late night bottle – the complete baby food they said, Ostermilk – so he was always asleep when we pushed him home in his dazzling new Silver Cross pram – a present from Joan's mam and dad.

Mam would mind him on a Saturday afternoon too, so Joan and I were soon watching United again. Unfortunately no more home FA Cup games that season, they were drawn away in every tie up to the semi-finals. Tottenham 3-0, Swansea 1-0, Portsmouth 4-2. Wolves were then beaten in the semis and once more we were listening to Raymond Glendenning commentating at Wembley; this time we were against Arsenal.

Even with Arsenal down to ten men from early in the game, it took Newcastle most of the match before Robledo scored the winner. But we'd won the cup again. Our cheers at the final whistle woke up little Mark in his pram. Four-month-old Mark gave a cry, but not of delight, more of annoyance at being disturbed from his afternoon postprandial slumber.

"Da di da di da di da, da di da di dido."

It was one evening towards the end of August. Mark was in my arms; I was rocking him asleep to the tune of Barwick Green. Another episode of The Archers was ending.

Mark's "daa daas" had happily changed to snores. Cautiously, I walked into the bedroom and gently laid him down in his cot.

RAT-A-TAT, RAT-A-TAT!

"Damn! Who the hell's that?" I muttered. "Shush, Mark, shush."

I heard Joan at the front door. "Why, Stephen, love! What a surprise! Why this visit?"

"It's not a visit, Joan. I've come to stay."

15

THE RUNAWAY

Good – Mark was still asleep. I closed the bedroom door gently. In the living room, Stephen was sitting on the edge of the settee nursing a brown paper carrier bag. Joan was perched on the arm of an easy chair.

"What's all this, brother Stephen?"

"I've left home, Den. I've come to stay here. I think that's for the best. There're too many people at Mam's. There's Rob, Mam, Don, Cecil, the cat. I don't like cats. I don't like a lot of people. *And* those stairs, back and front. I don't like stairs either. Sometimes I feel I'm halfway to the sky. Cats and stairs – they're horrible."

"Since when have you thought this?"

"Since this morning when the cat scratched me and I nearly fell over the blooming animal and tumbled down the stairs. Look what the cat did!" he showed me a tiny scratch. "That was it, Den. That was it! I packed my bag and scarpered. I walked around the park lake for a bit. What was I saying? Aye! I walked around the park lake and sat on a swing. That was until the parkie came. He shifted me. Said I was too old to play on a swing. Where he got that idea from, I don't know. Anyway, I thought I'd come straight here. I've got everything in the bag. Everything I need, Den."

"Does your Mam know you've left home, Stephen, love?" said Joan, gently. "You can't just walk out you know. She'll be worried."

"Naw, she thinks more of the cat, man. I just sneaked out. Last week, Ephraim said I should leave home. He said go and stay with your brother Den, there's not as many people there."

"Did he now? But you can't stay here, Stephen. We haven't got room for one thing. Besides, *we've* got steps, steps up to the front door."

"Just a few steps though, and no cat." He frowned and looked around the room. "You haven't got a cat, have you? No, you haven't. Of course you haven't. You wouldn't have a cat with a babby. But I know you've got a spare room though, Den. I know you have." He turned his head, "Through there, isn't it?"

"No, Stephen, that room's not spare. Mark will be moving in there soon."

"You could give Mark to Mam, Den. Mam would have him. She would think it was a good swap. Mark for me! Hee-hee. Look, I've brought my things." With a flourish, he emptied the contents of his carrier bag onto the floor. Out fell the belongings he'd brought for his stay: a crumpled shirt, three socks, a drawing book which fell open to display sketches of matchstick men; two stubby pencils, an old tennis ball, and what had once been a colourful tinplate humming top, but was now battered and losing its paint.

I knelt at his feet and gathered the pitiful collection together. I bent my head to hide tears I found difficult to control and returned his pathetic belongings to the bag. I brushed wetness off my cheek and turned to Joan. She was snuffling into her hankie.

Stephen frowned, "Why have you put them back in the bag, Den?"

I stood up and put my hand on Stephen's shoulder. He looked up at me expectantly.

"Look, old pal. It's no good. Your place is at home, don't you see that?"

"Can't I stay the night, Den? I won't be a pick of bother. It's just that cat, you see. I've gone right off that cat. It scratched me. Look," he said, as he again showed me the tiny mark.

"There's no point in you staying the night, Stephen. I'd have to go along to Mam's and tell her you were here, otherwise she'd worry. So I might as well just take you back with me."

"Can't you see, Stephen? Your mam will be at her wits' end right now, wondering where you are," said Joan.

He giggled then, his face beamed happily. "Do you think so? Do you think she'd really worry? Do you think she'd miss me?"

"I'm sure she will, Stephen. She worries about you a lot, you know."

"Oh, in that case then, Joan, I might go back home. And bugger that cat. Bugger that cat," he chuckled. "Ee, sorry, Joan. It just slipped out. It's that Ephraim. He says it all the time."

"That Ephraim's a bad influence, Stephen," I laughed. "Come on

Castle on a Cloud

then, let's get started back to Mam's." It was a slow walk, Stephen, despite his built-up shoe, still limped badly, a limp I noticed more than ever that night. Poor devil.

"So *there* you are Stephen! Where's he been Den?" Mam sounded anxious, but relieved. There she was, standing in the scullery doorway, at the top of the stone steps leading down to the yard. From this position Mam must have been scanning the back lane approach to the house. Stephen always used the back way for his comings and goings. "I've been worried sick. He's been out since two o'clock. I would have sent Cecil out to look for him, but he's gone straight from work to see 'The African Queen' at the Odeon. Of course, Don had to be on a late shift when I wanted him. Come in, come in, Stephen."

"He's been to our house, Mam. He tells me he was leaving home, apparently, he doesn't like the cat."

"You daft lump, Stephen. You have me worried sick. I don't know what's going to become of you." She turned to me. "I've had him to Doctor Bloom's; he's making an appointment at the hospital for him. Rob says it could be serious. Don't you Rob?" she asked as we entered the parlour.

"Well, he's not getting any better is he?" said Rob from the depths of his armchair.

Already, Stephen had lost interest in this discussion. Instead he had plonked himself on the settee, and immersed in a fit of giggling, was stroking the cat.

"Good pussy, good pussy."

"I feel awful, Paul," said Joan on my return, "but we couldn't have him, could we?"

"Don't look so guilty, Joan, no of course not. I'm afraid he needs treatment though. Mam's taking him to the QE for a check-up."

"I can't help feeling that we could have done something all the same. He looked so forlorn."

I slept little that night, an image of Stephen emptying his carrier bag of its pitiable cargo of bits and pieces haunted my thoughts.

The minute she came through the door, she fell into Joan's arms sobbing. "He's got schizophrenia."

It was Mam. She'd called around on the evening of that awful day. The day the hospital consultant had broken the news. "Poor bairn, poor bairn, and he only sixteen," she wailed.

Joan hugged her, attempting to comfort her. "Come sit down. Tell us about it."

She slumped on the settee. "There's not much to tell. I suspected it was something serious. They don't know why. They don't know why. Whether it's something to do with his dad's illness – the TB. Whatever, whatever. There is no history of anything like that in either family."

She started sobbing again. Then laughed as she wiped her eyes. "I'm ruining my make-up."

"Paul, get your mam a cup of tea, love."

I was glad to busy myself in the kitchen for a few minutes and assimilate the news. To be honest, it was no surprise to me. Stephen had acted strangely, irrationally, for many years. His condition had just worsened.

"Here, Mam. Have a cuppa."

"Ta, Den." She took a sip and sniffed. "They didn't say much about treatment. They say he'll probably have to go into hospital eventually. I know myself that if he gets much worse, I won't be able to look after him, I won't be able to control him, Joan," she sobbed.

"Let's pray that he'll stabilise, then. He might go into remission you know. It's possible," said Joan.

"I don't know, Joan, I don't know, Den. I just don't know what to think. I don't even know whether he'll be home at Christmas."

Stephen didn't go into remission. Instead his condition worsened. He wasn't at home at Christmas. Instead he was in Stanningley Mental Hospital in the wilds of Northumberland.

The catalyst? It was a Friday. Just a few weeks since the visit of the runaway. I was in the office and had just finished making up the weekly pay packets when the phone rang. Freddie, incompetent Freddie, who at eighteen was still an office boy in all but name, shouted from the booth, "It's for you, Mr Potts." (Inept, but respectful Freddie.)

A phone call? For me? On a Friday afternoon?

"Paul, we've got a problem here." The voice was mellifluous, a Rosemary Clooney quality, only more so. For a moment I was puzzled. "Can you hear me, love?"

Stupid me. It was Joan. On the telephone. To me. For the first time.

Castle on a Cloud

I'd got accustomed to her pleasant voice, but to hear it over the wires triggered in me an unexpected shaft of pleasure.

I closed the door to the booth. "Sorry, love. It's just that you sound so nice over the phone. What is it?"

"It's serious, Paul. I wouldn't ring you otherwise. Stephen is missing. Don's just been around on his way to work. He's been away all day. Can you go straight to your Mam's? See what you can do. Cecil works late on a Friday and there's no telling when Rob will be in. Your Mam must be worried sick. You might have to call the police."

Half of me was listening to the music of her voice, at first confusing the seriousness of her message. "Police? Oh, police. Right, Joan. Old Patterson will let me off straightaway when I tell him it's important."

"Good."

"'Bye then. I love you, Joan."

"I love you too."

I caught one of the new buses, the clattering Gateshead trams now things of the past. Thankfully, it was not yet peak time and the Saltwell Park bus sped up Bensham and along Coatsworth Road. Mam must be in a turmoil I thought, though I doubted what help I could be. Where would I start? Stephen could be anywhere. Despite his limp he seemed to wander for miles with that Ephraim lad. Ephraim? Did Mam know where he lived? That could be the solution.

I heard voices as I climbed the steps to Mam's flat and entered the scullery. Strange masculine voices; then a giggle. A giggle? Stephen? What was all this?

'All this' was two policemen sitting on the settee, their helmets on their knees. 'All this' was Stephen perched on a dining chair. 'All this' was Mam pouring out cups of tea.

A freaky scene.

"Den! What's brought you here?"

"What's brought me here? Joan rang me, that's what brought me here! What's he done?" I said, looking at the Bobbies and then at Stephen.

Mam turned to the policemen. "This is Dennis, Stephen's brother."

The elder one, the one with three stripes, the one who reminded me of the avuncular Jack Warner playing Sergeant Dixon in that film the 'Blue Lamp', spoke up. "Nothing serious, Mr Potts. Nothing criminal as such. Apart from wasting the time of the police, I suppose. But we won't say any more about that," he said, taking a cup of tea and settling back comfortably. "It's all settled now, sir. Stephen's mam is taking him back to the doctor to sort things out. Is that right, Mrs Hall?"

"Yes, he told me to go back to see him if I had problems. I'm sorry for the trouble, Sergeant. He's a worry."

"But what's he done? I presume you were called out to deal with some disturbance. Was he in Saltwell Park? Was an older lad with him?"

The sergeant took a sup of tea and laughed. "Ho, ho! Saltwell Park? That's here in Gateshead, isn't it? No, no sir, not Saltwell Park. He had just come out of South Marine Park when we spotted him. That's where we found him, limping along the sea front in a torrential shower of rain, and him with no coat, just a pullover." He turned to the constable. "That's right, George?"

"Aye, Sarge, there was thunder and lightning, he looked lost and frightened."

"No sir, we're not from Gateshead, Mr Potts. We've driven up from South Shields."

"South Shields! What was he doing in South Shields? That's ten miles from here. How did he get there? He didn't have any money. He didn't Mam?"

"No, not a penny."

"No, he didn't have any money when we picked him up. He came quietly, no force was needed."

"Not a pick of bother, Den." Stephen giggled, suddenly taking an interest in the goings-on. I noticed that he had a dry jersey on now. "How did you get to South Shields, Stephen?" I asked.

"We asked Stephen that. He said something about an aeroplane, but that seemed far-fetched. He told us his name – Stephen; then we found a letter in an envelope addressed to a Stephen in his pocket. From somebody called Ephraim. I said to Constable Dawson here, I bet that's where the lad lives. Didn't I, George?"

"That's right, Sarge. Then you said we'd follow the clue up rightaway." He turned to me. "The sarge was right. The sarge was spot on."

"Then it was just spur of the moment, sir. Let's take him back right now, I said, and here we are."

The sergeant drained his cup. "Thanks, Mrs Potts. We'd better be getting along, George; our shift finishes in an hour."

Castle on a Cloud

The hospital people said he would get treatment. They said there was hope. Treatment seemed to be crude – mainly electric shock therapy. Hope seemed to be just a will-o'-the-wisp. In truth, his condition worsened. Most times, when Joan and I visited him, he failed to identify us. His mam and Don were the only souls he consistently recognised in his new world. Except for Harry – a male nurse. Harry had the patience of Job. Harry was his confidante.

"Harry's me mucker," he would say.

16

GROWING PAINS

"Blub blub blub blub, blub blub blub."

No, it wasn't Mark, he was eighteen months old now; he didn't gurgle any more. It was Joan, shivering and spluttering, as she dunked her face in the washing-up bowl. She'd gone into the kitchen, filled the bowl with cold water, then to our mystification had plonked it on the dining table.

Now, she reached for the towel. "There, that should keep me awake for a bit."

She had no stamina these days. It was only a quarter-past-eleven on a Monday night in June. Looking out over the roofs across the lane, the sky was still diffused with the pink of the sunset afterglow, yet Joan was flagging.

Until this bizarre interruption we had been playing cards; Joan, her dad, her mam, and me. When she'd failed to trump her Mam's king of spades, I had blown my top. "Joan! You're falling asleep!"

She'd put her hand to her mouth. "Oo! Sorry, love," she'd said, rubbing her eyes.

"That's another penny down the drain." I moaned.

"We'll just have another 'alf hour, Joan. Aa'm enjoyin' this whist lark," her dad had said.

Her Mam had piped up then. "No," she yawned, "if you're tired, luv, we'll go to bed. Aa know what your Dad's game is. He wants those pints he had at the Cannon to go through him, so he won't have to get up in the middle of the night and go down the backyard to the lav."

"I'm alright, Mam," Joan had said. "I know what I can do to keep awake."

That's when the bowl of water appeared, creating general merriment when she started ducking her face in it.

That's when I began to feel guilty. She'd lost a deal of shut-eye these last few weeks with Mark now teething. There were nights, when, unselfishly, she had shooed me into the spare room so that I would get some sleep and be fresh for work.

Her reward? To hear me give her a rollicking for losing a penny. Not only that I'd joined in the general laughter at her antics.

Well, it was funny.

"There, Mam, I'm fresh now. Deal the cards."

"Alright, luv," said her mam, shuffling the pack. "That's the second laugh we've had today, Joan." She turned to Joan's dad. "That was a good coach trip we had, weren't it George? By, there's some luvly countryside up here, Joan, and that Bamburgh Castle! But that chap in the front seat. He was a queer one."

"He was that, Joan," laughed her dad. "It were fair enough when he cem around 'olding out his bowler 'at, shouting 'Tips for the driver, folks'. By, that driver did well, mind, Aa saw somebody put a 'alf crown in that tidfer."

"Getaway!" said I, picking up another trick and thinking – keep talking Grandad. I hadn't expected to win that trick with a Jack – there was a Queen lurking in somebody's hand and it wasn't in Joan's – she'd thrown away.

"Aa'm not kiddin' – a 'alf-crown! Nobody goes putting 'alf-crowns into bowler 'ats for engine drivers. Not even thruppeny bits, even though we drive people a 'ell of a sight further than Bamburgh. Why not, I ask?" He chuckled to himself. "That would be a good idea don't you think, Paul?"

"You mean going along the train holding out your railway cap?" I said, picking up another unexpected trick.

"Honest, though, Paul, Aa didn't really mind him raising money for the driver, Aa put a tanner in meesen. But would you believe it, just when we drove into the coach station and we were all in a hurry to catch our buses, didn't this chap stand up! 'Ladies and gents,' he shouted. 'Let's give three cheers for the jolly old driver.'"

"He didn't," I laughed.

"'Ee did, Paul."

"So did you give three cheers, Dad?"

Castle on a Cloud

"Well, what could we do, Joan?" said her mam. "When he shouted, ''Ip, 'ip', we all shouted, "Ooray', like a lot of daft buggers."

"Mam!" Joan whooped.

"Pardon my French, but that's what we must have sounded like, weren't it, George?"

"Not only that," chuckled George, "but he weren't happy with three 'oorays. He wanted another one. 'One last cheer for the jolly old driver,' 'ee said."

Why were we playing cards at nearly midnight on a Monday and me up for work in the morning? Because Joan's Mam and Dad, were having a week's holiday with us. This was their second day and if they were going to keep us up every night until midnight and beyond playing cards, *I* would be a wreck by the end of the week, never mind Joan. I hoped the coach trips would tire them out. Hoped in vain.

A few weeks later, we got our revenge – our holiday base was Joan's Mam's. Her Dad was on early shifts that week, but nevertheless we made sure he joined in our card games on a night. Mark wasn't keeping us awake now, tired out as he was with toddling on the beach, laughing as he knocked over Joan's flawless sandcastles, and splashing in the sea at Scarborough and Whitby. We made the most of our British Rail runabout tickets that holiday.

It was a great week, weather glorious every day. A great week until we went to the Ashes Test Match, leaving Mark in the care of his gran. Up at seven, sandwiches made, thermos filled, off we went on the crowded bus to Leeds.

Headingley! First time for me, but not for Joan. After queuing for an hour, we entered the famous ground. The ground where Don Bradman had scored that record 334. Today, Australia and England were scrapping it out for the Ashes, the first three Tests had ended in draws, this game was destined to end the same way. Nevertheless the cricket had been absorbing, with flamboyant Denis Compton, playing an unusual, back-to-the-wall, defensive innings.

"I wonder how Mam's got on looking after Mark today," said Joan on the bus back to York. "He's getting to be a handful, always looking for mischief."

"She'll have enjoyed it, Joan, remember what she said last night? 'Get theesels off t't'cricket. Aa'll luke after the little lad?'"

"Gerraway, she doesn't talk as bad as that," she laughed, "you're exaggerating."

As we entered the parlour, Gran came in from the kitchen. Hot and bothered from cooking, as usual. But something else; I detected a pallor lurking behind her flushed countenance; a look in her eyes, unusually troubled lines etched on her face, no friendly smile to greet us.

Joan too, must have noticed something wrong. "Mam! What's the matter? You look awful."

Her Mam suddenly burst into tears. "Ee, lass, Aa'm sorry, but Mark's 'ad an accident."

Just then her dad appeared behind her and put a comforting hand on his wife's shoulder.

"My God!" cried Joan. "What's happened?"

"Don't worry, lass. Ee's alright in 'imself," said her dad. "It's just that your mam 'ad to tek 'im to the 'ospital."

"What happened?" I asked, "Which hospital is he in?"

"No, Paul, luv," her mam, snuffled. "'Ee's 'ome now. 'Ee's upstairs sound asleep. Aa blame meesen. Aa' was gettin' a bit of breakfast. Aa'd only taken my eyes off 'im for a minute, when 'ee ran out the backdoor and fell down those two steps."

"He's cracked his head?!" gasped Joan.

"No, but 'ee's broke his ankle, luv," said her Dad.

"Aye," her mam said, "the doctor says 'ee'll be alright. Thank goodness for that, but the poor bairn! A right granny Aa've turned out to be. Aa didn't know how to face the two of thees. Aa've bin worried all day."

"There'll be no lasting damage, though, Gran?"

"That's what the doctor said, Paul. It's been a bad day all round, for the little bairn."

"How is that?" asked Joan, anxiously.

"Well, when Aa got back from the hospital Aa found the postman 'ad been. You know that lovely photo of Mark that ye gave me? Aa sent it to that bonny baby competition in the paper."

"You mean that one of him with the cuddly dog? I didn't know you'd done that."

"No, Aa was keepin' quiet about it. It was goin' to be a surprise when 'ee won. I was sure 'ee would, Joan. What a disappointment it was when Aa found 'ee 'adn't. The poor bairn."

I laughed then, "I don't suppose Mark's bothered about that."

Castle on a Cloud

"Anyway, we'll go up to see him, Mam."

"Right you are, luv. I'll get you something to eat."

Recovery came quickly for Mark, much slower for his gran. So for me, 1953 wasn't to be remembered for the Coronation, nor for Hillary and Tensing conquering Everest, nor for the death of Joseph Stalin, nor for myxomatosis (though old Davidson would miss his rabbit pies), nor even for England's cricketers regaining the Ashes. No, 1953 was the year that Mark Jet Potts broke his ankle and the year that his maternal grandmother nearly broke her heart.

"Naw, you're not my brother. I don't know you. He's my brother. Don's my brother. And who's that little fellow on your knee?" The little fellow was Mark, now just turned three. We were in the communal room of Stanningley Mental Hospital. Our visits to see Stephen seemed almost worthless these days. We'd hoped that Stephen would regain that part of his consciousness that seemed to have been extinguished – the ability to recognise Joan and I, and indeed, Cecil, as part of his family.

Cecil had accompanied us this day, Don was there too. Don had recently qualified as a bus driver and had wangled the Stanningley shift. The weekly bus from Gateshead to the mental hospital was a cushy number. Sunday overtime included the two hour rest before the return journey. Don used those two hours not only visiting Stephen, but chatting *to* Harry, and chatting *up* any canny female nurses who were daft enough to be in the vicinity.

"I'm not your brother? Don't be silly, Stephen. You must remember me playing football with you in the backyard?"

"Naw, Don's my brother, though."

"And you don't know who this is, either?" I asked,

Mark was looking at a 'Jack and Jill' comic.

"I know, it's a little laddie. Of course. He's a little laddie. What's he doing here? Can I have a look at your comic, little laddie?"

Mark looked doubtful.

"Let him have a look, pet," said Joan.

Reluctantly, he passed it across.

Stephen glanced at the comic. "It's not any little laddie, Stephen. This is Mark. You remember Mark?"

He frowned and scrutinized Mark for a moment. "Gerraway, that's not Mark. Mark's a little babby."

"You know, Mark, then."

"Why aye. That's not Mark. You're having me on."
"Do you remember me, Stephen – Joan – Mark's mother?"
"No, pet. I don't remember you. Joan? I don't know a Joan. Thanks for coming, anyway lass. What are you doing here, though? You're not Mark's mother. Mam is Mark's mother. She swapped me for him, you know." he giggled. "What's this fella doing here?" he asked, nodding at Cecil.
"I'm your brother, Stephen. I'm Cecil."
"It's all a pack of lies," he laughed. "Don's my brother. Where is he?"
"He's over there," said Joan, "talking to that nice nurse. That one who's yawning – see?"
"Aye, she's alright, but Harry's the best. He's my mucker."
Just then, Don came across. "She's a canny lass, that one. Her brother is in the RAF Regiment, my old unit. I was telling her about that time in Lossiemouth, but she had to go and see to a patient."
Stephen seemed to stand up quickly then. "Lossiemouth? It's about time you were going, isn't it, Don? Nice to see you, mind." He turned to Cecil and me, "Brothers!" he said, shaking his head. "Brothers! Daft buggers more like it." He gave a giggle, "Ta-ra, let yourselves out. I'm going to find Harry," he added as he wandered off.
That was us dismissed.

"Mammy."
"What love? Give me your hand, there are cars going along the drive."
"Who was that, Mammy?"
"That was your uncle."
"Like Unca Don and Unca Cecil?"
"Yes. And Uncle Philip in York."
"Do you know he's taken my Jack and Jill?"
"He hasn't, Mark!" said Don.
"He has Unca Don."
"I'll go back and get it off him, Mark."
"No, it's alright. I've read the pictures, Unca Don. He seemed to like it. Let him have it."
"Come on then, Mark," I said, lifting him up. Let's get the bus. "You've read all about Sunnybrook Farm, have you?"
"And all the other pages, Daddy. Mammy read them to me coming

Castle on a Cloud

here. Have you forgotten? You were talking to Unca Cecil about football, weren't you?" he chuckled.

"Don't be cheeky, young Mark," I laughed.

I turned to Cecil. "Stephen's not getting any better, is he?"

"He's getting worse, Den. I can't see him coming out in a hurry. Whoops." For no apparent reason, Cecil had stumbled.

"Careful, Cec." shouted Joan. "What happened there? I thought you were going to fall."

Cecil steadied himself. "I've done that once or twice, lately. I think I've got a weak ankle or something."

"Aye, you stumbled the other day, Cecil," said Don.

Mark piped up then. "I've got a weak ankle Unca Cecil. I broke it you know. Didn't I Daddy?"

"That was a long time ago. I don't think it's weak now, the way you run about, Mark."

"Look, Daddy. There's the bus. Put me down. I bet I can beat you to it."

"Right, you're on," I laughed. "Ready, steady, go."

He beat me by a whisker.

17

TALKING FOOTBALL

Cecil and me talking football on the bus to Stanningley? Of course we were talking football, weren't Newcastle United in the semi-final of the FA Cup next Saturday? Wembley beckoning them again?

On the Friday evening Joan, Mark and I landed up at her mam's in York. The plan? Leave Mark with his gran, then onward travel on Saturday morning to Hillsborough Stadium, Sheffield. That's where the semi-final was to be played. The opponents? None other than York City from the lower reaches of the Football League. York City – Joan's home town team.

Cecil had been sitting across the aisle on that bus to Stanningley. "You're going on a football coach from York? Joan's dad got tickets for the two of you?" Cecil seemed awestruck.

"What's wrong with that, Cec?"

"You're going to Sheffield with a bus-load of York supporters and you ask what's wrong with that? I'll tell you what's wrong with that, you'll be lynched!"

"No, no, Cecil, I won't be wearing a black and white scarf."

"You'll wear a red one?"

"No, no. I'm not a traitor. Good Lord, no!"

Joan, who had been reading those Jack and Jill stories to Mark on the inside seat, had chimed in then. "*I'll* be wearing a red scarf, Cec," laughed Joan. "I've told Den to shut up on the coach, just let *me* do any talking."

"No change there then, love!"

"Just for that remark, Den, I'm going to support the City. Mark, your Daddy's cheeky."

"Cheeky Daddy."

"Anyway, Joan. I can't be silent all the way! I'll just have to talk Yorksheer."

"Like 'Ilkley Moor bahtat', Den?" asked Cecil.

"I'll biff the pair of you in a minute. Anyway, he'd never get the dialect right, Cecil."

"I would, Joan. Listen to this. 'Ee by gum, Aa'm lukin' forward t't' City wallopin' yon Geordies. Think on, lass, we could be tittlin' off t't' Wembley in May!"

Joan gave me a dirty look. "No, Den, I think it'll be better if you just keep quiet."

"I'll tell you what, Den," laughed Cecil. "I once read a story about a British airman who was shot down over France during the war. He'd got some civvy clothes from a friendly Frenchman and was trudging along a lonely country road heading for the Channel coast when this truck pulled up by him. It was full of German soldiers."

"What's that got to with anything?"

"Well, I'll tell you," he laughed. "The driver wasn't your usual Nazi and he knew a bit of French. 'Liftez, hitchez to the next ville?' he said, or something like that. You know, German-French for climb aboard. Well this airman, we'll call him Bill, this airman who could hardly speak a word of French, and the only German he could think of was 'Gott im Himmel!' clambered on the truck amongst all these Jerries. You can imagine he was in a bit of panic. Then he had this brilliant idea. With a silly grin on his face, he pretended to be deaf and dumb, pointing to his tongue and his ears, then grunting. You could do that on this coach next Saturday, Den, eh?"

"Don't be daft, Cec."

"Ah well, it was just an idea, but don't worry, I'll come and visit you in hospital."

They say it's not far from York to Sheffield, about a couple of hours by road. Two hours didn't *sound* much, but sitting in my window seat on that coach, I began to think that trying to hide my Geordie 'nationality' for 120 long minutes amongst this happy crowd of York City fans would seem a lifetime. And then there'd be the return journey after Newcastle had thumped the City. How could I hide the smile of victory in what

Castle on a Cloud

would be a sombre bus-load of broken-hearted fans? Hang on though! God forbid! What if York won? Impossible! But what if the impossible happened? It would be my doleful face that would give the game away then.

Cecil was to blame for my trepidation. When Joan had suggested this trip, I'd looked forward to travelling with a crowd of York hopefuls, prepared to treat them with a friendly superciliousness. Cecil was a canny lad, but why did he have to go on about blasted Airmen Bill, surrounded by hostile Germans? Deaf and dumb? What a stupid idea. He had me thinking that if I as much as opened my mouth I'd feel a hand on my shoulder and a harsh Yorkshire voice saying, 'The game's oop, lad.'

I buried my head in the morning paper – the Yorkshire News – it was full of York City's big chance of Wembley glory. I passed it to Joan in disgust. "What a load of codswallop, Joan."

She was in the aisle seat; the plan was that she'd shelter me from discovery. She looked around anxiously. "Shh, Paul!"

Too late. I'd botched the plan. The nosey chap sitting opposite, with a rattle on his knee, looked across. "Did thees cum far to catch this coach, lass?" he asked suspiciously

"Oh, just from Burton Lane, up by Clifton tha knows," said Joan, as quick as a flash.

"Aa see, lass. It's just that your 'ubby didn't sound from rownd York way."

"'Ee was in India a long time."

"Oh! Anyroads, lass, W'shud wallop the Geordies th'safternoon. They've bin lucky to get this far. They've bin rubbish, lass."

"Hang on, lad. Rubbish or not, they'll wallop York City."

Who said that? Who said that? Was that was my voice! What had I done? I'd blown it, that's what I'd done.

The fellow leaned forward across the aisle to take a closer look at this blasphemer. "What's cum over thee, lad, doan't tell me tha's a Geordie?"

Joan, bless her, tried to make the best of it. "Well, 'ee came from Tyneside, originally, but I'm fra' York. Sometimes 'ee gets carried away."

Originally? Like yesterday did she mean? But I had no time to ponder further. Our friend was chortling now. "Gets carried away? He'll be lucky if he doesn't get carried away by an ambulance, lass."

He stood up and shouted down the coach. "Hey lads, we've got a Newcastle supporter on the bus!"

"What?"
"Weer?"
"Bloody hell!"

For a moment there was a hint of pandemonium as people got to their feet to see where the alien sat. A few came down the aisle to look at this phenomenon, this strange creature with the crimson face.

A stout chap, who seemed to be the organiser of the trip, struggled through the melee.

"Mek way, lads. Let's 'ave a luke at this stowaway. Eh, lad, ye've got some gumption. And thee lass, what about thee? Are thee a Magpie?"

"Oh, no. Aa'm York born and bred. Aa'm supporting the City," she said.

The female Judas Iscariot! She'd been a disciple of Newcastle United for nigh on seven years, and now, and not even for thirty pieces of silver, she'd denied her team to this inquisitor. What could be her defence? That she'd been a City supporter before seeing the light? I'd make an allowance for that, but I was on my own now, and too late to act deaf and dumb.

"So you're a York lass? I suppose we'll 'ave to forgive thee for marryin' a Geordie," he laughed. "As for thee lad, don't fret, we'll 'ave to look after thee. Shall we look after 'im, lads?" he shouted.

What a jolly face, and what a kind remark. I listened to their banter and started breathing again.

"Ee'll be gettin' the train back when 'is lot lose, Sam. 'Ee won't dare t'get back on this bus," said the big chap in the seat in front.

A squeaky voice piped up. "Aa don't know, but 'ee's got some nerve."

"Make him wear yor City scarf for 'is impidence, Sam," shouted someone from the back.

I boned Joan as we stood on the terraces before the match. We'd found a spot away from the coach-load of sarcasm. "Fine wife you turned out to be, letting me down like that!"

Joan just laughed. "I knew the game was up, love. You blabbed. You should have acted like Airmen Bill. Anyway, you know I don't care who wins. If York did win, they would be the first little team ever to reach the final."

That was true.

They didn't win, but big surprise! They drew. I wasn't too

Castle on a Cloud

disappointed, we'd clobber them in the replay, plus there would be a truce between little me and forty-odd Yorkies on the return journey.

A truce perhaps, but certainly not peace, next Wednesday's replay at Sunderland would settle the dispute – surely in the Magpies favour?

As we alighted from the coach at York station, stout Sam was waiting on the pavement. He held out his hand. "Ta-ra lad, Aa might see thee at the replay next week. Aa'll luke out for thees. If thee sees us ont' terraces, cum and join us."

I didn't look out for them at Roker Park, Sunderland, even after the final whistle. Newcastle had won two goals to nil; I didn't want to rub it in. They were a canny bunch I suppose.

So United were bound for Wembley again, this time to play Manchester City.

"What shall I wear?"
"When?"
"A week on Saturday."
"What do you mean?"
"For the Cup Final."
"Well, how about a black and white woolly hat and a black and white scarf?"
"Don't be funny; we're going to your boss's in Gosforth, not to Wembley. I'm not sure that I want to go anyway, even if it is to see the match on television."
"And why not?"
"Well, if they live in snooty Gosforth they're sure to have airs and graces."
"Old Patterson doesn't have airs and graces."
"No, but I bet his wife does. I'll need some new clothes. And look at my hair, it's months since I had a perm."
"Your hair looks nice, Joan, I like that soft look. As for clothes what about that smart black skirt? You'll wow old Patterson with that skirt and the white blouse that you made. The one with the rolled-up collar."
"What white blouse?"
"You know, the one you wore on Easter Sunday."
"You're full of blarney, Paul," she laughed. "It's the Irish in you – soft look – wow the boss. Right, I'll wear that blouse and skirt, but I want a new jacket. We'll go to the shops in town on Saturday."
"Aw! You don't mean Newcastle?"

- 153 -

"I certainly do. There's more choice – there's only Shephard's in Gateshead. Fenwick's or Bainbridge's may have a reasonably priced jacket, or we could try Farnon's. We'll have to get Mark a tie as well."

"Mark a tie? He's only three-and-a-quarter!"

"I saw a black and white one which will go with his white shirt and his blue V-necked pullover."

"Hi! We're not going to see the Queen. I'll tell you something, Joan; I'm not wearing a suit."

"No, your sports coat and flannels will be alright. As for the perm, you can give me one."

"What!"

"Well, it's cheaper than paying pounds at the hairdresser's. I saw a Toni Home Perm for ten and six in Boots."

My ears pricked up at news of a ten bob perm. "Oh. Do you think I could do it?" I asked.

"I'm sure you could, love."

"Who's talking the blarney now?"

The boss had been going on about his telly for months. He was proud of all sixteen inches. The programmes that he went on about were just names to me; Qatermass, Panorama, The Good Old Days, What's My Line. And what a fine picture he obtained. Very proud, he was. Hence his invitation – "Come and see the Cup Final, Paul. Bring Joan and the laddie."

"What's your name little boy?" Mrs Patterson's pleasant voice hinted at Edinburgh origins in contrast to the boss's touch of Glaswegian.

Mark was sitting between Joan and me on the settee in front of the television set. Our hostess had pulled up a coffee table which was now laden with tea, biscuits and cream-cakes. Mark's attention was torn between the fascinating black and white pictures from a place called Wembley, far far away, where the Guards' Band was marching and the Queen and Prince Philip were waving; and that near-at-hand trayful of cream-cakes.

"Will Prince Philip be supporting Newcastle?" said the commentator. "Perhaps; remember he once commanded HMS Magpie!"

That was something I hadn't known. I didn't find out much more.

Joan, sitting up primly, determined to show she was at ease in this

Castle on a Cloud

world of coffee tables, china teacups with matching plates and saucers, lush settees and state of the art sixteen-inch TVs, turned to Mark. "Tell the lady your name."

Mark looked up at the cream-cake lady. "Mark," he said shyly.

"Would you like some lemonade, Mark?"

"Oo, yes," then remembered his mam's intensive morning coaching lesson. "Yes, please."

"What a polite boy, Joan. It is Joan, isn't it? I'm terrible with names." Joan smiled contentedly and sat back. Things seemed to be going well.

"It's a pity you hadn't a television, Joan," Mrs Patterson continued, "I'm sure Mark would love some of the programmes – Andy Pandy and Watch With Mother are two excellent ones. I just love Looby Lou." She started to sing, "Here we go Looby Lou, here we go Looby Ly."

"I'm sure Paul and Joan wud love to hear about Looby Lou m'dear, but some other time, perhaps?" said Patterson, from his easy chair as he picked up another cream-cake. "The match is aboot to start and I'm sure oor guests wud like to watch it. Ye'll be pleased to know, Joan, I'll be supportin' Newcastle. Y'see, Bobby Mitchell's ma favourite fitballer. And you young fella," he added, "we want the team in black and white stripes to score."

Mark looked quizzically at this funny speaking, craggy-eyebrowed stranger, and then at his wife who was now sitting on the arm of Patterson's chair. She gave him a smile – he smiled back and accidentally tipped half the contents of his glass of lemonade onto the rug.

"Oh, Mark!" shouted Joan in horror.

"Don't worry, Joan, I'll get a cloth."

"Goal!" cried Patterson. He was the only one who had kept his eye on the screen during the commotion.

"What! Goal? Have they kicked off? Who's scored?" I gasped.

"Forty-five seconds – Jackie Milburn – and a header!"

"A header? He can't head the ball." I turned to Joan who had taken the cloth from Mrs Patterson and was now on her hands and knees mopping up the lemonade. "Did you see the goal, Joan?"

"No, I didn't, Paul," she flustered, rubbing away fiercely. "Don't stand on the wet patch, Mark, just sit down and straighten your tie. I don't know what Mrs Patterson will think of us causing all this upheaval!"

Our hostess laughed, "Don't worry, Joan. Come into the kitchen, Mark and I'll find some more lemonade." With alacrity, eager to escape from the scene of the crime, Mark jumped down and took his new-found friend's hand.

Old Patterson took his eyes off the football for a minute and laughed. "Don't look so worried, Joan, I won't be giving Paul the sack over spilt pop."

"Oh! That looks bad!" I shouted.

"What? Damn me, don't say Manchester have scored?"

"No, but their full-back seems badly hurt. It looks as though he'll have to go off and there's still seventy minutes to go."

"They haven't played twenty minutes already, Paul? I haven't seen any football yet!"

Patterson laughed. "Well, Joan, you should see Newcastle win now – against ten men."

Win they did, but it was only after Manchester City had equalised that Mitchell and Hannah clinched it.

"I hear you were in the garden when the football match was on, Mark."

"Yes, Mammy. It was a big garden, bigger than Grandad's. I wish we had a garden. I wish I could ride on a trolley bus like this one everyday. I wish I could have lots of pop and cream cakes as well."

"You're full of wishes, Mark. Did the lady play with you?"

"Yes, Daddy. We played football; then she tried to catch me when I ran around the big tree. Then we talked."

"What did you talk about?"

"I told her about when you did Mammy's hair. I told her about, let's see, I told her about Mammy with all those funny red things sticking in her head. I told her about you and me laughing, Daddy."

"You didn't, Mark! You shouldn't have told her about Daddy doing my hair. Did you say they had a big tree?"

"It was called a willow, I think. The lady said it cried. I didn't believe her. All the same I wish we had a garden with a big tree that cried, Mammy."

"So do I, Mark."

18

GIRLS PLAY NETBALL

Joan plonked herself beside me on the settee. "That's Mark tucked up in bed, and I've washed the dishes seeing it's your thirtieth birthday. Is there much on the wireless?"

"To tell you the truth, Joan, I haven't looked in the Radio Times. I would be surprised if that Bill Haley noise isn't played some time tonight, though. How people can prefer him to Frank Sinatra or Bing, I just don't know. Rock Around The Clock? More like Racket Around The Clock!"

Joan laughed, "You *are* getting old, love. The Archers are more up your street. What did you think of them tonight?"

"I don't know, I wasn't really listening. I've been browsing through this Wisden you bought me."

"I don't think The Archers is the same since Grace Archer died." She sounded wistful.

"You're not still in mourning?"

"Don't be daft. So you like the Wisden, then? I nearly bought that new word game – Scrabble. I changed my mind when I thought how you'd crow if you beat me!"

I laughed. "You're safer with this Wisden, love. It's the first I've got my hands on since Cecil and me got the 1937 edition. Fancy, eighteen long years without cricket's bible!"

"You two bought a Wisden? I thought your family were on the breadline in those days?"

She snuggled up to me. The pleasing aroma of her perfume prompted me to put an arm around her. I sniffed. "You smell good, Joan – and what's with all this nuzzling?"

"I'm just being nice to you on your birthday."

"So I'll think that there's not another wife like you?"

"I couldn't put it any better I, love."

"It's back to being nasty tomorrow, then?" I asked, ducking my head to evade a thump that never came.

"Don't be horrible. I mean being extra nice, I'm always nice to you. Last night, for example."

"What happened last night?"

"You *are* asking to be bashed," she said, getting in a surprise low blow to my thigh.

"Ow! Do you want to hear this story of the Wisden?"

"If you must."

"Well, Cecil and me ordered it from the paper shop at the top of Derwentwater Road. Correction, *I* ordered it – Cecil did pretty much what I suggested in those days."

"No change there, Paul, you're still a bossy boots."

I pretended to sink my teeth into the back of her neck, but finished up kissing it. "Can I go on with my story?" I asked.

She giggled. "Yes, if it'll stop you doing that."

"Well, we didn't ask the price, but we'd saved up more than enough – one and fourpence to be precise. In fact I thought we'd probably have the fourpence left over. Not many books in those days were more than a bob. Every week we'd call on our way home from the Saturday matinee at the Bensham: 'Have you got it in yet, sir?' I'd ask the chap. You know him, Joan, he's still has that shop."

"You mean that tall, nice man who looks a bit like Alastair Sim?"

"Aye, he does, I suppose. Anyway, we must have called half a dozen Saturdays, me ready every time with the money in my hand. Then came the day that he rummaged under the counter and came up with that Wisden. I could hardly wait to get my hands on it. I've always loved statistics."

"More than me?"

I thought for a moment. "No, not quite, pet. Anyhow, I knew the Wisden had reams and reams of records in it."

"So how much was it?"

"'Five bob, lads,' Alastair Sim, said. *I* was gobsmacked, but you should have seen Cecil's little face."

Joan laughed, "Five! That was a king's ransom!"

"It was to us, but do you know, he let me take it home if we promised to pay him fourpence a week."

"Gettaway! He trusted you?"

"Well, we had honest faces."

"I'm not so sure about that."

"Anyway, bang went our Saturday matinees for the next ten weeks. We only got thruppence pocket money in those days, so we just had a penny left every week for things like a ha'porth of black bullets, a stick of Wrigley's chewing gum, or a second-hand Wizard."

Joan laughed. "You poor things."

"Aye, lass, times were hard."

"Hang on, though Paul, ten weeks? It would have taken eleven weeks to pay for the book."

"By, you're quick at arithmetic, but you're wrong, he let us off with the last fourpence. We dashed straight from the shop with our tuppences and just made it to the Bensham in time for the matinee. Cecil was tickled pink that he'd not be spending any more of his spondulicks on a mouldy old book. Mind, we didn't half get wrong off Mam that day. She'd been having fifty fits wondering where we'd been."

"He let you off with the last instalment? I told you that he seemed a nice man."

"Aye. Mind, it's funny. Just seeing this Wisden cover brought back that memory. I can't wait to read this one. I'll take it to bed tonight, Joan."

"That sounds exciting," said Joan, yawning.

She took my hand. "Paul, love."

"Mmm?"

"We're both thirty."

"Really, is that so?"

"Mark's nearly four."

"Yes, I had an idea he was. Did you know Winston Churchill's eighty-one?"

"And he hasn't got a baby sister."

"Who, Winston? Oh! Mark, you mean? He hasn't got a baby brother either."

"You had brothers; I had a brother and a sister."

"Perhaps Mark doesn't want a brother or a sister."

"Of course he does."

"How do you know?"

"I just know. He'll want one when I tell him what he's missed these last few years. Anyway, it was always part of our grand plan. I think we should strike whilst the iron's hot."

"The iron's hot? What makes you think that?"

"Your iron's always hot," she laughed, stroking my thigh.

"You don't mean?"

"I do mean. I want to give you a birthday treat. I want you to read your book another night."

"You mean, you mean, you mean, like last night?"

"Uh huh. Well, *something* like last night."

"But you don't mean, yes you do mean! Crikey! But what about a house with a garden? That would have to go on the back-burner if you had a baby now. And what about the willow tree?"

"Blow the willow tree!"

"Blow the willow tree? This *is* serious. This is sudden, this is very sudden, Joan. Let me think about it."

She laughed. "Look, while you're thinking about it, I'll go and have a bath."

"But you'll spoil your perfume!"

"I'll spray some more on, here and there – seeing it's your birthday!"

I lay back on the pillow with a smile like a cat that's just drank a saucer of cream. "Will it be a boy or a girl, do you think?"

"Who says it'll be anything yet?" murmured Joan, cradling her head on my chest as I stroked her bare flank.

I smiled, contentedly. "I just know... I just know."

"That's high enough, Dad!" Mark laughed.

"That's high enough, Paul."

A Sunday in June, we were in the park on the crowded playground by the lake. We'd been to see the bunnies, the guinea pigs and the peacock, we'd fed the ducks with stale bread, watched the rowing boats circling the island, and ran away from a jealous swan protecting its young. It had been an exciting afternoon. Now Mark was on a swing.

"Can I push the little boy? And can I have his swing when he's finished?" A girl some eight or nine years old, dressed in her Sunday best, her hair in a pigtail, looked up at Joan.

"Can the nice girl give you a push, Mark?" Mark had a dubious frown on his face, but nodded his head. Joan watched anxiously,

Castle on a Cloud

monitoring the situation. At last she seemed to be happy with things. The girl seemed a canny lass, she was pushing him gently.

Joan turned back to me. "I've been thinking lately, Paul. Our baby will be here in a couple of months."

"And you'll be back to shape, love," I laughed.

She shook her head and looked down at the bulge under her flowery maternity frock. "I'm going to have to watch myself; I think I've putting on too *much* weight. What I was going to say is; that expecting your mother to look after two children while we go to the pictures will be asking too much of her."

"Oh, I don't know."

"You know it will, now that she's lost Rob. She still hasn't got over his death. That heart attack came out of the blue. Besides, Rob would always play with Mark. I know Don and Cecil entertain him, but they're often out."

"What are you getting at?"

"We should get a television, people tell me there seems to be lots to watch these days, plus ITV will be coming up here soon. That girl we see in the park sometimes with her man and her kiddie, you know, Mary – the one who lives down Dunsmuir Grove – they have a telly."

"But can *we* afford it? Tom and Mary are both working. Their girl, Alice, is eight now."

"Can we afford it! That's all you can say! Your salary isn't bad especially with your bonuses."

"The bonuses may not be there forever. The shipyards aren't as busy these days and in any case welding's taking over from riveting. Rivets are half our business."

"Don't be so pessimistic, love. Your firm will find something else to sell. We don't have to *buy* a set, we could rent one. Radio Rentals are advertising tellies for a few shillings a week. Just think, there's a lot of sport on; cricket, rugby, racing."

My response was stifled by Mark's anxious cry. "Mam, Mam, Dad, look, I'm brave! I'm going high!"

Mark's expression did not manifest bravery to me, more a kind of counterfeit courage, and even that tenuous look was dispelled as he went higher still. The sensible little girl had had a relapse – a relapse into stupidity. She was pushing Mark fiercely now.

"That's high enough," cried Joan, brushing the girl aside as she attempted to steady Mark. The impetus of the swing however, was too strong for Joan. Mark landed on all fours at my feet and the swing seat caught Joan a glancing blow.

The canny little girl? She had done a bunk.

Mark, at first dumbstruck by the shock of a four-point landing, was now bawling. Joan was rubbing her side. I picked Mark up, but Joan was my first concern. "Are you alright, love?"

"I think so," she said, feeling her stomach and hip. "How's Mark?"

"Shush, Mark, you've just scratched your knees. You'll be OK."

Mark's crying subsided into sniffling. Then he looked down and saw blood. "Dad!" he wailed, "Don't send me to hospital. Say I won't have to go to hospital."

"No, Mark, but your mam should go to the doctor's tomorrow, you could go with her, eh?"

"I'm not going to the doctor's, Paul. I'm OK."

"Why did you rub your tummy, then, Joan? The swing caught you, didn't it?"

"Not really. Doctor Bloom will think I'm stupid, always worrying about my babies."

"Doctor Bloom will think nothing of the kind. Look, Joan, I'll make you a bargain. You go to the doctor's and I'll agree we get a telly, right?"

"OK, OK. If it'll make you happy, I'll go."

"Aye, it's good, Den. That Billy Cotton Band Show was great. It was just like going to the Empire, even if it was a black and white picture."

Don was puffing on his pipe. He and Cecil had come down to see what this TV lark was really like when viewed from close-up seats.

Joan and I sat back proudly. It wasn't everyone who had a television; they weren't ten-a-penny objects around our neighbourhood. "They say colour tellies will be here in a couple of years, Don. We'll be able to upgrade then, Joan, won't we?"

"Listen to him, Cecil. He said he didn't want a telly a couple of weeks ago."

"I was just having you on, Joan."

"I think *we* should have one, Don. We could club together and rent one, eh? Mam would like it."

Don stood up and knocked out his pipe in the tiled hearth. "Aye, Cec, we'll do that."

"Are you alright after that bang from the swing, Joan? You were going to the doctor's weren't you?"

Castle on a Cloud

"Old Bloom thinks she'll be OK, Cec. We're keeping our fingers crossed."

"I go back next Tuesday for another examination, Cecil. I feel alright. How are you though? How's your leg?"

"Well, it's both legs – just now and again one will seem to give way and I lose my balance. I went to the doctor the other day. He said give it a few months to see if it rights itself."

"You're not with old Bloom?"

"No, we changed to Rob's doctor, Dr Williams, a couple of years ago. He's nearer."

"Joan swears by old Bloom, Cecil," I said.

"Well, Cecil, Den may laugh, but I bet he would have sent you for tests before now."

"It's a funny little thing, Mam. It's got a funny face."

Joan smiled, "She's just been born, Mark. You were her size when you were born."

"Did you say *she*, Mam?" Mark asked, crestfallen.

"Yes, it's a little girl, Mark," I said, "and you're her big brother. You'll have to look after her as she grows up. You can play with her."

"But girls don't play cricket or football, Dad."

"Some do," said Joan.

"*You* didn't, Mam. You told me you played netball all the time. You told me about that teacher who kept you in after school, and you nearly missed the big cup game, but you didn't, and you scored a lot of points, and your team won. You told me that story a lot, Mam. It was always netball though," he said sadly.

Joan laughed, "I've only told you that story once or twice. It's your dad who's always telling you about the football match when he was in the army and he scored twice."

Mark frowned, "But that was *football*, Mam."

"Anyway, Mark," I said, "Your Mam's tired, I'll put the baby in the cot and we'll go and have a quiet game."

"Can we play soldiers, Dad? A big battle? Will the baby play soldiers one day? Do girls play soldiers, Dad?"

"Questions, questions, questions, Mark. If you can be quiet we'll play soldiers, but we'll have to be very quiet. We'll have to listen for a knock on the door. Your Gran's coming up from York."

"Why, Dad?"

"She always comes when your Mam has a baby, that's why I've hidden the mustard."

"What's mustard got to do with Gran?

"It's a secret. So whatever you say, Mark, don't mention mustard to her."

"I won't Dad."

"That's a good boy."

"So what are ye going to call her, Joan?"

Joan was sat up in bed, nursing our daughter. "Well, Mam, we thought Anna Jane, didn't we, Paul?"

"That's right. By the way, do you want me to go to the registry office this week to get the birth certificate?"

"I don't think so, love," she said firmly. "It might be better if I go myself next week."

"Ye givin' her two names, love? Yet Mark's only got the one?"

"Mark likes his name, don't you, Mark?" I said evasively as Joan gave me a certain look.

"I don't want to be called Anna, Dad!" Mark laughed, clambering onto our newly acquired second-hand ottoman by the window and standing up.

"Be careful, Mark," shouted Gran, "Ye'll fall, like ye did on that swing."

"I *jumped* off that swing, Gran, I didn't fall."

"You little fibber, Mark. You cried when you saw the blood."

"No, Dad. I jumped off, just like this." he said, landing on all fours. "Ouch, Gran. That hurt." He looked at his knees. "Dad, I've broken my scab, look!"

"Well, you should stop showing off."

"Anyroads, Mark, luv. It's about time ye were going up the wooden hill to Bedfordshire."

"What does that mean, Gran?"

"It means it's time for bed," laughed Joan. "Look, Anna Jane's asleep."

"We're not going to have any more babies, though, Mam?"

"No, we're not going to have any more, Mark," I said, fingers crossed.

19

HE BAD MAN

"Ooh! Get off!" Joan was leaning over the cooker, making the nape of her neck vulnerable to a kiss. "Enough of that at this time of the day, Paul. Have you had a good pay day? No shortages from the bank this week?"

"No, no shortages; but not a good day. I'm glad it's the weekend. Oh, hello, Mark, good school today?"

"Not really, Dad, I'm glad it's the weekend."

Joan laughed, "You're copying your dad."

"And what are you doing crawling over my shoes, young lady?"

"*Anna's* probably glad it's Friday, too, love. She's got her daddy to spoil her now."

"Come here, Anna Jane. Whoops, up to the sky!" Anna chuckled as I lifted her high. A chuckle that helped to allay some of the disquiet I'd felt all day.

"You're a cheeky live wire, Anna. What have you got in your little hand?"

Mark took an interest now. "She's been rummagering in my soldier box, Dad. She's got one of my cowboys, Dad. It's the one who's always the boss of the bandits when I play Lone Rangers with my soldiers. Tonto says 'HE BAD MAN, KEMO SABI'. Take it off her, Dad."

"She hasn't been rummagering, Mark, she's been rummaging. Besides, you shouldn't have left them where she could get them. Anyway, she's not doing any harm, Mark."

"She is, Dad. Look," he said, pointing. "His head's fell off."

"It must be on the floor, Mark. We'll look for it after tea and I'll put it back on with a matchstick. You can do that with these old toy soldiers."

"You can't with my new plastic soldiers, Dad."

"Their heads don't come off in the first place, Mark," I laughed.

"I hope she hasn't swallowed it, Paul!"

"You wouldn't do that, Anna, would you?" I said. "Give the soldier to me. There, thank you, Anna. He bad man. Where's the bad man's head, pet?"

Anna pointed to the headless cowboy and screwed her face up into a ludicrous scowl. "Ppp!" she blurted, "Baba!"

"What a face, Anna! She seems to be saying she spit it out, Joan."

"I hope so; we'll have to find it after tea. You said you'd had a rotten day, love. What's happened?"

"I was called into Patterson's office first thing. Straightaway, he came out with it! 'Instructions from Head Office, Paul. Make up four weeks pay and P45's for Charley Boon, Sam Nixon and Danny Hall, and the same for their three feeders and three pickers-out'."

"They're three of your rivet-making teams, aren't they? You don't mean he gave them all the sack?"

"Aye, I do. 'Lack of orders, Paul. This bloody welding craze,' he said. 'We can't just stockpile rivets ad infinitum'. It's sad, Joan, when you think that they were crying out for rivet makers during the war. It was a reserved occupation in those days."

"That's about a quarter of the workers in the Rivet Shop going, isn't it?"

"I think there'll be more, Joan. It's Sam Nixon I feel sorry for. He's got three youngsters already, with another one on the way."

"They'll get other jobs, surely. Cheer up, love, let's hope that it's a one-off, eh? Come on, Mark, come to the table for your tea. And you, Anna, up into your new high chair."

"It's not new, Mam, it's *my* old one isn't it?"

"It's new for Anna, Mark."

"Can you pass the salt, love?" I asked, as Joan sat down, but my thoughts were not on food. My mind was still dwelling on those sackings and the images of shocked faces.

"Here you are. Do you want the pepper? And don't look so worried, love. Things at work will settle down."

"I'm not so sure."

There were three of us crawling all over the floor; two of us were searching for the baddie's head, the other one was just making a

Castle on a Cloud

nuisance of herself. She'd got the impression it was a new game. The fourth member of the household was washing the dishes – there was something to be said for this rooting about on the floor lark. Besides, it was relaxing after the upsets of the day.

Joan, drying a plate, poked her head in. "Any luck?"

"Not yet, Mam. If we can't find it, can I get a new bad cowboy, tomorrow?"

"We'll – oh, Paul! Look! What's Anna got in her hand? Put it down, Anna; nasty, nasty!"

I sized up the situation and scrabbling on all fours, reached the bairn just as she was about to put the head – Stetson and all – into her mouth.

"Phew!" Joan gasped.

"Thank you, Anna."

She smiled, "Da, da. Ba, ba."

"Morning, love, you're up early!" I said, wandering into the kitchen in my pyjama bottoms, bleary eyed and half awake. "It's Saturday, you know, and it's only eight o'clock. I've missed our cuddle."

Joan was beavering away in the sink, rubbing and scrubbing fiercely in the soapy water. I brushed off a bubble that had floated onto her nose and replaced it with a kiss.

"What are you washing?"

"Anna's nightie and her cot sheets. She was vomiting her heart out during the night, Paul. Did you not hear her?"

"No. When I eventually dozed off, I must have been dead to the world. She was asleep when I got up just now, bless her."

"I'll give her something to eat when she wakes up. I hope she's not sickening for something," Joan said, sorting the wet things and loaded them between the rollers of the Acme wringer.

"Hello, Mark."

"Did you fix my soldier last night, Daddy?"

"Old one track mind, Mark," I laughed. "Yes, he's on the mantelpiece, out of your sister's reach. There, next to the photo of you and Anna, in between Happy Mullet and Ruddy Glow. He's just like new now."

"Why do you call those two little ponies by those names, Dad?"

"Well, when I was in York on holiday, your grandad told me to back two racehorses called Happy Mullet and Ruddy Glow, and they both won. So with the winnings I bought those two trinkets for your Mam."

"Why did you back horses, Dad? That's gambling isn't it? I'm not going to gamble when I grow up, Dad."

"Well, sometimes your grandad, and sometimes your mam, leads me astray, Mark."

Joan came in at the wrong time. "You devil, Paul. It's the other way about!" cried Joan, swiping me with a damp cot sheet.

Mark picked up the toy soldier and examined it thoroughly. "No, it's not as good as new, Dad. I can easily pull his head off the matchstick."

"Well don't pull then."

"Are we going to the shops today, Mam?"

"I don't know, love. Anna's not well. I don't want to leave her. Your dad might have to go and get some bits and pieces. You can watch the television later."

"There's not much on, Mam. I wish Crackerjack was on on a Saturday, Mam. It was good last night. I like Double or Drop. I wish I could go on Double or Drop, Mam, and win all the prizes off Namon Andrews, Mam."

I smiled. "It's not Namon, Mark, it's Eamonn. But you can't go on the programme, you're not old enough. You couldn't hold the goodies in your little hands."

"I could, Dad," he said indignantly, "If I can carry Anna, I'm positive I could carry a pile of toys."

"I'll tell you what; I'll let you help me mend our shoes later."

"With your new first, Dad?"

"Are you trying to be funny? You mean last," I laughed. "That's not new either, Mrs Dawson upstairs, gave it me after Mr Dawson died. It was no good to her."

"Ladies can't mend shoes, can they Dad? I'll mend shoes when I grow up, but Anna won't be able to."

"Don't you believe it, Mark, Anna might mend shoes better than you. I bet *I* can mend shoes better than your Dad."

Mark laughed. "Why don't you then, Mam?"

"Because your Dad likes to mend shoes."

You learn something new every day.

"How's Anna?"

"No better, Paul. She had a few bites of Shreddies for breakfast, but she's been sick again. She's got diarrhoea now as well. I've put her back in her cot. Later, I'll try her with just milk."

Castle on a Cloud

"I nearly went into Gale's the chemist when I was on Coatsworth Road."

"There's no point, we don't know what she's got. She really needs the doctor, but it's their Sabbath."

"I know, they were all milling about on Bewick Road near the synagogue, all dressed in black. They're very religious. I saw a queer thing, though. A woman with two dogs walked right through the middle of them and they seemed to part like the Red Sea. It made me think. I don't think I've ever seen a Jew with a dog. Have you?"

"What a funny question! Come to think of it though, *I* haven't either."

I shook my head. "It's queer, when you think about it!" I dumped the shopping basket on the table. "I've got everything on your list, Joan, plus I got our Saturday cream cake at Carrick's. You forgot about that."

"I don't think Anna will want any cream cake today, poor bairn."

"Kids are funny, Joan, she might be right as rain in a few hours. Anyway, I've just remembered love. I've promised, to let Mark help with those shoes, but I'd better get the ladders up in the backyard first. I want to paint the old girl's upstairs windows while I've got my courage up."

"We should get somebody in to do them, Paul. I know you don't like heights. Even Mam's worried about you going up the ladders."

"What makes you say that?"

"Well, I told her in my letter last week that now you'd done all the downstairs paintwork, you'd be up the ladders this weekend. Her reply came this morning." She picked up a letter from the table. "Here, listen. 'Tell Paul not to go up that old wooden ladder and him not liking looking down. Your dad thinks the same as me, and him with those two lovely bairns. He said what would they do without a father?'"

"Hi! Come on Joan! That's going overboard a bit. Tell them thanks; I wasn't looking forward to it in the first place, even less now that you've read that out."

"So, you won't do it?"

"Of course I'm going to do it. I'm not chickening out now. All I ask is that you hold the ladders while I climb up. I'll be alright after that,"

"Phew! I'm glad that's over for a year or two."

"You're shaking; give me that paint pot and brush."

"I'm not shaking."

"You are! Look at your hand. Go and lie down on the settee."

"Don't be daft. The worst part was when this face appeared at the window."

"Face?"

"Old Mrs Dawson. A shadowy face through the glass. I nearly fell off the ladder when she opened the window and started talking. I found out one thing – I don't like having chats about the price of greens these days – not at the top of wobbly ladders. It was alright for her, she had a firm wooden floor under her feet. Then I had this thought; if she didn't like her landlord, she just had to give the ladders one big push and I would be no more."

Joan laughed, "Don't be daft!"

Anna showed no signs of improvement through the afternoon. I tried to blank out my concern by hammering Blakey's segs into the heels of shoes and applying rubber stick-on soles with 'help' from Mark. Mark gave my thumb a whack with the hammer.

"What's happened?" asked Joan when she heard a yelp, "Is Mark hurt?"

"No, Mam. It's Dad. He put his thumb under the hammer and I hit it by mistake."

"Oh, that's alright, if it was a mistake."

The throbbing took an hour or two to subside, to be replaced by a nagging feeling. It was now evening, we'd put Anna to bed, but she seemed worse. She'd kept nothing down – not even water. Feeling her brow, she didn't seem to have a fever, but her little eyes appeared to have a glazed look and her naps were spasmodic and short-lived. A stray beam from the declining sun illuminated her pale face. She cried out weakly in her sleep.

"What shall we do, Paul?"

"We could take her to the Emergency Department at the QE."

"But it might be nothing serious – just a bug that will pass over."

"Or, I could call at the doctor's."

"You'd have to wait until the sun had set, Paul."

"I think he would come before that, don't you? No? Alternatively, I could go for him in the morning."

Joan stifled a sob. "I don't know, I don't know."

"Let's drop the side of the cot and lift it next to the bed, love. I'll lie and keep an eye on her."

"No, Paul, *I* will. I'll try to comfort her."

Castle on a Cloud

For the first few hours, we slept in snatches, checking her condition regularly. Each time, there seemed to be little change. Unforgivably, about three o'clock I fell into a deep sleep. I awoke with a start.

I sat up to find Joan also sitting up, nursing Anna on her lap. Anna looked deadly pale, her breathing almost imperceptible. Joan was asleep, her head drooping as she dozed. She'd been crying, the tear stains were still wet on her cheeks. I looked at the clock – seven o'clock – and slid quietly out of bed. Not quietly enough.

Joan awoke with a jerk. "What?" she gasped, "Oh, what time is it?"

"Seven, love," I whispered. "She's no better is she?"

Anna stirred. "No, she was sick before, it was shortly after I gave her a drink of water, but she had nothing to bring up. Just saliva."

I pulled on my trousers and reached for my shirt. "I'll go get Dr Bloom – now."

"But it's Sunday, Paul."

"It's not *his* Sunday, love." I said, fumbling with my shoelaces.

Joan wriggled over the side of the bed and gently put Anna back in the cot, trying not to wake her. "I'll get dressed then. Be quiet when you go out, Paul, let Mark sleep."

I knew so well now this route up Bensham Road, this path that I had trodden more than once to the doctor – along our cobbled back lane, then onto the main road. Twice it had been a walk of eager anticipation – the thrill of the imminent arrival of a new baby in our home – but at other times it had been a walk filled with foreboding.

None more so than now. Please God, let Bloom be in, and please help him quickly diagnose this sickness and set Anna on the path to recovery. She had looked so ill this morning, so ill and lifeless. How quickly had she deteriorated! How could thirty-six hours bring such a change? With such thoughts jangling, I rang the bell on the big old door of the big old rambling terrace house. Part of the house had long since been converted into a surgery. I looked at my watch – it was barely seven-thirty. I stepped back uncertainly. What was I doing ringing someone's doorbell at this unearthly hour? And on a Sunday, too. The answer was simple – Anna needed help – urgently.

I heard doors slamming and footsteps approaching. I stood my ground. The door opened and old Bloom himself, a dressing gown over his shoulders, looked at me; at first with displeasure, but then with a tired smile, perhaps realising that this worried looking young man had never asked spuriously for his help.

"It's little Anna, doctor," I blurted out.

"Come in, come into the vaiting room," he mumbled, "It's chilly at the door at this time of the morning. Now vhat is it? Vhat's wrong with her?"

We sat on one of the bare wooden benches, as, haltingly, I explained her condition. The doctor interjected at frequent intervals, always with a query on his lips. 'Why are we wasting time?' I thought. 'Just say you'll come, and now – please...'

At last he stood up. "I can see that she needs a visit, Mr Potts. Give me half an hour. You've dragged me out of bed, you know," he smiled.

"Vhat has she been doing this last forty-eight hours, Mrs Potts? Vhat has she been eating, and vhat has she drank, eh? I believe the clue lies there." The doctor had painstakingly examined Anna; to me, his face appeared to be even more serious than usual.

"Well, really, she's had nothing since Friday. She had her usual meals prior to that. Now, even water and milk have come straight back up. Isn't that so, Paul?"

I nodded. Then saw Mark in the doorway. "Go and play in the backyard for a bit, Mark."

"It seems, Mrs Potts, that the baby is suffering from a form of poisoning. What it is, I don't know."

Poison!

"Dad!"

"Go and play, Mark." I almost shouted now.

"But Dad, Anna nearly ate the bad man's head. He –"

"Mark!"

"Wait a moment, Mr Potts. Do you know anything about this? The bad man? Who is the bad man?"

"A toy soldier, doctor," said, Joan.

"A lead toy soldier?"

"My God! We've been stupid, Joan!"

"You have, Mr Potts. To a baby, even more so than an adult, lead is very dangerous."

"I told you, Dad."

"Yes, Mark, now go and play. Please."

Castle on a Cloud

"What does this mean, Doctor?" asked Joan, her face, normally so glowing, now looked so gaunt.

"There's no hiding the fact that she is in a bad way. The most serious factor – she is very dehydrated."

"Does that mean you'll get her into hospital?" asked Joan tearfully.

"No. To move her would do no good. They could do no more for her than you can, Mrs Potts. Somehow, you must get her to drink, sips at first, then more. Every half-hour, or even more often."

"Will she keep the water down?" I asked.

"She must, she must. It's crucial that she does – today. You understand?"

We both nodded; there was nothing we could say.

"I'll be back at tea time."

All morning, Joan hovered over Anna's cot, and I was never far away. Anna slept so fitfully that it was never necessary to wake her to administer spoonfuls of water. But for agonising hours we took it in turns to comfort her, as, within minutes of every sip, she would retch pitifully. Watching her was so heartrending, that I took cowardly refuge for a time, seeking out Mark who was playing with a ball in the backyard. "Can you come in, Mark, please."

Mark looked up, "You don't want me to go and see Mam and Anna?"

"Don't you want to?"

"No, I don't like seeing Anna like that Dad. Will she die with poison?"

I bit my lip, and tears welled. Why did he have to say that? "No, Mark," I said, feebly, "But I want you to gather all your soldiers together and pick out the lead ones."

"I thought of that, Dad. The doctor said they were deadly poison didn't he?"

"We'll sort them out and throw them away, Mark, eh? You don't mind do you? I think we should, don't you."

A worried frown appeared on Mark's face. "I suppose so, Dad. Does that mean the bad man as well?"

"Especially the bad man, Mark. But I'll tell you what, Mark, we'll replace them with new cowboys and Indians, what do you say?"

"OK, Dad, I hope I can find a good bad man, Dad."

"We will, Mark."

"How is she now, love?"

Joan was sat on the bed by the cot. "I don't want to speak too soon, Paul, but I gave her two spoonfuls of water half an hour ago and she's kept them down." I sat beside her and took her hand. She burst into tears. "Oh, Paul! I hope she'll be alright."

"Look, love," I said, "I'll get you a drink and I'll make you and Mark a sandwich. You just lie back on the bed. You must be shattered. Shall I give her a little more water, first?"

"Yes, please."

"Sit up a little, Anna, water, eh?" I eased her up; she ran her little tongue around her cracked lips and held out her puny hand.

"No, love. *I'll* give you a drink, open your mouthie." This time she seemed to drink it eagerly, an eagerness in contrast to her earlier reluctance.

"Do you know, Joan, I think she's going to pull through," I snuffled, rubbing my damp eyes.

She reached up and hugged me tightly, sobbing against my shoulder.

"Mam, Dad, why are you crying?" It was Mark from the doorway.

"We think Anna's going to be alright, Mark," I said.

"Why are grown-ups so funny, Dad?"

"Just because, Mark... Just because."

20

THICK AND FAST

"Ee, come in lass, did you 'ave a good journey? 'Ow are you, Paul? By! You've grown, Mark! And come 'ere, Anna, come to your gran."

Hearty greetings in the kitchen from Joan's mother as she wiped her floury hands on her apron. Her dad, hovering behind her, expressed similar sentiments. His smoke-blackened face, his collarless shirt and his blue overalls gave strong indications that in the very recent past he had been on the footplate of a steam loco.

Anna didn't seem too sure about this strange couple. It was at Easter that she had last seen her gran, and judging by her puzzled frown, she had never clapped eyes on the black man who looked like a golliwog; a fearsome golliwog, not like the cuddly one that she took to bed every night.

Way back at Easter, she had been a year-and-a-half old baby. Now she was almost two. So would she remember this stout lady who talked funny? We'd told her we were going on a too-too to her gran's in York. Not in a push-chair to her grandma's in Gateshead. She'd been on a too-too, so surely she would have worked out that this must be her gran?

It appeared she did, for although at first, somewhat dubious and sucking her thumb for reassurance, she eventually toddled into Gran's welcoming arms and was lifted up for a kiss.

Gran turned to Joan, "She don't seem any the worse from that scare she 'ad last year, Joan. She's as bright as a button."

Joan's dad, nodding agreement, gave an Al Jolson smile, false teeth gleaming. "Ye are that, Anna, my luv. Coochie coochie coo." I don't know whether it was the coochie coo, or the black face, but Anna suddenly sobbed and buried her head in her gran's shoulder, much to the chagrin of Grandad.

"Ye'd better go and wash thy face in the sink, George, ye've frightened the poor bairn. There, there, luv, we'll go in t'other room. It's only ye dotty grandad."

"Why did you say as bright as a button, Gran?" piped up Mark, tugging at her apron. "*My* buttons aren't bright, look," he said pointing to the buttons on his little suit jacket, "they're black."

"It's just an old saying of your gran's, Mark. Your Grenadier Guards' soldiers have bright buttons, anyway."

"I suppose so, Dad. Hey! Gran!" shouted Mark, changing the subject. "Do you know I had nits last week? The nurse found nits in nearly everybody's hair in the class. My pal, Tommy, says Scruffy Wilson must have spread them."

"You stool-pigeon, Mark," I laughed. "We weren't going to tell your gran about the nits, she'll worry now."

Gran took time off from petting, Anna. "Don't be daft, Paul. We all picked up nits when Aa were at school; and fleas sometimes. That were before the First War tha knows."

"I think I've got rid of them, Mam. I've had the fine toothcomb on him, and washed his hair with Suleo every night. I don't like them, mind, they make me feel all itchy."

"Ah! Anna, here's your Grandad back – with a clean face. You know your Grandad, now, eh?"

Anna clapped her hands and beamed, "Grandad!"

"Anna's daft, Gran. I knew it was Grandad."

Gran laughed, "Anna's not two, Mark. She's not as clever as thee yet. But Joan, ye 'aven't said what you think of our new place."

"I haven't had much chance, Dad. It looks OK, though. I'm glad you got the council to move you. That Burton Lane house was too big for two. Not only that, Dad, that nice lawn means you won't have as much garden to look after."

Her Mam laughed. "Gerraway, lass. You'll make us feel like old codgers soon. We're just past sixty tha knows."

"I like the lawn, Gran," shouted Mark, going to the back door threshold, "And they've got trees just like that lady's house in Gosforth, Mam."

"They're not willow trees, like hers, though, Mark, they're apple trees."

Castle on a Cloud

"Aye, they're apple trees," said Grandad, proudly, his thumbs hitched into red stripy braces, visible now that he had dumped his overalls. "Not many people in the world 'ave got apple trees, Mark, but your grandad 'as. Come on, Mark, come on, Anna, let's see if Aa can find each of you a ripe red apple."

Mark was out of the back door in a flash, followed by Anna, content now to hold Grandad's hand.

"They'll be 'appy as Larry on that lawn, Joan, it's a pity you've only got a backyard for them to play in." She glanced at the big clock on the mantelpiece. "'Ee! Look at the time, Aa've got a pie and some veg in the oven for the lot of ye. I'd better see to it, luv."

"Look, Mam, I'll give you a hand, I don't want you knocking yourself up. Have you seen the doctor yet?"

"You mean after that bad turn, Aa had? Aye, Aa saw old Merryweather and told 'im the story."

"Is Merryweather still on the go, Mam? He must be ninety if he's a day."

"No, luv, don't be daft, he won't be eighty yet, 'ee was only a slip of a lad when he brought Liza into the world. Anyroads, 'ee says Aa've got to get some weight off. To tek the strain off my heart, tha knows."

"I could do to lose a bit of weight myself, Mam. It's been difficult since Anna was born."

"You're alright, Joan, I'll tell you when you're too heavy," I laughed. "What else did the doctor say, Gran?"

"'Ee gave me some tablets."

"You'll have to take it easy, Mam; you're always on the go."

"Nay, Joan, I can't just sit around."

"Is Merryweather sending you for a check-up, Mam?"

"No, 'ee didn't mention hospital. Just to go back if Aa 'ave a funny turn again."

"What kind of doctors are they these days, Mam? You know Paul's brother Cecil is going to hospital for tests? At last! He's been waiting months."

"How is 'ee lately, Paul?"

"Not very good. He sort of staggered and fell twice, just in the last few weeks, and he drops things sometimes. I don't know how he manages at the sweet warehouse. He goes into the QE the week after next. He'll be in a couple of days."

"Aa hope they can sort him out, luv. 'Ee's a lovely lad."

"He is, Mam."
"So ye're going to 'ave runabout tickets again next week?"
"That's what we're doing. Isn't it, Paul?"
"Ye should tek the bairns away to the seaside for a week tha knows. Though, by golly, don't think Aa'm not glad to see thees."
"Perhaps next year, Gran, when Anna's a little older."

We'd had runabout tickets on our annual holiday for a few years now – almost every day we'd be off on trips from York; Whitby, Scarborough, Bridlington. At least once, we would do the coastal cliff-top run from Scarborough to Whitby. That run, with its breathtaking coastal views was my favourite, although Joan thought the moors journey through Pickering, Goathland and Grosmont, then on to Whitby, equally as grand.

Mark preferred Scarborough, it was a shorter journey. Besides, it was the town of bustling beaches, Corrigan's Amusements, Peasholme Park. Peasholme Park with its Tree Walk and its sea battle enacted on the boating lake – a twice a week sinking of the evil German battle cruiser, the Graf Spey, by the heroic British cruisers. Scarborough was always our first and last trip. This year, on the train back to York on the Friday, Anna, too, agreed with Mark. "I like Scarbor' bestest. But not big bangs on the lake, Daddy. I was fwitened."

"That's because you're a girl, Anna," said Mark. "But the Scarborough trip *is* the best, Dad."

Even more so that day, he thought, when, on alighting at York, he ran along the platform to get a closer look at the engine that had hauled our train. It was noisily letting off steam, followed by a whoop-whoop from its horn. Strange! Locomotives didn't usually whoop after they'd stopped in the station. All was revealed when the laughing driver, joints creaking, descended onto the platform and lifted a startled Mark sky high. Grandad had spotted him amongst the crowd, the whoop was his greeting. Black-faced Grandad! Engine-driver Grandad! He had driven our train! That made Mark's day.

Not Anna's, though. She put her hands over her ears to block out the noise resounding within the confines of the station, screwed her face up and kept a wary eye on the engine-driver. I lifted her up comfortingly and from a distance waved to Grandad as he chatted with Joan. I felt a pang of jealousy as he helped his grandson to jump up onto the footplate, and returned Mark's excited salute with ill-grace.

Castle on a Cloud

It was the Thursday night after our return from York. Three days back at Caledonian Connectors following the factory's resumption after the holiday and 'Scarbor' was another memory. On the Sunday, at York Station, Gran and Grandad had seen us off. Gran, tearful at having to say ta-ra to her bairns, but at the same time looking much more chirpy than when we'd arrived.

Now, we were anxious to find out about Cecil and his hospital tests. I'd called at Mam's on the way from the office, hoping to hear the results, only to find her sitting miserably in her armchair, snuffling and sniffing. She thought she'd got a dose of flu; feeling her hot brow, I thought the same. "I couldn't face going to the hospital this afternoon," she'd croaked.

"Don's on late shift, this week, isn't he Mam? I'll go up to the QE after I've had a bite to eat, and afterwards, I'll call at your doctor's and leave a note asking him to call."

"We'll both go tonight, Paul," said Joan. "I'll leave Mark and Anna with Mrs Dawson."

"That's what I was going to say, love."

We spotted Cecil in the big ward, most of the patients were dozing, only a few had visitors; Cecil was sitting by his bed in his pyjamas. He glimpsed us as we approached and gave a tired smile. Joan gave him a kiss before perching on the bed. I noticed a couple of men look up with interest at the bonny young woman in her checked sky blue summer dress and navy blue cardy. "Sorry we haven't brought anything for you, Cecil, it's been a bit of a rush," said Joan.

"I went to see Mam, first, but she's not well. So we didn't have time to get a bunch of flowers," I joked.

"That's OK," he said, with just a glimmer of a smile, "I'm coming out tomorrow."

"Oh, that's good Cec, so what do the doctors say then? Have they got to the bottom of things?"

"If you're coming out tomorrow, that must be good news, mm?" added Joan.

"They've diagnosed the problem all right," he said.

"What is it? What's the treatment, Cec?"

He looked at each of us in turn; then took a deep breath. "Disseminated sclerosis is what it is."

"What's that?" asked Joan, with a puzzled frown.

"Aye, Cec, what did you say, disseminated sclerosis? I've never heard of that. Have you caught it at sometime?"

Cecil wiped the back of his hand over his cheek where a tear had appeared. "*I* know all about it, Den, I've had books out of the library. Multiple sclerosis is another name for it." He gave a muted sob. "Don't I know all about it? Don't I just."

Joan took his hand, "There, love. Tell us what it is."

He was trying hard to recover his composure, but I sensed that tears were just waiting to flow. "It's, it's...."

He seemed unable to proceed, and suddenly I awaited his words with dread. Disseminated sclerosis? Multiple sclerosis? His demeanour suggested it was a serious illness. I berated my ignorant self. If I had known of this thing, his painful explanation would have been unnecessary. At last he spoke, but so quietly, it was difficult to hear him. "I knew I had it. I've known for some time. It wasn't the doctor to blame. He wanted me to go for tests. I kept putting off. I didn't want the certainty. Then, at least I could hope."

I put my hand on his shoulder. "You shouldn't have kept this to yourself, Cec. Tell us what it means."

"It means," he took a deep breath, "It means, well, it's a disease of the nervous system. Eventually it means paralysis."

"You mean you would lose feeling in your legs?"

"Worse, Joan, it could spread. You know what I mean?"

"But surely there's treatment, Cecil?"

"The books say no, the doctors only say it can go into remission, but it will still be there."

Joan squeezed his hand, "What sort of time scale are we talking about? Years?"

Cecil sighed. A despairing sigh. "It could be just months before I would lose my mobility. It could be years. It could spread to my arms, and my hands, even my speech."

No longer could he hold back his sobs, quiet though they were. Joan arose and clasped his face to her bosom. "Come, Cecil, who knows a cure is not just around the corner? Hmm?" Joan said, anxious to be comforting. "Here, take my hankie, love."

Cecil sat up and gave a weak smile. "Sorry about that, I don't usually blub." He sniffed. "I suppose you're right, Joan. Where's there's hope, eh?"

"What did you say about remission as well, Cec? That could happen too."
"You must keep hoping, Cecil."
"I'll keep hoping, Joan." He smiled wanly. "I'm a stubborn sod."
"What are you going to do about work?" I asked.
"I'm going to work as long as I can, Den. I'm doing a lot more clerical work now. I don't hump boxes of sweets around much now. I haven't told you but I open and lock up, these days, second in command, I am." He laughed poignantly, "There's some good news about it, Den. They told me today that I will qualify for an invalid carriage, Den. I'll be getting a car before you!"

We called at Mam's from the hospital, telling her the news. I played down the full impact of the prognosis, omitting to tell her of the bleak prospect of a cure.
"Poor bairn, I hope it turns out alright. Thanks, Den," she said, through a sneeze. "You two had better go before you catch my flu. I hope I don't give it to Cecil when he comes home tomorrow."

The children were in bed. That afternoon, Joan had popped Anna into her pushchair and walked up Whitehall Road on a mission to the public library. We wanted to know as much as we could about the outlook for Cecil. Now, we were sat side by side at our dining table studying a voluminous tome. Joan had said that it would tell us more about this sclerosis thing.
We turned to the Ds.
"Ah, here," I said. "'Disseminated sclerosis' – see multiple sclerosis."
Joan flicked through the book. "This is it."
Silently we read the data. *Multiple sclerosis. A chronic disease caused by a virus, affecting scattered areas of the spinal cord and brain. Early symptoms; unsteadiness, tremors; then as the disease spreads so do the symptoms. Ultimately, in nearly all cases, ending in paralysis, incontinence, and speech problems. Periods of remission can occur in some cases. Extravagant claims for remedies, but no treatment of proven value.'*
I shook my head in grief for my brother. For a moment, Joan said nothing, but simply squeezed my hand.
"What a life sentence, Joan, and he will have no one to be by his side; not in the way that I would have had with you."
Joan took her hankie out of the sleeve of her cotton dress and wiped

her eyes. I put an arm around her as I struggled to read more, but the page was now just a blur through my tears of sorrow. It was then that a thought occurred to me, causing the sinking feeling in my stomach to intensify.

"What if it's hereditary, Joan?" You stupid so-and-so! Why did you say that?

She gasped, "You mean it may affect Mark or Anna? Or even you!"

I forced a laugh. "No Joan, I'm being silly. Even if it was handed down through the generations, there's no history in the family."

"Not your mother's, but you don't know much about your dad's side."

"Well, he never talked about any of his relations being crippled. Hang on love, I'm stupid. It says it's caused by a virus so it won't be hereditary. You pick up a virus, love."

"Are you sure, Paul?"

"It stands to reason, Joan," I said, hoping it sounded positive. "Then there's this bit where it says they are constantly searching for a cure."

"I can't help thinking of poor Cecil. I pray they find one soon."

I'd read enough. I closed the book, switched on the television, and sat down with Joan on the settee. Phil Silvers in Bilko had just started but most of the comedy seemed hollow this night. I picked up Joan's new magazine, Woman's Realm. Fourpence; it was a penny cheaper than 'Woman's Day', and a better read, Joan had said. I flipped the pages.

"You seem to be interested in the Morley Nylons advert," Joan said.

"Don't be daft. Look," I laughed, pulling up her dress, revealing cool white thighs, "her legs aren't as nice as yours."

"None of your flannel, Paul. I've got bare legs in this weather, anyway."

Still unable to concentrate, I picked up the 'Chronicle'. "What's happened to Yorkshire these days, Joan? I see Surrey are going to be county champions again. Fancy! Seven times in a row."

Her response to my teasing was stifled as a heavy rat-a-tat reverberated down the passage. "Who's that at this time of the night?" she gasped.

I tossed the newspaper on the floor and hurried to answer.

"Telegram for Mrs Potts," said the youth.

21

A SPADE A SPADE

"Thanks, lad," I said, but my heart dropped as I scrabbled in my trouser pocket for a threepenny bit.

"Ta, sir," he said, mounting his bike, anxious to depart the scene as quickly as possible. I understood his haste – how often must it be that these boys bring bad news. Pray let this be an exception. I closed the door and for a moment hesitated. 'Mrs P Potts'. It had to be from York. Should I open the envelope and read the contents?

"What is it?"

I jumped. I hadn't heard Joan come up behind me. "It's a telegram."

"My God! Let me see it!" she said, snatching the envelope from my gasp and tearing it open. With fumbling fingers she extracted the form and peered at the telegram, but in the fading daylight failed to decipher the words. She hurried into the living room to read the message, let out a cry of anguish, and slumped into a chair by the table.

"Oh, my God!" she wailed. "Mam, not you, Mam. Say it's not true, Paul!"

I picked up the telegram. Its printed message was displayed haphazardly on adhesive paper strips stuck on the Post Office form:

'MRS P POTTS, 31 DOVER ROAD BENSHAM GATESHEAD
=MOTHER PASSED PEACEFULLY AWAY THIS AFTERNOON
= LETTER FOLLOWING =PHILIP='

That was it.
Her obituary
Out of the blue.
Gran gone. Gone.
"Oh, love!" I said; that was all. Nothing else seemed relevant.
Joan got to her feet, turned to me, and buried her face in my

shoulder. I pulled her close and felt her form shaking with grief. I nuzzled her neck. "Oh, Paul! She's gone, I won't see her again. I wasn't there. I should have been there!" she sobbed.

"You couldn't though, love, could you? Philip says it was a peaceful passing."

She raised her tear-stained face. "He would say that. It must have been her heart, Paul, yet she seemed to be so full of beans on Sunday."

I kissed her forehead.

"I'll remember her waving on the platform. Forever. Forever." she sobbed. "Oh! Why did it happen?"

"Let's wait for the letter, love. We'll know more then. Come, Joan let's go to bed. We can't do anything tonight."

"I won't sleep, Paul," she whimpered. "Oh, Mam!"

"I'll bring you a cocoa, mmm?"

A brief, pathetic smile appeared on her face as she wiped away her tears. "I'm going to call you the cocoa man." Then, once more she succumbed to her sorrow. "Poor Mam. Poor Mam. And Dad, too, Paul! He'll be desolate tonight."

The letter arrived by first post next morning. In Philip's hand. Apparently she'd been off-colour. Determined to the last though, she had waited until Joan's dad had departed for work. His last words had been to tell her to leave the washing. His day off was on the morrow, he would help her. But Gran was obdurate, washing day would be today. Her man wasn't going to spend his free day washing the clothes. She had dragged the gas boiler out of the garden shed and along the path to the house. She hadn't made it to the back door.

That's where her neighbour, Maggie Butcher, who had come to borrow some sugar, found her. On the path. Lifeless. Too late for help. A massive heart attack the doctor said.

Philip had been called from work; Grandad was probably somewhere south of Doncaster at the time of her death, on his way to Peterborough, from whence he would bring a London express back to York. Unaware of the tragedy awaiting him.

Philip had made tentative arrangements. The funeral was to be on Monday. 'Please let me know, Joan, if you can't make that day,' he'd written.

"I'm going down tomorrow, Paul. I have to see Dad."

"Go today, love. I'll stay off and look after Mark and Anna."

Castle on a Cloud

"No, Paul, it's Friday, your paying out day. You can't."

"They'll have to manage."

"No, Paul. I'll go tomorrow."

"OK, love, if you're sure, if you think it's better, go tomorrow then, but I'll definitely come down to the funeral on Monday. Mam will look after the bairns for the day."

"Are you sure she can? She must be feeling low with the news of Cecil."

"Of course she will, love. Hopefully, having Mark and Anna will take her mind off things."

Joan's tears came again. "What a week this has been, Paul."

I hugged her tightly as her lips touched my cheek. "You'll fall asleep at work today, Paul. You were awake most of the night weren't you? Cuddling me."

Her hand brushed wet tears off the shoulder of my jacket. She tried to smile, it was a poignant effort. "You'd better get off to work, before I soak your suit."

"When will Mam be back, Dad?"

"Why do you ask that, Mark?"

"Because my boiled egg was hard, Dad, Mam makes me a soft-boiled egg on a Sunday," he said, lashing strawberry jam on one of the slices of toast that I'd piled on a dinner plate. "And this toast is burnt."

"I've got a lot on my mind, Mark. I forgot it was on the grill. I don't usually burn the toast, do I?"

"You don't usually make the toast, Dad," he laughed.

"You fibber. Anyway I was thinking of your mam in York with Grandad."

"Why do people die, Dad? Why did Gran die, Dad? I liked Gran even though she talked funny."

"Everybody dies sometime, Mark, and then they go to heaven if they've been good and don't complain about burnt toast."

"That was a joke, wasn't it, Dad?"

"I suppose so." I turned to Anna. "Come on, pet, drink up your milk and I'll put your shoes and socks on. We're going to see the too-toos at the big station."

I lifted her down from her high chair, sat her on the settee, and knelt before her. I grabbed a sock from a pile I'd brought through from her clothes drawer and wriggled it over a tiny foot. Then I picked up another.

"No, no, Daddy." said Anna, frowning.

"Yes, yes, Anna. Socks and shoes. Right?"

"Dad!"

"What? Can't you see I'm busy? Keep your foot still, Anna."

"Dad! They're odd socks, Dad. One's got blue rings, the other's got red rings! That's why she said, 'No, no'."

"Alright, clever clogs."

I picked up another. Anna clapped her hands and nodded vigorously. "Silly Daddy."

"Don't *you* start," I laughed.

"Dad, why are we going to the Central Station?"

"So I can see what time the train goes to York tomorrow."

"Are we all going to York?"

"No, you know you're not, Mark. You and Anna are going to your grandma's. You'd better take some toys to play with."

"I'll take my chemistry outfit, Dad."

"No, you'd better not, Mark. You might blow grandma up. Take your ball; Grandma will let you play in the backyard as long as you don't kick it over the wall. You could take your comic as well. And remind me to take Anna's picture blocks and her nursery rhyme books."

"I've read my Beezer, Dad."

"You can read it again. I'm only going to York for the day, Mark. To bring your mam home."

"You're going to Gran's funeral, aren't you? Why can't I go?"

"Little boys don't go to funerals, Mark."

"We didn't see many trains, Dad. Dad, what are you doing now?"

"We didn't have time for trains, Mark. I've got to get this letter to your mam in the post, so she can get it first thing in the morning. Go and play at the back with Anna for a bit. There's a good lad."

Peace descended for a while. 'My dearest Joan.'

I found it strange writing that. It was over ten years since I had written a letter to Joan – that was just before I'd gone down to York to marry her. There had been many, many letters before that – nearly two years of letters to her from India. My mind wandered; an ounce a letter; sixteen ounces to the pound; that's at least a pound a month; a stone and

Castle on a Cloud

a half of letters from India! All beginning 'My dearest Joan', or 'My darling Joan'.

I came back to earth. 'My dearest Joan, the train arriving in York at 1.27 is the only excursion, so I will come on that and go straight to the church. Mother's going to look after Mark and Anna. She says could you get a wreath or something from her tomorrow morning? Mark and Anna are OK.'

"What is it, Anna. Why are you crying?"

"Fell down, look, my knee, blood, Daddy."

"Just sit on the chair there for a minute, Anna. Daddy will mend it with Elastoplast. I must get this letter in the post, pet."

'Anna and Mark are OK, but I miss you very much. Your ever loving husband, Paul. xxxxxxxxxx.'

Anna was standing by my side now, the blood and the knee forgotten. "What are those, Daddy?"

"They're kisses for Mammy."

"Me do kisses for Mammy?"

"Of course, Anna, here, Anna, here's the pen."

'X@#§'

"Very good, Anna."

There was a crowd outside the church in Clifton, every man wearing a black tie, every woman in sober dress and all wearing hats. Some faces seemed familiar; distant cousins I'd seen at our wedding? Neighbours from Burton Lane? I stood on the fringe of the gathering. I guess I too was recognised, but at first, no one approached. Then a bent, frail, old lady, dressed in black from head to toe shuffled up to me. I got the impression she was wearing her everyday garb. "Tha's young Joan's man, aren't thee? Aa remember tha's weddin' as though it were yesterday. It were 'ere in this very church. By, it were a shock when I 'eered abowt Ida. She were a gradely woman, she were that. Aa remember *'er* weddin', she lived next to us in Aldwark. Those were 'appy times. They were that."

I never heard more about those 'appy times, because, just then, there was a stir in the crowd as the cortege came into view moving slowly along Clifton Road. As it halted outside the church Joan stepped down from the second black cab, flanked by her dad and brother Philip. Joan had acquired a veil covering the upper half of her face; and a hat. Strange to see her in a hat. She was wearing her navy blue suit with the straight skirt. My heart went out to her; how smart she looked, despite her wan complexion.

I stepped forward from the crowd and took her hand. She gave me a glance of thankfulness, but her eyes were brimming with tears, tears still to be shed. "How are Mark and Anna?"

"Fine, love, fine," I said squeezing her hand as we proceeded into the church.

The service seemed long to me, the sermon so full of platitudes. Echoes of similar services over the centuries. Echoes of the rituals of the Catholic Masses I had attended in India. An echoing hollowness that had made me renounce the formalities of established religion.

Interspersed in the parson's sermon was a brief, feeble eulogy. He spoke of Ida Speed as a good wife and mother. She was more than that, I thought. She was a good mother-in-law, a good neighbour, a good friend. Stubborn, independent, but kind-hearted, a straight woman, a 'call a spade a spade' woman.

As the service continued, memories flooded into my mind:

'Get stuck in, Paul. Tha looks as if a square meal will do thee good.'
'Why doant you tek lad int' front room, Joan? Ye can 'ave electric fire on.'
'That boid will tek some cookin''
'Get theeselves off t't match.'
'Aa've made thee some gorgy and mustard sandwiches.'

Through the service, Joan was outwardly calm – the flood of tears came at the graveside.

"Goodbye, Mam," she sobbed. "Goodbye."

22

ALL CHANGE

"Bruce is stupid sometimes, Joan."
Joan yawned. "He's stupid all the time, really, but he's canny."
"Canny? You're picking up the Geordie twang these days, love."
We were sat, slumped rather, on the settee, watching Sunday Night at the London Palladium. We'd had our new upgraded TV for a week now. We'd been slow to act; ITV, in the form of Tyne Tees Television, had been in the area nearly two years. We'd had enough of people telling us what we were missing – how great the new programmes were. They hadn't mentioned the adverts.

We'd been slumped on the settee many a time, but never before in our new living room in our new house. Well, it wasn't a new house as such, it was a pre-First World War terrace house, and we were still on Dover Road. Getting towards the posher end of Dover Road, though. Now we had a bay window and a front-doorbell; a doorbell, not a common or garden knocker. Now we were nearer to Saltwell Park; ever closer to Low Fell.

True to form, I'd been slow to agree to this move, despite Joan's urgings.

"We want another bedroom," she had said, "Anna can't sleep in our room forever. Besides, she's getting too big for her cot.""

It was a view that I couldn't continue to ignore, couldn't disagree with. Having Anna's cot in our bedroom, did cramp my modus operandi. Thus, here we were. True, upstairs, there were just two bedrooms, but now we had a spare downstairs front room where Mark would sleep.

Upstairs downstairs! An indoor toilet! A cellar! Even a tiny patch of garden in our backyard. We'd arrived!

We'd also got a bigger mortgage.

I sighed and looked at the horrible, psychedelic, deep blue, distempered walls of the living room. It was a blue almost as deep as my mood. The decor was an unwanted legacy left by the previous arty occupants. "Don't worry," Joan had said, "It will soon be sunny and bright. I'm going to start papering tomorrow."

I hoped it was thick wallpaper, thick enough to completely hide that garish blue.

But tomorrow? I sighed again. "What's wrong, Paul? You've been quiet all weekend."

I *had* been quiet all weekend, I'd been worrying all weekend, wondering how and when to break the news. I didn't know how, and I didn't know when; all I did know was that we *hadn't* been slow in getting new tellies and new houses, we'd been too quick.

"I know you, you're worried. Is it something at work?"

"Leave it be tonight, love, we're both tired. I know you're shattered, all that work making cakes and tarts for Anna's fourth birthday party. It was fun. Let's not spoil things. Let's get the weekend over, eh?"

Joan jumped to her feet and switched the telly off – right in the middle of Beat The Clock.

"What have you done that for?"

"I want to know what you're worried about. Out with it. Don't bottle it up."

"I was going to tell you tomorrow night, love. When I know more."

Joan frowned. "Know more about what?"

"They're closing the factory."

I'd planned to break the news gently, not to blurt it out like this.

Joan crumpled onto the settee. "My God! What does that mean? When? When?"

"It means I'll be out of a job, unless they keep an office open on Tyneside. We'll all be out of a job."

"How did you find out?"

"Old Patterson told me; just before I left on Friday. Apparently, young Crozier, you know, the Managing Director, is coming down from Glasgow tomorrow to tell the staff. He'll give us the details."

"Was that the first you'd heard of it?"

"Aye, sort of. I haven't told you, but I've guessed that something was

Castle on a Cloud

up for a few weeks now. Crozier's been down twice in a month. Not the usual smiley, smiley, 'How is everyone?' visits, though. This time, he would go out for an hour or two. Very mysterious, it was. 'Where's he gone?' old Miller would ask. As if I would bloody know."

"Don't swear, love."

"Sorry, pet. But business has been so slack, it was a worry. We usually see the MD in Gateshead about once a year."

"Why didn't you tell me about this before?

"It was all speculation – until Friday."

I gave a hollow laugh. "I might have been barking up the wrong tree – he could have found a girl friend down here, eh?"

Joan took my hand. "Don't be daft, but cheer up. You'll get another job, Paul, with your capabilities." She tried to sound convincing.

"I won't get a job like mine in a hurry. You know that, Joan. Wages, salaries, cash. I was lucky, dropping into it. I've no accounting qualifications to speak of. People look for certificates these days."

"Don't be so pessimistic. Ability counts."

"Mmm. If you say so." I sighed once more. "I've been well paid, what with bonuses as well. Now, at the wrong time, we're saddled with a whopping mortgage."

"Look, Paul, don't worry. I can get a job, can't I?"

"Now you're being daft. You have Anna to look after. You can't even get a part-time job until she starts school."

"What about a nursery school?"

"And where are they? There's none round here, is there?"

"OK, OK. I could work from home. What about that?"

"Ha, ha," I said. "What about Mam looking after Anna, though?"

"No, she's got enough on her plate and she's not getting any younger."

It was true. The factory was to shut down. The office was to close. Our dwindling customer base was to be serviced from Glasgow. Our jobs were gone. Patterson was to retire. To sit holding hands with his wife under a willow tree in Gosforth?

And me? Would they look after me?

Well, they tried. It transpired that Crozier's secretive outings were to nearby firms seeking openings for his redundant staff. He'd been able to place Sandra (who had long since been jilted by Algernon), and two of the staff from the works office in similar jobs. The rest of the staff, including Miller, plus the machinists and operatives, would be left jobless.

And me? In a similar job? With a similar salary? More difficult. Impossible.

Give him credit, he'd found me a vaguely similar job, yes – in the two-man staff wages office of the big engineering company across the road – to take over from the senior man in a matter of weeks. But salary? About two-thirds of my current pay – at most.

Tighten belts, Joan.

Goodbye Caledonian Connectors. Hello Tyneside Engineering.

"Up to me came Arabella Brown
Pulling up her railway socks
Good evening, Mr Winklepip
Come and have a dance
'Cos it's nearly twelve o'clock."

Grandad stopped singing to take another sup of Newcastle Brown.

"You're in your cups, Dad," laughed Joan.

"What a thing to say about your father, Joan!"

"Sing more, Grandad!" cried Anna. She was sat on the floor, jumping her dolly up and down to the tune. Her black dolly that Santa had brought only that morning.

Mark on the other hand, at the table, peering over the ramparts of his new toy fort, cast a sceptical eye on his grandad, perhaps thinking he was barmy.

I was proud of that fort; especially proud of the castellated battlements that I'd secretly sculpted for nights on end after Mark had gone to bed; almost as proud as Joan was of the colourful dresses she had rattled up on her sewing machine for Anna's piccaninny.

"Sing again, Grandad," said Anna, clapping her hands. With alacrity, Grandad responded to Anna's pleas.

"Right, love," he said getting unsteadily to his feet, his bald head shining, his face jolly, his cheeks red. "I'll do a little dance as well."

Nijinsky, he wasn't. Not even a drunk Nijinsky, but Anna wasn't a worldly-wise critic of the hoofer's art.

"Oh, it won't last very, very long
It won't last very, very long

Castle on a Cloud

Round we went till I shouted whoa!
There'll be trouble in a minute I know
'Cos I've got no buttons on me trousers
And the pins aren't over strong
Run away Mrs Brown. I can feel 'em coming down
And they won't last very, very long."

He took a bow as Anna chuckled gleefully, even Mark laughed, chortled even, at the thought of Grandad's trousers coming down.
"More, Grandad, more!" cried Anna.
"No more tonight, bed, young lady, and you too, Mark."
"Mam, not yet. Anna goes first."
"Half an hour then, Mark."

Mark and Anna were packed off to bed. We were playing cards – carrying on a twelve-year-old Christmas night tradition. We played three-handed games now. No more partner whist, with those measured criticisms after every deal. Remarks such as: 'Fither, ye should 'ave led hearts!' 'Paul, why didn't you trump Dad's king?'
No, now it was knock-out whist, or rummy, or pontoon; not the same somehow. You couldn't argue with yourself.
I shuffled the pack for another deal.
"'Ow's the new job, Paul?" A serious question. Grandad had sobered up a smidgen.
"So-so. It's different working in a big office, even though we have a little area partitioned off. "
"Partitioned off? Why is that?"
"Oh, just to keep staff pay secrets away from prying eyes."
"Are there some big pays, then, Paul?"
"God forbid. We're all poorly paid. The people on the shop floor get more than us unqualified clerks, what with their overtime and whatnot. I don't know how much the big bosses get – the departmental heads. The Chief Cashier, with AssICB after his name, or the Chief Accountant, FCA, handles *them*."
"Is there much chance of promotion, then?"
"Paul reckons not, Dad. As he says, the bosses are all accountants, qualified engineers, that sort of thing."
"Head of the Works' Wages Department – that could be a possibility, but the chap in charge is going to be there for years yet. So, senior clerk

in the Staff Wages Office, that's me – replacement for Charlie Roberts, retired. He'd been with them for 35 years, that's as far as *he'd* got."

"Look on the bright side. You've got somebody working for you," said Joan, as she sorted her hand.

I laughed, "Aye, little meek, Dick Dobson. Meek! 55 years-old and he didn't want the responsibility of being a *senior* clerk. Not for a pound a week extra, anyway. Do you know he calls me, Mr Potts? I'm waiting for him to call me sir, soon."

"He smokes a pipe, Dad."

"He does that. He's so puny that when he lights up he disappears in the smoke."

"'Ee sounds a funny chap. Anyroads, if you're not 'appy ye'll just 'ave to look around for somethin' else, Paul."

"Easier said than done."

"Aye, Aa suppose so. By gum, though, thee've got a job, Paul, that's somethin'. Mind thee, jobs don't seem to last these days. Aa was just thinkin' t'other day, Aa've been on't railways for fowty years this year – Aa'll be retired soon."

"Then you'll be able to stay longer at Christmas, Dad – not have to go back on Boxing Day, like this year."

"Aye, luv, Aa'm at work tomorrow night. Aa'll 'ave to be up sharpish int' morning. We'd better get to bed Aa suppose. Anyroads, Paul, Aa 'ope thee finds something better in 1961."

I threw the dishcloth across our kitchen bench, job complete. Tea dishes washed. It skidded across the surface. That dishcloth never used to skid across our well-worn wooden bench. It did now, though, now the bench was covered with Formica. Yes, Formica; just a cheap offcut, mind, and green it was. Not the colour Joan would have picked if we'd been bushed. But what do they say? Beggars can't be choosers? A bargain; Saul's, the hardware shop on Coatsworth Road, often had these snippets.

Cut to size and glued on by me. Who needs the advice of magazines like the Practical Householder when all one requires is a practical approach? I smiled, picked up the dishcloth once more and whisked it again. "Whee!"

"Are you talking to yourself," asked Joan as I came into the living room. She was pacing about; she seemed to be on edge.

"Of course not, I was just admiring the bench, love; it's good."

Castle on a Cloud

"It would be if it wasn't a manky green."

"Oh, I don't know, the colour grows on you," I said, picking up the Chronicle and flopping into an easy chair. "The forecast's good for the weekend, Joan, I hope this weather holds for a month. Fancy! Just two weeks to our holiday. Before we know it we'll be in York and dashing about on our runabout tickets again, eh?"

Joan gave a rueful smile. "I suppose so. It would have been nice to have taken Mark and Anna to Scarborough, though."

"We're going to Scarborough, Mam, aren't we Mam?" asked Mark, with just a hint of panic in his voice. He was at the table doing his homework. He liked to get his homework finished first thing on a Friday night. That left the rest of the weekend for play.

"Of course we're going to Scarborough, Mark, but we're not going to stay the week as we'd planned."

I got up and walked to the table. "How's your homework, Mark? I see it's your story book. You're doing English, eh?"

He laughed, "No, it's sums, Dad."

"Don't be funny. Can I have a look?"

"If you want. I'm writing a story about a cricket match."

"I see." I picked up the exercise book. *'there is a man bowling to a lady but the lady is going to be caught by a girl and a boy is wicket keeper a little boy is feellding as well when one team is all out they will put the roller on to straiten the pitch.'*

"Very good, except for spelling. You've also missed out capitals letters and punctuations – full stops and commas, Mark."

"Oh, don't worry, I'll go back and put them in before Monday morning, Dad."

"I think you're having me on, Mark." I scanned previous essays. "You've got some good marks."

Joan, who had been hovering, came across then. "Don't stop him, Paul. I'm waiting for the table when he's finished."

"I'm just about done, Mam, I'll leave the punctuation marks just now."

"OK." She turned to me. "Mark told me some good news when he came in from school. He's been made a prefect."

"Oh! That's very good. I'm proud of him."

Mark smirked.

"So what does that mean, Mark?"

"I have duties, Dad. For instance I have to fill the inkwells."

I laughed, "That may not be good if you spill the ink on your white shirt."

"He'd better not," said Joan, apparently seeing drawbacks to this prefect lark.

"Dad," said Mark, picking up his book and pencil.

"What?"

"Talking about ink. Can you answer me this question? How do you know when you've run out of invisible ink?"

"I don't know. Hang on though. Perhaps when you can see what you're writing, eh? But, Joan, what do you want the table for? Not for the sewing machine? On a Friday night?"

"Never you mind. You'll find out in good time."

Anna, who had been wheeling her dolly's pram back and forth, whilst at the same time humming a lullaby to black-eyed Susie, suddenly piped up. "It's no use, it's no use, Mammy. She won't sleep with all this noise. Let's do the paper hats."

"What are you talking about, Anna?"

Joan put her index finger over her lips. "Quiet, Anna. It's a secret."

What the devil was going on? Paper hats? Paper hats?

Joan went to the cupboard in the corner, came out with two big cardboard boxes, and plopped them on the table.

"What on earth are they?"

"I'm going to earn some money, Paul." Joan sat down at the table. Anna ran across the room and climbed onto a chair beside her mam. Mark too, showed interest and returned to his seat. I succumbed to this air of curiosity and grabbed the last chair.

Joan placed the boxes side by side and opened one, pulling out a rumpled piece of foolscap paper. From my seat at the other end of the table it appeared to be covered with squiggly designs. Were they instructions of some sort? In a businesslike confident manner she smoothed it out. We three waited with bated breath. Again she delved into the box and produced a pile of crepe paper squares, some red, some green, some blue. Now, she turned her attention to the other box – out came a string of tinselly tassels followed by paper festoons of cheery faces – doggies, pussies, reindeers, and yes, bunnies!

"Rabbits!" I shouted, "Just like David Nixon. Mam's a magician!"

Joan gave me a look. "Shut up!"

"What's it all about, Mam?" asked Mark.

"I'm going to make paper hats and earn some money."

Castle on a Cloud

"Where did you get these, love?" I asked in what I hoped was a mollifying tone.

"Well, you know Blenheim Street in Newcastle – where there are lots of little businesses?"

"Isn't that where that Persian Carpet place is? And isn't there a Chinese laundry, somewhere in it?"

"That's the street. Well, I was talking to Eddie the butcher on the corner saying I wished I could earn some money and he mentioned Ravi Prasad. Apparently one of Eddie's customers said he got people to work from home."

"Come on, Mammy, let's make some hats," cried Anna, picking up a red square.

"Wait a bit, Anna. Don't spoil them."

"You crafty so-and-so. You've kept that to yourself. You've been across this afternoon and carried these boxes back?"

"Yes, they're not heavy. I've got the instructions here. He was very well spoken. He's stocking up for the Christmas demand, he says."

"Blimey, he's starting early."

"Get cracking, Mam," said impatient Mark. "Let's see a hat. Then I can play in the backyard before it gets dark."

"Don't be in such a hurry. I'm going to practice with a piece of newspaper first. I don't want to spoil any."

She peered at the instructions and started folding half a page of last night's Chronicle. "First like this, then like that..... and then, and then a little tuck. No, that's not it. I'll start again. First like that, perhaps.... then like this, then fold here. Damn!"

Mark was leaning over examining the diagrams.

"Give me it, Mam, it's like this."

Joan watched, her face brightening. "You seem to have got it."

He hadn't. "Drat it, it's impossible."

"Like this, Mam," cried Anna. Her little hands made one or two lucky tucks.

"That's it!" laughed Joan, "That last tuck, see Mark?" She picked up the contraption gingerly and opened it out. It resembled a hat – a tent-like hat – a rickety hat.

"What happens next?" I asked.

"You put a dab of glue here, and here, and here."

"You've got glue?"

"Oh, yes. They supply Lion's Gum."

"That's good of Ravi. And then?"

"You stick these tassels at the front here and then a funny face on top to cover the ends."

"Me do that, Mammy. Me do the funny faces."

"Perhaps, Anna. Let's start, eh?"

I looked at my watch – seven o'clock. It would soon be Anna's bedtime. Let's hope they would get a hat finished soon. It would be a pity if Anna missed that wondrous moment. I stifled a yawn as they fumbled. By some miracle, the vague shape of a hat emerged from their efforts, then came a hitch. Ah! At last. There was a hat. An ungainly hat, but a hat nevertheless, complete with three tassels and a funny face. OK, the funny face was a smidgen askew and looked to me to be at the back of the hat, but hopefully, Ravi Prasad might be a complaisant individual.

Joan held it proudly aloft. I looked again at the time – 7.15. "Darling."

"Yes, Paul," Joan raised her eyes from this masterpiece.

"Darling, how much does Mr Prasad pay per hat?"

"A ha'penny. There's material for a hundred in these boxes."

"That would be four and tuppence, then?"

"As long as we don't spoil any."

"Do you know it took a quarter of an hour to make one? That's tuppence an hour."

Joan frowned. "That was the first one. Don't be so off-putting. I'm trying, aren't I? When I get used to it I'll probably make one in five minutes."

"Oh, great! That'll be sixpence an hour. At forty hours that would be a pound a week. That's slave labour. Even an office cleaner must get four times that these days."

From her expression I got this feeling that I'd vexed her.

"Don't be so nasty. I'm just trying to get a bit more money for extras."

"I know, I know, love. But I don't want you beavering away working for peanuts."

"Look, if I want to spend my spare time making a bit of money, it's my business," she cried, her face flushed.

"But love, it's stupid. It's slave labour!"

I was unprepared for her next move. She jumped to her feet and swept the boxes and their contents onto the floor. "You don't care, you just don't understand, I'm sick of having to skimp and scrape," she shouted, bursting into tears. "I'm going out," she cried, hurrying into the passage and grabbing a coat. "Don't dare to follow me."

As if I could. And leave the bairns?

The front door banged shut. A hushed silence followed.

Broken by Mark. "You've done it now, Dad. You have that. I think you've upset, Mam."

He was a shrewd cookie.

Anna looked stunned. "Is Mammy coming back, Daddy?"

"Of course she is, my love."

23

RIDES AND SLIDES

W*ill* she come back?
Don't be daft, of course she will.
But why were you so sarcastic? Why did you hurt her with your cynicism? OK, it was a forlorn scheme, but God! She was trying to help.

I know now. I know now.

Remorse? I was full of it. Bales of sackcloth, and ashes by the bagful. My mind was spinning; but there were things to do. Concentrate Paul. Things to do.

Things to do? Pick up those pathetic bunches of crepe paper, those tassels, those stupid faces that were scattered on the floor. Stuff them back into the boxes.

Get little Anna to bed. Tuck her up.

"I've been thinking, Daddy. Mammy will be back soon, Daddy. I know she will."

"Yes, Anna, she will. She's just a teeny bit upset. She's gone for a little walk. Have you got your golliwog? Goodnight, love. I'll leave the landing light on."

Anna sat up in bed, my tucking-up wasted. "But you don't know how I know that Mammy will be back soon."

"No, you tell me, then."

"Because she's forgot to take her handbag, Daddy." She smiled; a smile of satisfaction. "Night, night."

No handbag? No handbag? That bucked me up no end.

Things to do. Get Mark to bed. No problem there. He went quietly, no doubt still stunned by his mam's walkout. She never did things like that. Lose her temper sometimes, yes. But to walk out?

On my own now, I had time to think. I looked at my watch. She'd been gone over two hours. I went to the front door. I scanned the road for a sight of her. I stood there for ages, as one by one, the street lamps glimmered into life. Darkness approached, a darkness that was aided by storm clouds banking up in the night sky. Pools of lamplight contrasted more and more with the areas of purple dusk between their beams. I felt a cool damp breeze on my face. There were few people astir, just now and then, I heard footsteps. At their sound I peered into the darkness; anxious, but hopeful, waiting for the owners to enter the light. Each time, disappointment; each time, it was a couple, or a solitary man, or a youth that emerged from the gloom. Never Joan. Never Joan.

It began to rain – so much for the weather forecast. I heard thunder; then recalled that in her haste, Joan had flung a flimsy summer jacket over her shoulders. Not her raincoat. She'd be cold, wet and frightened when she did return. She hated lightning. I closed the door and went up to the bathroom. I checked the water heater. Switched it to on. Good, she'd need a bath to warm her. I skipped back down the stairs heading for my lookout post.

"Dad!" It was Mark from the front room.

"What is it?" I said poking my head round his door. "Are you not asleep?" I added stupidly.

"You're toing and froing, Dad, I can't get to sleep."

"I was just looking for your mother."

"She'll be at Grandma's, Dad."

"Yes, you're probably right. Goodnight."

I was sure he was wrong, though. Don was on an early shift this week, if Joan had sought unlikely sanctuary there, Mam would have sent him to me, telling me not to worry.

I wandered into the kitchen. I put the kettle on. She'd need a hot drink when she *did* return. I opened the kitchen cabinet and looked for the tin of cocoa. Ah! There it was behind the Andrews' Liver Salts. That good old standby – calming Bournville Cocoa.

The harsh ring of the doorbell made me jump.

Joan, I hoped. I hurried to answer. Joan, bedraggled, pushed passed me. Not before I saw that she'd been crying.

"The bath water's hot," I shouted as she ascended the stairs. There was no response. I closed the door, shutting out the rain, rain now coming down in torrents.

I made the drink and took it upstairs. I put my ear to the bathroom

Castle on a Cloud

door; I could hear Joan splashing in the bath. Cautiously, I tried the handle. She'd locked the door! She never locked the door, not after the kids had been put to bed. I crossed the landing to our bedroom and placed her drink on our lone bedside table. I switched on the lamp. It gave a subdued, muted glow to the room. A romantic glow, ha-ha! Then I hurriedly undressed and jumped into the cold bed.

"Brr."

No central heating, no electric fire. The room felt chilly, even on this summer night. Chivalrously, I rolled onto Joan's side of the bed to warm her place, then waited.

I heard the bathroom door open, heard her walk towards the bedroom. Next moment she appeared, wrapped in a bath towel, her hair all frizzy from the rain. Without a glance in my direction she went to the chest of drawers.

"I'm warming your place, Joan." No answer, not even a 'Humph'.

She seemed to be having problems in ferreting out a nightie. She slammed one drawer shut and tried another. Then came a 'Damn'. The drawer was stuck. She pulled fiercely with both hands, allowing her towel to fall to the floor.

She stifled a sob, and for a fleeting moment, just stood there. Naked and forlorn. My heart reached out in pity.

And yet, and yet.

There was also a stirring of desire for her, a desire for her that was never far away. But this time a want that was not only physical, but contained a need to encompass her whole being, to comfort her, to love her as never before.

She retrieved the towel, but now I was behind her. As she attempted to cover herself, I snatched the towel from her grasp and tossed it away; I enfolded her silky nudity and held her tight. My hand caressed softness, my cheek her frizzy hair. Hair still damp.

"Darling, I'm sorry. I've been worried sick about you. Can you forgive me?" I pleaded, my lips on the nape of her neck.

She said nothing, just shivered.

"Come to bed."

It was like the first time, it was like an echo of countless other times. Only better, only better. Despite our tears. Or because of them. Those tears of forgiveness. Those tears of joy.

"Your cocoa's cold."

"Mmm."

"I love you, Joan."

She smiled, a tired smile, a contented smile. "Even with my crinkly hair?"

I laughed, "Even more so. You reminded me of a poor waif, needing love."

"Thanks very much!"

"A lovely poor waif, darling," I said, brushing my lips over those tight curls. "I do love you."

"I know you do, you've just said so a thousand times."

I caressed her flank. "That's an exaggeration. But I'm sorry for being so nasty."

"You were right though, Paul. It was a daft idea."

Her warm brown eyes glowed in the subdued light, glowed with love. She smiled, and wriggled sensuously to my touch. "Can I ask you a question? How come, that when I dropped the towel, you were in bed, yet before I could cover myself, you'd grabbed me. How so quick?"

I laughed. "I had a second to act; you know, like the heroes in those kids' stories when they jump on the baddie – 'It was with one bound he seized his chance!'"

She giggled. "So I was the baddie?"

"No, love, the towel was the baddie. You were the maiden in distress."

"You're a crackpot!"

"Darling."

"Yes, Paul?"

"Shall I take your paraphernalia back to this Prasad fellow in the morning?"

"Yes, please." she held out her arms, "Yes, please."

"Please take the hats back?"

"Ah-ha. But that's just the first please."

"You mean, you mean?"

"Ah-ha. You're the Grand Panjandrum, aren't you?"

I wasn't sure about that, but I did get her two bob deposit back next day. Yes, two bob deposit for bits of paper. *And* Ravi didn't give me the ha'penny for the completed hat.

"Here's your two shillings, Joan."

"You want sixpence for bus fares then."

"No, no, love. I'll pay that out of my pocket money. Conscience money, eh?"

She laughed, "You cleared your conscience last night. You were the bee's knees."

"Mam," asked Anna, picking the wrong time to come in from the backyard, "What do you mean, the bee's knees? Why was daddy the bee's knees?"

"You call someone the bee's knees when they're nice. When they do something nice."

"You were upset with Daddy last night, Mammy. What did he do nice?"

"He made sure I had hot water for my bath, love."

Anna shrugged her shoulders almost disbelievingly. "Hot water! And that makes him the bee's legs!"

"Dad, you're back." cried Mark, barging open the back door and throwing his bat into the corner. "I've been waiting to give you a game of cricket. Anna's not much good."

"Not now, Mark. We're going to have our dinner and I think we're going to see North Durham play Burnopfield this afternoon," I said, looking enquiringly at Joan.

"Yes, we'd better go to the cricket today, It looks as though I won't be able to go with you on a Saturday much more."

"Why not? What do you mean?"

"*I* know why, Daddy."

"You're a little know-all, Anna. But what's all this, Joan? You like cricket!"

"I've got a Saturday job, love!"

"What? Where?"

"At the Post Office on Rectory Road. One pound, ten shillings! They knew I'd worked in the Pay Office. It was just chance. This morning, I went to buy that Premium Bond we'd talked about. They offered me the job – just like that! So I took it. You won't shout at me? They say when one door shuts another one opens, don't they?"

She was bubbly. *I* was knocked sideways. Was it good news, or bad? Good – the money would be welcome. Bad – guess who would look after the bairns? Even so, I wasn't going to shout at her, not after last night. On balance, it had to be good news – much better than the paper hats fiasco. I quickly calculated that she would have had to make 720 hats for that sort of money. At a quarter of an hour per hat, that would be 180 hours per week. The week would have had to be extended.

"Who's that toot-tooting in the front street?"
"I'll go and see, Mammy."
"You can't reach the latch, Anna."
"I can if I stand on tiptoe."

Joan was busy filling a Thermos; I was collecting Mark's bat and stumps. Mark was on his hands and knees, scrabbling for his old tennis ball which had rolled under the twin tub.

Anna came running into the kitchen. "Mammy, Daddy, it's Uncle Cecil! It's Uncle Cecil!"

"What do you mean, Uncle Cecil? Is Uncle Don with him? He couldn't have walked all that way on his own. Is he coming in?"

"No, Daddy, come and see, come and see!"

Come and see what? 'What?' was a car! An invalid car. A little three-wheeler. In the driving seat, the only seat, was Cecil. Smiling.

I opened the car door. "Cecil! You've kept this quiet!"

"You crafty thing," laughed Joan, from behind me.

"A s-surprise, eh? I got it on Wednesday. Taken it to work since then. Had a little ride this m-morning."

"Are you coming in?"

"Thanks, but I'm going to the cricket. Just thought I'd sh-show off first."

"*We're* just off to North Durham's ground too, Cec. You'll be there before us."

"You will that," laughed Joan, "A car! It'll be years before we get a car."

"Mammy, Mammy."
"What, Anna?"
"Can I have a ride in Uncle Cecil's little car?"
"No, love, there's no passenger seat, pet."
"There's space though, Mammy. I could sit on the floor, there, look!"

Cecil laughed. "She can c-come if you like. She can't interfere with the pedals. I haven't got any. It's all m-manual control, see!"

"Are you sure, Cec?" I was doubtful.
"Please, Daddy, please."

Always a soft touch when people said please (last night was a fine example), I glanced at Joan. She shrugged her shoulders.

Castle on a Cloud

"OK, Anna, but keep still. And mind Uncle's walking stick."
"Dad, can I have a ride. Why, Anna and not me?" Mark had come out to see what was going on.
"It's obvious, Mark. There's no room for a big lad like you."
"You're trying to pull the wool over my eyes, Dad."
There was no answer to that.
We watched as Cecil drove his car along the street and disappeared up Whitehall Road, It was a jerky performance; was the man or the machine to blame?
"I hope she'll be alright, Paul. Did you notice how his speech is becoming more and more affected?"
"I did. It's sad; he's so uncomplaining."

At the ground, a handful of motor cars and a coach; the Burnopfield team bus, occupied the makeshift grassy car park. I spied Cecil's puny three-wheeler sandwiched between two Morris Minors.
Anna saw us coming, and ran across the grass. She seemed to be rubbing her brow. "We nearly ran over a pussy, Mammy."
Cecil, steadying himself with his walking stick, shuffled up. He looked concerned. "Yes, Den. I had to swerve, the cat just shot across the road. I think Anna slid into the door."
"I'm not hurt, Mammy."
"Let's see." Joan took Anna's face in her hands. "You've got a little bump on your head, but you'll be alright, pet."
I stopped at the nearest bench on the boundary.
"If you want, we c-could go behind the wicket, Den."
"No, no, Cec, this is far enough for you to walk."
Cecil gingerly lowered himself on the seat. "I think that was a bad idea of mine, Joan. Anna had nothing to h-hold on to. No more lifts, Anna."
"*I* wouldn't have bumped my head, Uncle Cecil," piped up Mark.

The sound of ball on willow. The hopeful cries of "Howzat?" The scoreboard ticking over. The heat of the sun tempered by a light breeze. How restful, how relaxing.
But the tranquillity was soon disturbed. "Daddy, can I go and jump on the roller?"
"Of course not, Anna."
"But I'm bored with the cricket."

"Look at your alphabet picture book, then."
"I've done that; I know all the letters, Daddy."
"I bet you don't. What's D for?"
"That's easy, Daddy," she laughed, "it's Daddy."
"You should have brought your knitting, then, like your Ma – watch out, Anna!" The cricket ball hurtled past her and into the fence.

Mark recovered the cherry-red ball and threw it proudly to the waiting fielder. "Can I go over in the corner, Dad, and play with my bat and ball?"

"That's a good idea, Mark. Take your sister with you."

"Do I have to? Oh, come on then, Anna, but play properly this time, eh?"

"Oh, l-look, Den, here's Don coming in. He must have had an early finish."

"Hi, Joan, hi, Den. Has Colin Milburn batted yet, Cec?"

"W-where have you been, Don? It's years since he played for Burnopfield. He's playing for Northants, now. North Durham? He'll be playing for England soon."

"Oh, aye. Of course. Hey, I bet you lot won't believe this. I had that fella on my bus again today."

No one responded. We all knew about the fella on his bus. He always seemed to be on his bus these days. We knew the story. It started with "I says it's a nice day."

Don sat down next to Joan; she'd made the mistake of leaving a space. "Have I told you about him? What a turn he is. I says to him, 'It's a nice day, isn't it?'"

I turned to Cecil, and silently mouthed, 'He looks up at the sky.'

"He looks up at the sky. 'Aye,' he says, 'but look at that cloud on the horizon, that's ominous.' He's the opposite when it's cloudy. I says to him, 'It's not so nice today, is it?' And he says, 'Aye, but look – there's some blue sky over there.'"

Nobody laughed, except Don. And kind-hearted Joan.

"Aye, but listen to this. This is really funny."

"Oh, good shot," I cried, as our opening bat hit a straight six.

"A six was it? I missed that. Good shot! But this is really funny. It was a cloudy yesterday, wasn't it? Well, this woman who I'd never clapped eyes on before, got on my bus. I says to her, 'Where's the sun these days?' She says, 'Oh, he's working in Saudi Arabia now.'"

Castle on a Cloud

Joan and I laughed, this was a new one. Cecil didn't. He'd probably heard it a few times last night. As *we* would in due course.

"What do you think to Cec's car, Don?"

"It's good. Pity he couldn't drive it up the back steps."

"Do you have a struggle, Cecil?"

"A bit, Joan."

"A bit! He has to take them one by one on his backside these days. That's if I'm not there."

"That's only on a b-bad day, Don."

"What happens if you're there, Don?"

"I get behind him and lift each foot in turn. Sixteen steps up, Joan."

"Yes, but I pull on the banisters to help, Don."

"I think your Mam should be getting on to the council for an invalid house, Cecil. Where you'd be on the level – no stairs."

"Oh, I can manage, Joan. Some days I'm a lot b-better than others. I don't think Mam would want the upheaval of moving at her time of life. I can manage. I manage at work as well."

"You know what he does at work now, Joan? He goes up to the first floor in the lift, but up there, his little office is nearer the parcel chute. That's how he comes down."

"Down the chute, Cec?" I laughed, "You're a crafty so-and-so."

"Never mind me, let's watch the cricket, eh?"

24

BIG GIRLS DON'T CRY

"Careful, Anna. This baking tray's full of hot oil. You'll get burnt."
"What are you doing, Daddy?"
"You know what I'm doing," I said, wiping sweat off my brow with a tea towel. "I'm putting these Yorkshire puddings in the oven. Your Mam will be in from the Post Office soon. I'm also trying to watch the cricket on the telly, keep my eye on this piece of brisket, check the roast potatoes and turnip, boil the cabbage. I wish I'd never opened my mouth and said I'd cook a Sunday dinner on a Saturday. That we'd have two Sunday dinners every week."
"You seem to be busy, then, Daddy. I wish I was busy. I'm bored."
"Why don't you go and play with Mark? Where is he?"
"He's in the cellar with his gang. He won't let me in. You need a password – 'For seckuwity reasons,' he says."
"His gang? You mean Tommy Cooper from over the road and his little brother?"
"He calls them his gang, Daddy. He thinks he's the big boss, having a cellar with a light and seats."
"Seats? You mean those planks he put on the bricks?"
"He says he's going to make a table with some more bits of wood he's found at the back of the cellar. Then his gang will be Knights of the Square Table."
"He's full of bright ideas; he'll be planning to go up in space next. Like Yuri Gagarin and John Glenn and that lot. But Square Table? That's original. Hey Anna, if they going to be Knights of the Square Table you could be Guinevere."

"I wouldn't like to be called Jenny Vere, Daddy. There's a girl called Jenny in my class and I don't like her. She's stuck up."

"Not Jenny, love. Look, don't bother me now. Go and see Mark. He'll let you in. You see, I know the password, it's 'Kemo Sabi'. I heard Tommy Cooper knock on the cellar door and say 'Kemo Sabi' last Saturday. But use a deep voice."

"'KEMO SABI'. Like that, Daddy?"

"That's right love, just knock on the cellar door and say 'Kemo Sabi', he's bound to let you in."

"Ooh! Thank you, Daddy. 'KEMO SABI', 'KEMO SABI'. 'KEMO SABI'."

Now Anna was out of the way, I opened the oven door. Then I remembered Joan's golden rule and closed it with a bang. 'Don't let the oven cool once the Yorkshires are cooking.' Fair enough, but judging by the stife from the oven, the turnips and potatoes must be well browned. For a minute I hesitated, then boldly flung open the oven door again and whisked out the veg. Mission accomplished, I banged the door shut with my behind. Now pray that I hadn't disorientated the Yorkshire puddings.

I went into the parlour and dropped into the sofa for a bit of a break. I'd watch the Test Match.

Five minutes, eh?

Not blooming likely.

Anna ran into the house, crying her head off and wiping tears from her cheeks. She must have fouled up her foray into the gang's HQ. "Daddy, Daddy, Mark shouted at me."

"Don't cry, love. You're a big schoolgirl now, you're nearly seven. Big girls don't cry. Why did he shout at you, anyway?"

"Well, he opened the cellar door when I shouted Kemo Sabi, but he wouldn't let me in. He said girls couldn't join his gang. He wanted to know how I knew the password. I didn't tell him, Daddy. I'm no stool pijin."

"You didn't squeal on your Daddy? Good girl."

I jumped to my feet, the cabbage! Had it boiled dry? "Look, love," I said, hurrying back into the kitchen. "Set the table, eh? Your Mam will be in shortly."

I checked everything, including my watch – fine. The Yorkshires were puffing up proudly, the brisket was sizzling, the cabbage was OK. The time was 12.45.

Castle on a Cloud

No sooner had I turned everything off, than Joan walked into the kitchen.

"My!" she said, giving me a kiss on the cheek, "You look well organised. Is everything ready? It smells nice! Go and watch a bit of cricket, love. I'll put the dinner out. I've got over an hour before I have to go back to work."

"It's all a question of timing, Joan," I said smugly. "Have you had a good morning?"

"Cushy, really. Not like you, pet."

I plonked myself back on the settee. Damn! I'd missed two wickets. Just like the thing. A shout from the kitchen. "Paul."

"What, love?"

"Where's the gravy?"

"Hell's bells! I've forgotten!"

She laughed. "Not so organised after all! I'll have to mix a bit of Bisto. That'll have to do."

"Aye, love."

"That was nice, Paul. I'll wash the dishes in a minute. But you know, you shouldn't bother with a big dinner on a Saturday."

"No bother, love," I said, fraudulently.

"I've got some news, Paul. I hope you'll like it. Mr Logan wants to know if I can work part-time – five mornings a week. It shouldn't affect you and we'll have a bit more money. But you, Mark, and you, Anna, you're going to have to get up a bit earlier so I can get you off to school before I start work."

"No!" groaned Mark.

"But, Joan, you make me feel guilty. I should be earning more myself. I'll have to ask for that rise. They said they would look at my pay when I switched to Purchase Accounts; that was a month ago. Oh, by the way, I forgot to tell you we've got the bill for the roof repairs this morning. Old Scotty called with it. Three pounds fourteen. Most of it was made up of eleven bob for a dozen slates and thirteen and six an hour for labour. It's robbery, Joan – thirteen and six an hour!"

"That's the way it is these days, pet. Perhaps it's as well I'll be earning a bit of money to help pay these bills." She laughed. "We don't want Daddy going up on roofs. Do we, kids?"

"Not without a parachute, Mam," chuckled Mark.

"Talking about money, Paul, I saw an advert for a job in last night's

Chronicle. It's for a Branch Accountant – a firm called Pharma Supplies down Askew Road. If you get a chance, have a look at the thing this afternoon. I think you could do it. Anyway, I'd better do these dishes, Paul. You go and sit and watch the cricket."

Watch the cricket? Some hope! Down at the Oval, they were all trooping off the field for a bite of lunch.

"Did you have a chance this afternoon to look at the advert for that job, Paul?" Joan was standing in the kitchen door, drying a supper plate. The kids were in bed, I was watching The Black and White Minstrels on the telly. By, that Dai Francis was a canny singer.

"What? Oh, that. It's out of my range, Joan."

"What do you mean? You could do it."

"I'm not so sure about that. Anyway, I haven't got the certificates they'd ask for."

"Don't be a stick in the mud."

"It's not a question of that. Look who they want," I said, picking up the paper. "'Someone who can work on accounts up to trial balance and with experience of running a busy office.' Then they go on about purchasing, sales, debtors, creditors, cost accounting, wages, cash, pricing."

"You've done wages, you've done cash."

"Aye, petty cash."

"You're doing purchase accounts."

"Just passing purchase invoices, and that's only lately."

"You could do the job, Paul."

"I wouldn't get the chance. They're looking for somebody with qualifications. But me? Because of the war, I left school before I was fourteen. Because of the blooming war, night schools were put on the back burner. Because of the blooming war, before I knew it, I was called up."

"Because of the war, you met me, love!"

"Thanks to the war, Joan," I conceded.

"Anyway, you've got those certificates from the Army."

"They not exactly what's wanted," I said, exasperated. "Can't you see?"

"Look, think about it, Paul. You've got nothing to lose."

"Humph."

Castle on a Cloud

"Have you thought any more about applying for that job, Paul?" said Joan, slipping on her jacket and picking up her handbag. She was all ready for our Sunday walk. God! She was like a dog with a bone. She'd got her teeth into this idea and wouldn't let go.

"I'm ready, Mam. I've washed my face. Where are we going this afternoon, Mam?"

I picked up my checky sports coat. "No, Joan, I've told you, I'd just be wasting my time."

"So you won't do it? You won't please me?"

"It's not worth the effort, Joan."

"Mam, are we going out or not?" asked Mark, waiting in the passage.

"Yes, we're going to the park, Mark, eh?"

"Can we go on a rowing boat?"

"Why not?"

"Joan, Charlie Lawton told me the other day, that there's a nice walk near Winlaton Mill, you get the Rowlands Gill bus, why don't we go there for a change?"

"Yes, Mammy, let's go to the mill," piped up Anna.

"*You* go with him if you like, Anna. Your Dad's got big ideas about walks but that's as far as his big ideas go," Joan said sharply. "Come on, Mark, if you're ready, we're off to the park. Come on. Your Dad and Anna can please themselves."

Mark looked dumbstruck. We never went separate ways on a Sunday.

"Are you coming, Mark? I'm off."

Mark shrugged his shoulders and shook his head as his mam stormed to the front door. Still shaking his head, he followed.

The door banged shut.

For a moment there was silence, then: "Daddy, what's happening?"

"Well, Anna, it looks as though Mam and Mark are going to the park."

"I guessed that, Daddy. Are we going to the mill?"

"It isn't a mill, pet. It's a walk."

"I like this walk, Daddy. There's just you and me and no other people. Not like the park. I bet Mark would like to go on this walk."

"I bet Mammy would too, Anna."

"Why didn't she come, then Daddy? Look, there are cows over in that field."

"They've been in this field too, Anna."
"How do you know, Daddy?"
"Because of these.... Watch out, Anna! Because of these cowpats. Don't stand in them. I'll really be in the black books if you do."
"I won't, Daddy. Oh, Look! Look at all the pretty flowers in the field."
"They're buttercups and daisies."
"I know what they're called. If I get some daisies will you show me how to make a daisy chain, Daddy?"
"I don't know how to, pet."
"Mammy knows how to."
"Yes, I wish she were here. But I'll tell you what, Anna. Why don't you pick some flowers? We could take a big bunch home for Mammy. I'll help you."
Anna laughed. "You want to get into Mammy's good books again. Why don't you tell her you'll have that big job, Daddy? Mammy says you can do it."
"It's not so simple as that, Anna."

Not even the first part.
We were home before Joan and Mark. I was at the table with Friday's Evening Chronicle when they came in. "Hello, Joan. Where's the writing pad?"
I thought that I'd asked about a writing pad. Maybe it was just my imagination. Joan didn't seem to hear me. "What's that smell, Anna? What's that on your shoe? Where have you been?"
"Just in some fields, Mammy. There's a surprise for you in the kitchen, Daddy and me have picked a bunch of flowers. I'll go and get them."
"Did you get on a rowing boat, Mark?" I asked, looking up from the paper.
"No, Mam said that she couldn't row. I said *I* could but she said no. I had an ice cream instead. We walked for miles."
"Here, Mammy. Daisies and buttercups. I picked the daisies."
"The *daisies* are nice. But come here Anna, take that shoe off. Did your Daddy not tell you to be more careful? You've stood in a cowpat."
"Just a little bit, Mammy."
So, evidently, Joan knew I was around, but it seemed she didn't like my buttercups.

Castle on a Cloud

I thought I'd try again. "The writing pad, love. Where did you put it?"

Joan stomped across the room, rummaged in a drawer and threw the pad on the table. I'd made contact!

Of a sort.

"Mark, Anna, let's go and have some bananas and custard and a drink of pop, we'll go in the backyard in the sun. Leave your Dad alone."

"Good idea, Mam, I'm thirsty," said Mark.

"Me too."

I heard Anna hopping along behind Mark. With one shoe off, the other shoe on, she clumped down the backyard steps. Silence descended. For a minute or two, I rattled my teeth with my biro pen. How should I begin?

'Dear Sir.' Yea, that's a good start. But why hadn't *I* been offered bananas and custard?

'I am writing in response to your advert.'

Not only that, Where's my drink?

'I feel that the position advertised would give me the sort of dynamic challenge that I would relish. Having just turned 37 years old....'

Thirty-seven! I'm getting old! What about my hair? When I'd looked in the mirror this morning I'd noticed grey here and there. If I did get an interview my grey hairs might turn them straight off. I'd better get Joan to get some Grecian 2000 tomorrow. That is if I can make contact with her. Perhaps I could send her a note.

'I am fully conversant with trial balance.'

(I could be by the time I'm interviewed if I can get a bookkeeping treatise out of the library.)

'Bla-de-bla-de-bla.'

I'm getting into the swing of it now; cost accounting? A doddle! Debtors? Creditors? Bring them on two at a time. This letter would keep Joan happy. Surely? But could she not see that there was no chance of me getting the job? It would surprise me if I got an interview.

But, by golly! I was thirsty.

It was as if by magic. A tumbler of amber liquid appeared in my eye line. "Would you like a shandy? You must want a drink."

Was that Joan speaking to *me*? I took the drink without a word, gulped a mouthful, and placed the glass on the table.

She leaned over, her face inches from mine. "That looks a great letter, Paul."

"Mmm," was all I said.

So suddenly, things were hunky-dory, were they? Because I was writing a letter? Not so fast, Joan. You're not going to get around *me* so easily. *I* hold the high ground now.

Still, the kiss, when it came, on the cheek was welcome. "I love you, Paul."

OK, OK, Joan. Come up and join me on the mountain. "All the time?"

"All the time, even when you're stubborn."

I swung round on the chair and pulled her down on my lap. She wiped a tear from a cheek." "Now look what you've made me do!"

"Stop it love," I laughed. "Big girls don't cry."

25

WOULD YOU BELIEVE IT?

Visiting night at Mam's. We climbed the steps to the back door, Mark leading the way. As usual, the door was unlocked.

"Hi, Grandma. Hi, Uncle Cecil," said Mark, running through the scullery into the parlour.

"Hello, Grandma. Hello, Uncle," said Anna.

Mam put aside her book. "Hello!"

Cecil, smiling, turned his attention from the television.

"Hi, Mam," I said, then noticed the telly. Steptoe and Son had just finished. The credits were rolling on the screen.

"Steptoe, Joan! We forgot about Steptoe!"

"It wasn't so g-good this week, Den."

"No, Joan." said Mam, "I went back to my novel. Anyway, how are things with you?"

"OK. We've got bits of news. Den's applied for a new job," said Joan, as she sank into an armchair.

"Oh! What's wrong with the one you've got?"

"I've told you before, Mam. One, I don't like the place much, too many snidy characters. Two, the wage is poor." I took the last seat at the table, Mark and Anna had already grabbed chairs either side of Cecil. Brother Cec always sat on a dining chair these days, getting up from an easy chair was well nigh impossible.

"I suppose it's a pity your old place closed, Den," said Mam.

"Uncle Cecil, can we have a game of cards again?"

"N-not cards, Anna, I would drop them tonight. Get the dominoes out of the games drawer in the sideboard. I think I can play with them."

"Well, the old firm did close, Mam. The other news is that Joan's going to start work mornings at the post office from next month."

"Oh! You'll be rolling in it if you get this new job as well."

"T-turn over the spots, Mark, and shuffle them."

Rattle-rattle-rattle.

Mam screwed her face up at the noise.

"Anyway, Mam, I might not even get an interview, they want somebody with accounts qualifications."

"Well, it's your own fault, Den. You could have gone to night school. I kept telling you, but you took no notice."

"Uncle, you've knocked some of your dominoes over," laughed Anna. "I can see what you've got."

"I know, Mam, I know. Anyway, how are you, Cec?"

"P-put them up again, Anna. N-not so good, Den. I'm giving up work. I can't cope. They're just carrying me these days; I'm getting p-paid for nothing, really."

"Uncle," laughed Mark, "You can't put a double-six against a five!"

"Daft me. Wrong end. Put it at the other end, Mark. Thanks." He turned to me. "My boss, old Smithy, has been very g-good; he's had to get a lad in to do the manual part of my job. I've been struggling just to do the clerical side. Some days, handling a pen is a problem." He laughed poignantly, "Never mind a domino."

"You'll get benefit then? Disability Allowance it's called, isn't it?"

"It's you to play, Uncle," said Anna.

"Play the one on the l-left for me, Mark. That's right. Benefit? I think so, Den. Someone f-from Social Services is coming to see me next week."

"Benefit is all well and good," butted in Mam, "but that will hardly keep him. Thank God for Don. He works quite a bit of overtime these days and he's very good at helping with money."

"Domino!" shouted Mark, plonking down a double blank.

"What about your car, then, Cecil?" asked Joan. "Can you still manage that?"

"Deal me some dominoes, Anna. St-stand them up to face me, but don't look at them. Car? Oh, I'm n-not so bad at driving. I k-keep to the side roads. I'll be able to get out during the week on my good days, the days I can m-manage going down the back steps."

"What about going up them?"

"I'll plan to come home when Don's in to h-help me. Play the second from the right, Mark. No, m-my right. That's the one. I drove up past Lamesley last Sunday, and on the way to Sunniside I found a

Castle on a Cloud

nice s-sneck at the top of the hill. I'll be able to sit there for hours and l-look over the countryside. You can see the Cheviots in the distance and most of Newcastle and Gateshead as well."

Joan looked puzzled. "What's a sneck?"

Cecil laughed. "W-weren't you educated, Joan? It's a hidey place. You know, your own little patch. I can s-sit there and forget about my worries."

Poor blighter. How could he manage to forget?

"Uncle, it's your turn."

"The one on the end next to you, Anna."

"Will the social worker look at your mobility needs, Cec? One of these houses equipped for that sort of thing?"

Mam sat up then. "He can manage at the moment, Den. I don't think I'm well enough to handle a move."

"We would help you to move, wouldn't we, Den?"

"Of course. You say you're not very well, Mam? What's wrong?"

"I keep getting terrible headaches."

"Have you been to the doctor's?"

"No, Joan. They're a waste of time."

"Our cat's got kittens, Grandma."

"That's not as bad as headaches, Mark," said Mam. Mark frowned. He couldn't see the connection.

"Mammy says Tibbles and the kittens have all got cat flu, Grandma. She's giving them honey."

"Wrapped up in a five pound note, Anna?"

Anna laughed. "Like the Owl and the Pussycat, you mean, Grandma? No, Grandma, she doesn't give them money. Just honey."

"Come on, Anna," cried Mark, "it's you to play."

The honey didn't do any good; the kittens all succumbed, as did their mother, all in one night. There they lay, in their basket, still and lifeless.

"Put them in the coalhouse just now, before Mark and Anna come down, Paul. If they see them like that it will only upset them. We'll sort something out later."

I threw their old blanket over the basket and carried the pathetic burden down into the yard.

Just in time. "Where are the kittens, Mam? Where's the basket?" asked Mark, rubbing the sleep from his eyes.

"I wasn't going to tell you until tonight. They've died, love, and the cat too."

Anna arrived downstairs in time to hear the bad news. "What, Mammy! Tibbles as well? I liked Tibbles, except when she scratched me."

"Yes, Tibbles as well, love, I'm afraid. She was getting old, Anna," Joan lied. "Cats don't live forever."

"So we've got no pet now, Mam?" asked Mark.

"Everybody has a pet, Mammy."

"Look, children, we'll get one soon."

"A little puppy, Mammy? Like the one we saw on the Quayside market the other Sunday? The one I wanted and Daddy said no, because we already had a pet pussy?"

"No, love, not a puppy, Daddy's not keen on dogs. He had a scary experience with a dog many years ago."

"You're not scared of dogs, Dad?" laughed Mark.

"No he's not scared of them," said Joan.

"No, kids, I'm not scared of them. I'll tell you what. We'll get a budgie."

"A budgie!" said Mark.

"A budgie!" said Anna. "You can't take a budgie for walks!"

"No, but you can let them out of their cage and they can fly about the room." It was then I had a rush of blood. "You could have a goldfish as well."

Joan gave me a quirky look. "I'm not sure about this flying about the room business," she said.

"You'd get used to it, Joan. But just think kids, two pets – a budgie *and* a goldfish!"

"They're not as good as just one doggy, Daddy."

Joan butted in then. "Anyway come on, eat your breakfasts. You'll be late for school."

"Listen, there's the postman, Paul."

"I'll go and see what he's put through, Mammy."

"Eat your cornflakes, Anna, I'll go," I said, getting up from the table.

"It may be for that job interview, Paul."

"To say thanks, but no thanks?"

"Don't be a pessimist."

There was just the one envelope in the lobby. A local postmark. I wandered back to the table and sat down, studying it for a clue.

Castle on a Cloud

Joan stood in the kitchen doorway, her hands round a cup of tea. "What is it?"

"It's for me. I wonder what it is."

"Well open it, you'll find out."

I followed her instructions.

"It's from Pharma." I read on, as Joan came to peer over my shoulder.

"My God! You've got an interview!"

"Aye, next Monday at eleven o'clock."

"There you are! I told you that you'd written a good letter. What you have to do now is to make an impression," said Joan, suddenly aglow with enthusiasm.

Too much enthusiasm at this early hour.

"I'll press your best suit. There's no time to get a new one made to measure. Both Jackson's and Burton's take weeks."

"Even if we could afford it."

"We've still got a bit of money in the post office, Paul. We'll get you a new shirt and tie. Plain light blue will go with your navy pin stripe."

She took a sup of tea and warmed further to the project. "And your shoes, they're getting a bit battered; besides they're brown. We'll get you a pair of black shoes. I've told you for ages brown shoes don't go with that suit."

I could see advantages in this job-seeking lark, new shirt, new shoes. But also snags. "I'm thinking, Joan. Do you know I've never had a proper interview for a job? I was the only one sent from the Labour Exchange for that office boy job at Cally's; we didn't get interviews for positions in the Pay Corps, not in my time, anyway; and my present job was just arranged by old Crozier."

"So?"

"I'll panic."

"You won't. Even if you don't get it I'll still love you," she laughed.

"You'd better get it, Dad," said Mark, fastening his shoe laces, "Mam might change her mind."

"*I'll* still love you, Daddy!"

"Gee, thanks, Anna."

"Come on, kids. You're going to be late for school."

Pharma Supplies was located down Askew Road. Askew Road where I was born and bred. Our old street was long demolished; slum clearance they said. I never thought of it as a slum; we had our own backyard, our own netty, our own scullery, our own tap.

The foundations of our old house were now under Askew Business Park, possibly somewhere under the custom-built premises of Pharma. Possibly under this very lobby where I was sitting on a two-seater settee. Sitting next to a sleek, horn-rimmed spectacled, jet black hair parted in the middle and plastered down, young man. The epitome of a whizz-kid.

"Mr Potts? I'm sorry we're running late," the willowy redhead had said, coming out of her little office to welcome me. "If you could take a seat next to Mr Smart."

Smart? First name Alec perhaps?

Smarty spoke. "I think there's been a hitch, it's very irritating. I hope I'm not going to be held up. I've got another interview in Newcastle this afternoon. Cost Accountant – job sounds better than this one."

'What are you doing here then?' I thought, but just said, "Mmm."

"Mind, the chap in front of me seemed to be genned up, too genned up. He had a new briefcase. Not like my battered one. New briefcase signals showy, battered briefcase, signals well used."

"Why would you want a briefcase for a job interview?"

"First impressions. Look organised. CV handy if required. People are wanting CVs these days. Although this lot didn't ask for one."

"Oh, aye, CV. Sent mine with my letter."

"By, that was crafty!"

CV? What the hell's a CV? I was a novice at this job hunting lark.

Just then the door marked 'Branch Manager' opened. A brash looking guy, about twenty-five, and dressed as though he'd come straight from Carnaby Street, and yes, carrying a spanking new briefcase, appeared. He was followed by an older man.

"We'll be in touch, Mr Eager," said the second man.

This man was bald, in his mid-forties, probably the Branch Manager? No dress sense though – navy blue suit with brown shoes. He turned to the whizz-kid. "Mr Smart? Sorry to keep you. Won't you come in?"

So there I was, left on my own. I couldn't browse amongst the contents of my brief case, not having one, so I settled down to twiddle my thumbs and try to prepare myself. I'd have to appear smart and look eager. Ha-ha. Smart, Eager and Potts. Potts didn't sound right. No chance for Potts. Ha-ha.

Castle on a Cloud

"Did you say something, Mr Potts?"

I hadn't noticed the tall redhead come out of her office carrying a folder, and heading for the door marked 'Warehouse'.

"Eh? Oh, no. But may I ask if there's just the three of us for interview?"

"No, there're three more this afternoon."

"Oh." I twiddled my thumbs again. Then for a bit of variety, I felt my pulse. It seemed to be racing.

I jumped as the Branch Manager's door opened and Smarty and the boss appeared.

Now it was me.

"Will you come in, Mr Potts?"

Here goes. It might be a waste of time, but I'll come in.

"Take a seat. This is Mr Murray, our Regional Accountant, up from York. I'm Jones, Branch Manager. Mr Murray will be exploring your accountancy knowledge. I'll be assessing how you will fit in here."

(Oh, I'll fit in alright. Just give me a desk and a little office.)

Then came the inquisition. My previous and my present job. My forces service.

"In the Pay Corps, eh?" asked Murray.

"Yes, Income Tax in York. Handling officers' accounts in India. From second lieutenants right up to generals. Even a Field Marshal – Auchinleck. Japanese Campaign payments – the lot."

"You were in India, with Auchinleck, by Jove!" remarked Murray, settling back in his chair. I was taking a liking to this Murray fellow. "Mind if I smoke?" he added.

"No, no," I said, magnanimously.

"You were in York, too. Strange that our Regional Office is in York. Pay Corps, eh? Funnily enough, after getting wounded I was transferred to the Pay Corps during the war."

"Wounded?" I said, commiseratingly.

"Yes," he laughed. "That was when I was in the KOYLIs. Broke a leg walking up the gangplank to go to France in 1939. Major Murray, that was me; never got out of Blighty. Never saw active service." Major Murray? That was no surprise with his military moustache and general bearing.

"Let me see," he added, inspecting my letter. "This other stuff; from your application I see that you've got a wide experience of accounts, both with your present employer and with Caledonian Connectors, eh?"

"But no formal qualifications?" asked Jones.
"No, the war spiked my guns a bit there. (Spiked my guns! Murray would like that.) But I've handled accounts up to trial balance stage," I lied.

"And staff?"

"Yes, at Caledonian Connectors, I was responsible for all levels of staff in the office. Responsible to the Branch Manager."

True: all levels; clerk, typist, office boy. One of each.

"But no qualifications?"

Why does he keep going on about qualifications?

"Do you know anything about computers?" asked Murray.

"Not at first hand."

"Not many people do," laughed Jones. "But the guys at Head Office are investigating the possibility of using them in our business."

"That sounds exciting," I said, "I would like to get in on the ground floor on that sort of project."

Computers? Ground floor? Project? Who was this talking?

"It's the young chaps that are leading the way these days, not old guys like me and Mr Murray. Let's see, you're going on for thirty-eight?"

"That's so, Mr Jones, but I try to keep abreast of these new developments. Punch cards, comptometers, that sort of thing."

Like I'd read about them in library books last week for example.

"Mm, but no qualifications, Murray," said Jones, looking at his colleague.

"True, true."

Jones got up and held out his hand. "Anyway, Mr Potts, thanks for coming. We'll be in touch."

"How did you come on, love?"

I slumped onto the settee. "Horrible. The manager, a chap called Jones, kept going on about diplomas. Why did he ask me to go for an interview in the first place?"

"Well if you remember, Paul, you didn't mention qualifications or the lack of them in your letter."

"Then I kept talking rubbish."

"I don't believe it."

"Plus, the other two applicants I saw there were in their twenties. *And* there were three more coming this afternoon."

The sound of the doorbell interrupted my ranting.

Castle on a Cloud

"Now, who's that?" I cried, hurrying along the passage.

I opened the door, saw no one at first, then glanced down at a four-foot-something laddie, sporting a tanner-all-off haircut, a green pullover with holes in the elbows, and tattered plimsolls.

"Mister Potts?"

"Uh-huh?"

"Yor brother said see if you're in. He said gi' him a message. He said tell him A'm stuck on Saltwell Road near the Stirling House. He said tayk this message and ye would gi' me a bob."

"A shilling?"

"Well, naw, he said a tanner, Mister. Aa was fibbin' when Aa said a bob."

Joan, wondering what was going on, had joined me at the door. "Is he in his car?"

"Aye, Missus. If you can caall it a car."

"Right," I said, fumbling in my pocket and pulling out a sixpenny piece, "I'll go and see him."

"Thanks, Mister. By, it's a good job for yor brother that Aa bunked oot of school today."

Joan accompanied me down to Saltwell Road. There was his car. It had mounted the pavement.

"Hi, Cec, what's all this?"

"Thank God you're h-here, Den. A kiddie ran right out from behind a bus. I swerved over this high kerb and got stuck. I can't reverse out."

"Let's have a look." I saw the problem. The council workers were in the process of re-laying the pavement. They'd lifted the old paving blocks, replaced the kerbstones, but left the job unfinished. The high kerb, coupled with his car's puny power had prevented Cecil from backing off. He was stranded there, helpless.

"I think we can get you off, Cecil. You get into reverse, I'll try to lift, and Joan, can you push?"

It didn't work; the little car was heavier than I thought.

"That's no good," I panted.

"Want a hand, mate?" I looked up. It was a burly fellow, well over six feet, vaguely familiar.

"Yes, please. We're trying to get the car over the kerb here."

"Nee problem. Are you in neutral, mate?" he shouted, then turned to me. "Yee grab that side, I'll grab this. Right?..... Lift and gan!"

We went. Onto the road. Just like that. Easy.

"Thanks," said Joan, gratefully.

"Think nothin' of it, lass. Nee bother. But yee, mate," he laughed, "Divvent drive on any more paths, eh."

With that advice he disappeared up the steps to the pub.

"Are you OK now, Cec?"

"Thanks, I'm fine now," he said, popping his head out of the window.

"Where are you off to?"

"I'll go up to my sneck, Joan. Thanks again. I'll be alright. It was just that kid."

We watched as the invalid car laboured into motion and chugged out of sight.

"I'm worried about him, Paul. I'm sure that car is getting too much for him."

"He'll be gutted if he's got to give it up."

"I know. He'll be virtually trapped in that upstairs flat."

"Wasn't that funny, though, Joan? Do you believe that families can share one guardian angel?"

"You mean a guardian angel with a broken nose?"

"It was him alright. Weird, wasn't it?"

26

PAPER CHASE

The envelope was on the doormat. I stifled a yawn, picked it up, and wandered into the living room. Still sleepy, I tore it open and fumblingly extracted the contents. A sheet fell to the floor and Joan, coming in from the kitchen, picked it up. Bleary-eyed, I tried to focus on the letter inside.

"You've got it! You've got it!" cried Joan, "This is asking you to sign your acceptance."

"Blimey! You're right. Listen to this: £900 pounds per annum, annual bonus, four weeks holiday, non-contributory pension. It's all confirmed!"

"I told you, I told you," laughed Joan, as Anna came tumbling down the stairs and into the room.

"What's the fuss, Mammy?"

"Daddy's got the job, that's what." She took Anna's hands and waltzed her around the room.

"Daddy's got the job, Daddy's got the job!"

"What on earth is going on?" asked Mark. He was at the door, struggling into his pullover and looking half-asleep.

"Your Mam's gone mad, Mark. She's prancing about and I haven't got my toast yet."

Jones and I walked through that door marked 'Warehouse'. Into a bustling scene.

"Before I take you to the Accounts Office, I'll show you around the operation," he'd said.

Young women and girls were assembling orders, hurrying and scurrying between rows of shelving. The shelves were encircled by a rattling roller-conveyor. Small crates, empty at first, except for three-part order sets, were taking a ride round the system, stopping at assembly stations, and then, orders complete, at their final destination. There, a mountain of cardboard cartons enabled packers to transfer the orders into a box of suitable size.

Drivers in insipid green uniforms, were humping those cartons, or pushing laden trolleys onto an outside gangway. We followed a gangly fellow and his trolley. Sensing us behind him, he turned round.

"Mornin', Mr Jones. How are you keeping? Did Aa tell ye that me little lass starts school this mornin'? Aa've got her photo in me pocket. Would you like to see it?"

"Not just now, Sam." He ushered me away as though from an unexploded bomb. "Watch that fellow, I've seen that bloody photo a dozen times already," he muttered, "He'll ambush you at the drop of a hat."

"This is our van fleet," he added, waving his hand proudly.

There were a dozen or so sickly-coloured green vans lined up. The row of vehicles put me in mind of the starting rank of a Le Mans 24 Hour Race.

Inside again, we continued or tour. "On your left is the Security Room, controlled drugs in there. Along here is Goods Inward. And this is the Returns Section. It may seem a shambles, but it all works."

Not perfectly, I thought looking at the "Returns' benches. They were piled high with what I guessed were goods wrongly supplied.

"Here, we have the Hospital Department," he said, walking into a small office. "Morning, Claude. Morning, Sally. Claude's our pharmacist. It's a Head Office rule – a pharmacist at each branch. This is Paul Potts, Claude. Our new Branch Accountant."

Claude had a long thin face and a shifty look. He gave me a weak handshake.

"Now this," he said, moving onwards, and closing the door on Claude, "is an empty office – designed for an Assistant Branch Manager. A couple of years ago, when this place was just a project on the drawing board, all our new branches were to have ABMs. Halfway through the construction, didn't the powers that be change their minds? Put it all on hold. Too late to change the ABM office plan. I suppose that with these expensive pharmacists an ABM was a luxury they couldn't afford. I know which I would rather have." He laughed, but I had the feeling that

Castle on a Cloud

he had a thing about chemists intruding into the wholesale business, particularly ones like Claude.

"This is the Tele-Sales Office. Morning, Deirdre."

I was greeted by a clatter of typewriters as a bevy of girls chattered on headphones. Deirdre, older than the rest of the Tele-Sales staff, her hair mousy and straight, her look troubled, mumbled, "Morning, Mr Jones."

"And this is our Buying Department," he said, bustling ever onward. "Morning, Jeff, morning, Matt. Morning, girls."

Matt and Jeff were poring over flip-card files. "Morning, Mr Jones," they shouted, almost in unison. They could almost have been twins. At first glance I could only tell them apart, because one, Matt, I think, was wearing a bow tie. Both were in overalls – white coats – both were wearing heavy-framed horn-rimmed spectacles.

"Now we'll go into Accounts, but you get the picture? Orders typed onto three-part sets – control copy to security – delivery note to the customer – invoice to the Pricing Department – then to your lot. It'll be simple for you, eh? Then of course there's the suppliers' accounts, wages etcetera, but with your experience you'll suss all that out."

'It'll be simple for me?' 'My experience?' I must have conned him somewhere along the line.

At last, the Accounts Office. "Morning, girls. This is your new boss – Mr Potts."

It was like a dawn chorus – "Morning," they twittered. They were all at their desks, ready and waiting for this. I counted eight females of mixed shapes and sizes, various ages, diverse dress styles; from tight sweaters and lacy blouses, to staid frocks and cardigans.

"Your office is at the end, Paul. Let's go in there for a chat," he said. "Take your seat; I'll sit in one of your visitors' chairs."

Golly, I had visitors' chairs! *And* my chair was an executive model. I resisted the urge to swivel.

"We weren't completely open at your interview, Paul, Murray and me. By the way, in private call me Ivor."

"Not completely open, Ivor?" I said, unable to conceal an anxious frown.

"Well, whoever we selected was going to be thrown in at the deep end. You see, Charlie Watts, your predecessor, had a nervous breakdown six weeks ago. Job too much for him. Handed in his resignation. We didn't tell you that. You didn't ask. The Accounts Office has been limping along since. So we needed an experienced man. I think we got an experienced man. Experience – and a man who wouldn't flap."

My mind wandered for a moment, I nearly looked over my shoulder to see who this fellow was. Until he said, "You gave us the impression you would fit the bill."

He laughed. "I was goading you at your interview – remember? Qualifications, qualifications! You didn't flap there. That was it for me. But to the present. Old Murray's been coming up for a day every week, but you can't do much in a day. He'll be up again on Wednesday to help you settle in." He looked at his watch. "Is that the time? I'll have to leave you. Just feel your way in, OK?"

With that, he up and left.

For a while, I just sat. In a bit of a daze. My head spinning. My fingers drummed in agitation on my desk. A pristine desk. Except for a blank foolscap pad. I'd never sat at a desk so pristine. I swivelled nervously in my chair. Now my fingers were beating out a rhythm. I started singing to myself.

"Who wears the bow tie?
Matt wears the bow tie
Who gets the invoice?
Pricing gets the invoice
Who gets the control copy?
That's a very good question
Who is the shifty one?
Claude is the shifty one
Which one is dreary?
Deirdre is dreary.
And what do you think to Ivor?
Ivor is a skiver."

A knock on my office door brought me back to a confused reality. I jumped. Never before had I had an office to myself. Never before a door for people to knock on.

I cottoned on to my next move pretty quick. "Come in."

It was a buxom lady in an overall with three chins. No, I was getting confused, it was a buxom lady with three chins. She was wearing an overall. "Good mornin', Mr Potts, I'm Molly, the dinner lady. Would you like tea or coffee?"

Castle on a Cloud

"I'll have coffee, please."

I stood up, walked to my office door, and looked into the big office. "Where's everybody, Molly?"

"They're on their tea break, Mr Potts."

"All at the same time? They don't stagger their break?"

"Mr Watts let them go together."

"Oh! Did he?"

Molly closed the door behind her. I returned to my seat and pulled open a drawer. Empty except for a folder marked – 'Vade Mecum, Branch Accountant'. Vade Mecum?

I scanned the pages, I'd found the Holy Grail! But why did they call it Vade Mecum instead of Holy Grail?

Yes, I'd found the Holy Grail. It was all there. Procedures for final invoices, posting to ledgers, production of statements, chasing of debtors. Passing of suppliers' invoices against delivery notes and copy orders. Wages. It appeared so straightforward. It was if a heavy burden had been lifted from my shoulders. I listed the salient points on my pad. Right, let's get cracking.

I heard the staff return and then the rattling of office machines. Strike while the iron's hot, Paul Dennis. I stepped into the outer office. "OK, girls, let's find out who's who and what's what, eh?"

Nobody seemed to hear. I grabbed a ruler from a nearby desk and banged hard. The clattering stopped. There was a spooky hush. Everyone looked up. I cleared my throat nervously and repeated my message.

With pen in hand I looked at my list. "Extending and totalling invoices?"

"Me," said a shy looking girl. "Me," said a bonny kid of about sixteen. Stupid me. Those big things on their desks were comptometers, weren't they?

"And you are?"

"Patsy,";"Hilda," were the replies.

"Right, Patsy, Hilda – calculations." I scribbled down their names. "Posting to ledgers, statements?"

"Me, Rita Spark," piped up a fussy looking woman at an NCR machine.

"Debtors?"

"I handle the debtors, produce lists for you, Mr Potts. *When* I get the information," an older woman said, giving Rita a frosty look. "My name is Miss Jean Parker."

I was getting into the swing of things now. "Purchase invoices?"

"I'm Gloria, I've got those – more than I can cope with and it's not my fault, Mr Potts," said a blonde girl.

God! She looked ready to cry. "We'll have to look at that Gloria." I said, passing on quickly. "That leaves?"

"Me, Emily, queries. Mountains of them," said a plump girl, not to be outdone.

"Me, Wendy – wages," said the bright looking brunette.

"And you're the typist, eh?"

"You're the clever one, Mr Potts." The girl, sitting at the desk on which was a typewriter, laughed. "My name's Lillian."

"Right," I said, "I've got all that. So I can let you get on with the job. But don't forget, any queries, I'll be on hand."

I closed my office door, plumped back on my seat, and mopped my brow. I thought I'd handled that pretty well, all things considered. What next? I opened another drawer. Not so lucky this time. God! It was bunged up with a pile of papers. I scooped most of them out onto the desk. They were letters, letters from customers, together with their neatly typed replies signed by C. Watts, Branch Accountant. Nothing wrong there – but why weren't they filed? Hang on though, the replies were not copies. Yes, the copies were also there, but these were the originals with the Pharma Supplies letterhead. The letters hadn't been posted!

I looked at one, 'Dear Mr Lane, thank you for your letter complaining that you were overcharged'. The date, 2nd June, 1963. We were into September! I picked up another 'Dear Mr Lewis, sorry you did not get a reply to your letter dated 27th April, please accept our apologies.' The date, 28th May.

Murray had gone off ill in the middle of July, yet these letters were still in his drawer. I delved into the drawer again. This time I came up with just a bundle of letters from customers. These customers apparently, had not yet been pampered with the bonus of an unposted reply. I banged the drawer closed. Watts had been gone six weeks. Had no one discovered these legacies to his successor? Had Murray not investigated?

Fearfully now, I opened a third drawer. Another clutter, this time of

Castle on a Cloud

letters to and from suppliers. Charlie had a system! Sales one drawer, purchases another.

Congratulations, Charlie! You were on a winner there! What's more, you wrote some good letters, but why the hell didn't you post them?

I consulted my list and opened my office door. "Lillian," I beckoned, "Can you come in?

"Yes, Mr Potts?"

"These letters," I said, waving a hand at the pile. "Did you type them?"

She leant over the desk and picked up a couple of sheets. For a moment, my attention was distracted by her lacy blouse and the subtle pink of her polished fingernails. Just for a moment. "Yes, see the reference CW/LB – C. Watts – L. Blair," she said, a mite condescendingly.

"Oh, Lillian Blair? Well, do you happen to know why these weren't posted, Lillian? And where are their envelopes, eh?" I asked.

"I haven't a clue. I would have typed them, but I wouldn't be surprised if Charl.. Mr Watts has posted empty envelopes. Can I just say that Mr Watts seemed to change those last few months, shouting and raving and talking to himself."

"Watch out, Lillian. I might be shouting and raving myself if I find much more of this. Anyway, thanks for now."

"Just one thing, Mr Potts, Gloria's gone home."

"Gloria?" I glanced at my list, "Purchase Invoices? Is she ill? Why didn't she see me first?"

"No, she's not ill. She just threw a folder of invoices on the floor and stomped out. We had just picked them up when you called me in. I think she was upset. And scared. She was crying. The job was getting too much for her."

"Another nervous breakdown, eh? Will you gather her work and bring it in? I'll have a look at things."

I drew a deep breath. They say deep breathing calms one down. I looked at my watch, twelve-thirty. A knock on the door and Lillian returned carrying two tatty folders. "Here you are, Mr Potts, where shall I put them?"

I spied a stout briefcase on a filing cabinet in the corner of the office. I got up, brought it back to my desk and said a prayer. My prayer was answered; the case was empty, no more skeletons just yet. I grabbed the papers off my desk, stuffed them inside the briefcase and snapped it shut.

Lillian looked puzzled. "What are you going to do with them, Mr Potts?"

"Ha-ha, careless talk cost lives. I have a plan." I said, giving her a wink and tapping my nose.

The look she gave me was full of concern. Did she think I was cracking up already? She could be right.

"There, Lillian. Clear desk! Just stick the folders down." It was then I heard raised voices. "Is someone shouting out there?"

"Oh! That's Jean and Rita having a bit of a barney. We get used to that." Bloody hell! What was this job I'd taken on?

On my own again and with those voices subsiding I opened a folder headed 'Invoices To Pass'. No surprise there; invoices one, two, three months old. The second folder was thinner, the one labelled 'Delivry Notes, Orders Recevied'. Where were the delivery notes for all the invoices? Where were the copy orders? Action required, Paul!

But what? I had two choices; (1) Grab my coat and follow Gloria out of this madhouse, or, (2) Do something.

Do something? I had two choices; (1) Move the folders to one side and bang my head on the desk, or, (2) Go and see somebody.

I chose number two. But who do I see? Ivor the skiver would be out. He had told me he was lunching with a prospective customer – a chemist in Durham City. So who would have delivery notes? Goods Inward! Let's go. Which way though? Follow your nose, Paul. Follow your nose. Left – right's Goods Out.

Here we are, these piles of cartons still unpacked, the trolleys heaving with Benylin, Lactulose, Codeine, Gaviscon and suchlike. Ah! Here was a lad checking packages.

"Where's your boss?"

"'Ee's roond the corner, mister, 'avin' 'is bait." He was. Munching into a homemade stotty-cake.

"Hi there, I'm looking for completed delivery notes – old ones."

"And who are yee?" he asked, through a mouthful of dough.

"I'm Potts, the new Branch Accountant."

"Why, that's funny. Aa'm the new Goods In Supervisor, Ben Gunn. Been in the job aboot fower weeks. Ha'd on a tick, Aa think Aa knaa where yee might find some. Aa saw some owld paypers the other day."

Castle on a Cloud

He went into a drawer of his battered desk and pulled out a bunch of crumpled forms. "Cud these be what yer lookin' for, mate?"

I looked at them. "Yes, I think so. These are all you've got, eh?" He nodded. "Are you passing the current notes into accounts?"

"Oh, aye. Aa give them to that Gloria. She's a bit of aalreet that blonde. A bit highly strung, mind."

"You can say that again."

I wandered back into my office. These delivery notes might help, but they didn't seem enough of them to match the number of invoices. There could be problems there. Ha-ha.

I looked at my watch again – two-thirty. Old Jonesy should be back from his blow-out by now. Let's go and see him. If I didn't pluck up my courage now I never would. I picked up the briefcase and grabbed the folders.

"You're not going out, Mr Potts?" It was Emily, the plump girl.

"I don't think so." (Not unless Ivor gave me the sack.) "I'm going to see Mr Jones. Why?"

"I've got some queries. Some problems."

Problems? Join the gang!

"Yes, Mr Potts?" It was the willowy redhead, Ivor's secretary – Dolores. At her desk. Dolores? Yes, that was her name.

"Is Mr Jones in?"

"Yes, Mr Potts, he's just got back."

I knocked. "Come in."

Jones was just slinging his jacket on the back of his chair. He looked pleasantly flushed, a flush that extended to his bald head. I guessed he had both lunched *and* imbibed in good measure.

"Ah, Paul, sit down," he said dropping into his seat. "That was a job well done – old Simpkinson is going to give us some business. A new account, eh? What can I do for you, though?" he asked, suspiciously eyeing the briefcase and folders I'd placed on the desk.

"We've got a problem, Ivor," I said.

My next move was uncharacteristic, it was almost flamboyant. I don't know what came over me, but boldly, I opened the briefcase, turned it upside down and let the contents cascade all over Ivor's smart mahogany desk.

"Whoa! Steady on, Paul! What's all this?" he cried.

"What's all this?" I asked. I picked up a letter at random. "Look, a letter typed, signed by Watts, not sent, date 26th May, another 28th May, not sent, 16th April, not sent!"

"OK, Paul, I get the gist. I get the gist."

I wasn't finished. No, no, I wasn't finished. I opened a folder. "Look, Ivor. Suppliers' invoices – May. One here April."

"Not paid?" he said leaning forward. "A Glaxo invoice, April, not paid? They'll be stopping supplies. Either that or Head Office will come down on me like a ton of bricks!"

"Not only not paid, Ivor. Not passed for payment."

"My God! I didn't know things were that bad. Where did you find these?"

"The letters? In Charlie's drawers. The invoices? In Gloria's desk. The girl's gone home. Ben Gunn will be most upset," I added irrelevantly.

"What the hell has Ben Gunn got to do with this?"

"Nothing really. But you get the picture? The branch accountant has a nervous breakdown, the purchase invoice clerk goes home bubbling, not to mention Jean and Rita having a ding-dong. Things are not stable in the office."

Jones took out a handkerchief and wiped sweat off his bald head. Sweat tasting of best Burgundy, perhaps? There was no doubt I had disturbed his postprandial euphoria.

"It seems a bloody mess to me. What's old Murray been doing? He hasn't even looked in Charlie's drawers."

My first interpretation of his remark was that such an action could have been construed as being too intimate, but found that was wrong when he resumed his tirade. "Murray's let this get out of hand. Wait till he comes up on Wednesday. Give me a report on the state of things. He can't expect you to sort the backlog out. Meantime, see what you can do on purchases. We don't want supplies to be threatened."

"What on earth's the matter, Paul? You look like something the cat's brought in!"

"We haven't got a cat, Mammy."

"I know, pet, but your daddy knows what I mean. What's that you're carrying?"

"It's Charlie Watt's briefcase. I'll tell you the horror story, later. Let's have something to eat, Joan," I said, flopping into a chair.

Castle on a Cloud

The kids were in bed. I'd given Joan a résumé of the day's events. Then, for the first time ever, I'd had a bath without a song on my lips. Now, we were sat on the settee.

"It was bad?"

"It was frightening, Joan. It's a shambles. I think I've made a mistake. It's too much. What am I going to do?"

"You know what I think, love? You'll sort it out and if I can help I will," she said, putting an arm around my shoulder. "Jones said he would get something done on the backlog, didn't he?"

"Jones has had six weeks to get something done!"

"You've got to make allowances, Paul. He obviously knows little about accounts."

"Yeah, even less than me, I suppose."

"Look, give me the briefcase. I'll sit at the table and try to match stuff up. Before I worked at the Pay Office I did a bit of this sort of thing in York Co-op. You do that report that Jones wants for Murray."

Joan went to the table and opened the case. "My God!" she cried.

"Ah! You see now!"

"Leave me be. Here's your pad. Just turn the telly off, we'll have to miss Eric Sykes."

"He's not on tonight, is he?"

"Shush, just switch it off, love."

I'd roughed up a report that afternoon following my meeting with Jones. It told of staff that had received no guidance for months, it told a tale of chaos with creditors, a shambles on sales, confusion on correspondence, disorder with debtors, questions with queries. To sum up in one phrase – Anarchy in the Accounts Department.

I condensed my comments into a two-page report, then sat back and admired my handiwork. I'd never written an appraisal of this kind before. And getting the problems down in writing seemed to help. One thing for sure – nothing was understated.

What would Jones do when he read this? Would I get the sack for blowing the whole thing out of proportion? Would I get a rise for unearthing the mess? Ha-ha.

"How have you got on, love?" I asked, looking over her shoulder.

"You'll be pleased to know that a lot of the invoices match up with this batch of delivery notes."

"Good."

"The bad news is that there's a dozen old ones that don't. About £10,000 worth. You know what I would do?"

"What?"

"I would pass them. Start with a clean sheet. If there was a problem later they would blame Charlie."

I sat on the arm of the settee. "Do you think that would work?" I asked, brightening up. "It seems the only way to clear the backlog."

"Just imagine, Paul. You could blame Charlie for months to come. Not only that, anything you do would be an improvement."

"Thanks very much!" I said, "But I see what you mean. I don't like admitting it but you're a gem, Joan." I was warming to the idea. "We could start afresh. That would please Gloria if she comes back."

"This Gloria. Is she a blonde?"

I laughed – first time today. I even broke into song to a tune spinning round in my head.

"Charles will get the blame
Yes, Charles will get the blame
It could be unfair
But I don't care
If Charlie gets the blame."

"You daft cracker," laughed Joan.

She got up and gave me a push. I collapsed backwards onto the settee. She jumped on top of me and found my lips with hers. "Stop it, Joan, I'm shattered." I breathed.

"You'll be even more shattered by the time I've finished with you tonight. You deserve a treat poor thing. But you see? Nothing is as bad as it looks. In three months time you'll wonder what you were worrying about."

"In three minutes judging by the way you're behaving!"

27

MEN AND MACHINES

Three months? More like three years. No, I exaggerate – after three months the department *was* on the mend.

Give Ivor his due, he chivvied old Murray into getting in a 'body' to clear the logjam. The 'body' was a retired accountant from one of our southern branches. He was a most meticulous fellow called Bert Devlin, so the shock of finding such a shambles hit him hard. He bravely rallied, however, and soon settled into a corner of the main office and slaved away assiduously. For six weeks he ferreted, foraged and fished; his nose hovering over ledger cards, debtors' records, copy invoices, from morn till night.

"Leave purchase invoices to me, Bert," I had said. "I'd like to tackle them."

"Right, Paul," he had agreed. "I'll report to you each Friday on my progress on the rest of the problems."

'Leave purchase invoices to me.'? Of course leave purchases to me. My short cut to clearing the backlog must remain a secret. But 'report to me each Friday'? This fella reporting to me was a Chartered Accountant. *I* was a phoney! He confirmed what I knew – systems in the Accounts were suspect. Accounts staff had lacked guidance. One, Rita Spark, gave a week's notice just before Bert began his investigation into the sales ledger. There, he found clangers of awe-inspiring proportions; but the worst was over.

Was the best yet to come? Well, not through the remainder of that year, nor in 1964, or 1965. The sheer volume of paperwork generated by the pressure of healthy sales contributed to an unhealthy turnover of staff.

I had this vision of the ideal scenario – a utopian fantasy: experienced tele-sales girls, superbly-typed invoice sets, faultlessly assembled orders, perfectly priced and impeccably totalled. Invoices posted to the sales ledger without error. In this daydream, even the most recalcitrant chemist customers would pay their bills on time.

Then there was reality.

But what about 1966?

"Computers? Will they catch on?"

"Oh, yes, they will!" said Tony Higgins.

"They'll catch on, and your branch will be in the vanguard," said Tom Williams.

I forced a laugh. "Whoah! I was only kidding." We were in Ivor Jones' office. I'd heard about the new Computer Centre and dismissed its possible impact on Gateshead branch. It'll just be a Head Office thing, I thought. Until Ivor told me that Tom Williams, Computer Centre head, was coming to the branch. Ivor would want me to attend a meeting in his office...

"In the vanguard?"

Ivor reclined in his chair and beamed. "Yes, Paul. These guys tell me that the Board are planning a computer revolution in the company, and Gateshead are to be the guinea pigs. A feather in our cap, eh? And your role will be crucial."

I held back a frown. No; not that I minded playing a crucial role. No, no. But on the other hand, I wasn't a great advocate of change, certainly not dynamic change. Old-stick-in-the-mud Paul Dennis; that was me. And after all, things were running quite canny, really. All things considered.

My expression must have displayed a hint of dubiety as we formed a semicircle around Ivor's desk. Tom Williams, sitting opposite me, leaned forward; his face, the face of a zealot. He was a white-haired, fifty-something chap. How could such an oldie show so such fervour for this newfangled computer thing? "Yes, Paul. Have you had any experience of computers?"

"Well, three years ago at my last job, one of our suppliers – Baker Perkins – was being computerised. Their computer-produced invoices were a pig's ear, just a confusion of numbers, no item descriptions. Impossible to pass for payment. We sat on them until they could translate them. If the same thing was happening with their other customers, their cash flow must have been in a hell of a mess."

Castle on a Cloud

"Ah," said, Tony, confidently, "That's not going to happen with us. Not with the help of Ivor and you, and of course all your people. I've heard you have a good crew."

(Good crew? Well, I suppose the branch hadn't sunk yet.)

Tony seemed a likeable lad, even though he had a Beatles haircut; full of enthusiasm, but that was understandable, he being in his mid-twenties.

"I believe, Tom," Ivor said, "You and Tony would like to have a wander round the branch, suss up the set-up here and then discuss things in some depth?"

"Yeah," said Tom, "we've both had experience of branches, but we'll need to check closely to see if you have any local foibles."

I laughed inwardly; they wouldn't need magnifying glasses, that was for sure.

"Right then," said Ivor. "Paul, can you stay a minute? One or two things to discuss."

"Good news for you, Paul. On top of the usual annual rise, you're to get another hundred. Recognition of the help the computer lads are going to need."

"Thanks, Ivor, "I said. "This computer thing – it's going to mean redundancies?"

"Some, Paul. Mainly in the Pricing Department, I fear. That's what I gather, anyway."

"Not good for some, eh?"

"That's great news, Paul!" We were at the table having our tea.

"Aye, the rise will be handy, Joan. But don't mention redundancies if you meet any of the girls."

"Of course I won't."

"Dad?"

"What, Mark?"

"Dad, if you're getting a rise. Are we going to get a car? A lot of the other kids' Dads at Heathfield have one."

"A lot of the Dads will be well off at your grammar school, Mark, bankers, bosses, that sort of thing."

"Well, Dad, you're an accountant."

"That's enough of that, Mark. Your Dad isn't a proper accountant."

"Gee, thanks, Joan."

She laughed. "Anyway, you'd better get ready, love. Don't forget we're going to see The Sound of Music tonight. We promised Anna. I'm looking forward to it, myself."

"Are you coming, Mark?"

"He hasn't got over that boat trip to the Isle of Man, Daddy. I don't know why he wants you to have a car. He even thinks the bus ride to the Odeon will make him sick."

"Don't be stupid, Anna. I'll give you a thump in a minute. I've got homework to do. Besides it sounds like a cissy picture. People prancing up mountains."

"Will this computer thing be difficult for you?" asked Joan, climbing into bed.

Reluctantly, I put down my P.G. Wodehouse. "Well, Tom Williams and Tony Higgins explained the plan. It's weird, really. Difficult to explain. I hardly grasp it myself yet."

"Try me."

I put the book down. "Well, just imagine – there's this big ICL computer room with machines the size of wardrobes capable of the most complex operations. The computer lads input a separate code into the works for every product stocked by Gateshead branch."

"You've got thousands of different lines. Tom and Tony will take ages to put them all in!"

"Don't be daft. They've got minions."

"Millions?"

"You're acting stupid now."

"Oh, go on, tell us more. I'll behave myself."

"For example take two litre Benylin, the code might be BEN12. They type that in together with the description and price. So there it is, this clever wardrobe. It's just there in this big room with all the other wardrobes waiting for someone to ask it what BEN12 stands for. It's just dying to tell them it's Benylin at twelve bob a bottle."

"Hang on, what if somebody means to ask about BEN12 but types in BEN22 by mistake?"

"Ah, Tom explained that. I forgot to tell you. Each code will have a check character; BEN12C, for example. Then BEN22, which might say, be Benylin 100ml will be BEN22F. So if someone types in BEN22C the wardrobe will just say 'Don't be a dope, there's no such product.' A foolproof system, Tom says."

"This computer talks?"

"Ooh, stop!" she laughed as I grabbed her neck. "OK, Paul, I'll buy it. But how do the codes get onto the orders?"

"Rubber stamps! There'll be a coded rubber stamp beside each product on the shelf. The theory is the girl picks up the goods and stamps the line on the order. Hey presto! It all sounds a bit far-fetched to me, mind."

"What if she drops the two litre bottle when she's struggling to stamp the order? And where does the ink for the rubber stamp come from?"

"I didn't ask that. I was getting a little bemused by then. Anyway, there's a lot of preparation to be done by the Computer Department, they'll be working in the branch for months before it gets off the ground."

"I suppose there must be a lot more to the system other than what you've explained. Better you than me though. Anyway lights out, Paul, eh?"

I lay quietly for a while unable to sleep. Joan was tossing and turning. "Paul, are you still awake? I can't get off to sleep, I was thinking about all that input. Imagining hundreds of operators beavering away, and these big computer wardrobes trying to deal with them all at once."

"Come here, love," I said, "Forget about that sort of input." I pulled her close. "Would you like some input from me, instead?"

Joan giggled. "You *are* awful, but I like you!"

"Paul. You know what Mark asked about last night?"

"What was that?"

"When he said, why don't we buy a car now that you've got this rise?"

I put my book down again. At this rate, I'd never get Jeeves read. "I can't drive, Joan."

"I have a plan."

"You always have a plan."

"Listen to this. You have, say, six lessons from Harry Lomas. You know him. Amanda who owns the cake shop round the corner – her husband. He's a driving instructor."

"Hang on, love. I'll need more than six lessons. I'm a doddery forty-year-old and I can count on the fingers of one hand the times I've been in a motor car."

"I don't know about you being doddery, though I wish you were sometimes," she laughed. "But I know what you mean about six lessons. Just listen will you? After six lessons we buy a car. We've got a bit in the bank now. I'm sure that Tom Foley will come with you so you can get more practice."

"You mean Mary's Tom? Tom down Dunsmuir Grove?"

"Yes, Mary said he wouldn't mind."

"You've got it planned, you devil. OK, I'll give it a go," I said, dubiously. "I haven't told you this but Ivor keeps asking me when I'm going to learn to drive."

"There you are, then!"

Just being in a car was uncanny, I was a lot nearer to the ground than when sitting in the front seat of a bus; the lorries, coaches and vans zooming around seemed much taller, making me feel almost Lilliputian. Then there were all those controls.

And just a measly one-hour lesson a week!

Then I had this idea. That old dining chair upstairs with the curved wooden frame and the circular shaped seat! That old walking stick in the landing cupboard!

As, hands full, I came through the parlour door, Joan put aside the Chronicle and looked over the top of her new reading glasses. "What on earth are you doing with those?"

"Aah, hah," I said, "just watch this!"

I leant the back of the chair against the settee, climbed astride, and grasped the round seat.

"You're going to play motor cars, Dad!"

"I'm going to get some practice, Mark. Pass the gearstick."

I had hours of practice. "Brr, brr," I would buzz. (It was a noisy car.) "Coming up to Coatsworth Road, change down, brake, into neutral. Brr, brr. Road clear. Into first, accelerate, into second, now third. Damn, I've dropped the stick!"

"Watch out, Dad!" Mark would shout, "Mind that dog!"

I'd slam on my brakes.

Anna would just give me a supercilious look. Probably tell her schoolmates she had a queer Dad.

"Prince Consort Road. Turn left – spin the steering wheel. Damn!" The chair leg always cracked against my ankle. "Now into second, brr, brr."

"Hand signal," Joan would laugh. "You forgot hand signals!"

I drove all over Gateshead in that fake car.
Then we looked around for a proper one.
'Morris Minor, one careful owner. £85 o.n.o.' The address up Lobley Hill. Tom drove us there in his old Austin. "It looks alright, Tom."
"I don't like red," said Joan, shaking her head.
"75,000 miles, Paul," said Tom, shaking his head.
"Careful miles," said the vendor, his face was as red as the car, his nose more a maroon shade. "One thing to watch oot for though. Yee cannot get furst gear. But Aa manage aalreet. Ye winnet get a better buy for 85 quid."
Tom took me to one side. "You don't want this, Paul. No first gear!"
"Is that a problem, Tom? I've started Harry's car in second many a time. He didn't like it, mind."
Tom gave me an old-fashioned look.
"OK, OK." I turned back to red face, "We'll think about it. We're not sure about no first gear, are we, Tom?"
In Tom's car I consulted the Chronicle again. "I ringed this one, Tom – 'Ford Anglia tip-top condition – £100'. That's our upper limit, isn't it, Joan? It's in Saltwell Road, Tom."
"I hope it isn't red, Paul."
There it was, parked outside the house in Armstrong Street – the only car to be seen – a black Anglia of indeterminate age.
"I'm not all that keen on black, Paul."
"It's a nice black, Joan."
Tom gave me another funny look.
A ginger-haired fellow opened the door. A problem here, Joan had a thing about redheads as well as red cars. "Aye, Aa've had this car for years. It's been well looked after."
Tom sat in the driving seat, scrutinising the dashboard. Then he turned his attention to the gearstick. "It just has the three gears, Paul. First, second and third. But that's OK. Except that when you change down, you'll have to double declutch."
I have a lot to learn about this motor car lark, I thought. The Morris was no good because it just had three gears, now all of a sudden three gears was OK? And what the hell was this double declutch thing? Still, if Tom said it was OK, that's fine by me. I just want a car – tonight!
Ginger-hair was hovering around as Tom got out and checked the tyres, then Tom fingered the exhaust pipe. To pass the time, Joan went round to sit in the passenger seat.

"It burns a bit of oil, mate," Tom said, looking at his sooty fingers.
"Aye, a bit, but not a lot for 70,000 miles, yee knaa."
"Well, what do you think, Tom?" I asked, keen to get behind the wheel.
"It's not bad, Paul, but a hundred pounds seems a bit steep."
Joan had now rejoined our group, "What do you say, Joan?"
"Well, the passenger seat was comfortable."
I turned to Ginger, "We'll give you ninety for it."
"Done, mate."
The alacrity with which he took my money made me think that it was me that had been done.

I passed my driving test at the second attempt – failed the first on my emergency stop. No Mark around to shout "Mind that dog!"
Now, it was the week after England had won the World Cup. We were on the road to Ilfracombe, Devon. The holiday of a lifetime. We'd remember this summer.
"It's further than the Isle of Man, Mark," said Anna, But you'll be pleased. You won't get seasick."
"Will you stop going on about the Isle of Man. It was something I ate, Miss Clever Clogs," said Mark pushing her into the car.

"Dad, why are going so slow?"
"Because I can see a big cloud of blue smoke in my mirror when I go faster."
"But you're only doing forty miles an hour."
"I'm going uphill, Mark. I go forty-five on the flat."....

"Daddy, there's another Ford Anglia passing us. Why?"
"He's got a newer car, Anna, and he has only one passenger. There's four of us, plus lots of luggage."......

"Paul what's that red light on the dashboard?"
"God! It's the oil warning light. We'll have to stop and get a can of oil at the next garage."...

"Daddy, are we there yet?"
"No, pet. We're only at Doncaster. Daddy's a new driver, he can't go any faster."

Castle on a Cloud

"It's not because I'm a new driver, Joan, it's because I've got a bloody old car!"
"Language. Paul! Keep you eyes on the road, love."....

"Daddy, I want a wee."
"So do I, Paul. Can we stop at the next garage?"
"Why didn't you go when I got the oil?"
"Why are you clenching your teeth, dear? Anyway, you need more oil, the light's on again."...

"Dad, I've been studying this map, I reckon it's twelve inches from Newcastle to Ilfracombe. We're getting near Stratford, that's about seven inches. By my calculation we've got another five inches to go. Now let's see, we set off at nine o'clock this morning. Say we stopped an hour for oil and wees."
"We stopped to have those sandwiches I made, Mark."
"I'm counting that, Mam. What time is it now?"
"It's seven o'clock."
"That's nine hours for seven inches. I reckon the other five inches will take approximately 6.225 hours plus more stops for oil and wees. Say seven hours. It'll be two o'clock in the morning when we get there."
"OK, Mark, we know you're getting a maths O-Level."
"Never mind maths you two. Right, that's it, Paul. We'll have to stop soon. You're not driving in the dark, you must be shattered."
"I'll carry on a bit longer, Joan. I want to break the back of it."
"You'll have a *break*down if you're not careful."...

"Stop, Paul. Look! There's a fish and chip shop."
"Stop, Daddy!"
"Dad."
"What, Mark?"
"I've banged my mouth on the back of Mam's seat."
"Are you alright, Mark?
"I will be when I get my fish and chips, Mam."....

"Did you get to sleep in that layby, Paul? I nodded off. Mark and Anna were snoring."
"*I* don't snore, Mammy."

"Yes, I did sleep, Joan. But I've got a stiff shoulder. It's getting daylight now. I'd better push on."
"Yeah, Dad, there's still three inches to go."...

"You've been asleep in that deckchair all day, Paul."
"Daddy, aren't we going to see what there is to do?"
"Tomorrow, Anna, eh? We've got six days holiday left."
That garage in Nether Stowey was wonderful. We'd only travelled about an inch on our way home, when the noise became apparent. The clanking started just as we approached the outskirts of the town. As if by a miracle, there it was; 'Blackwell's Garage, Ford Agent'.
They replaced our broken crankshaft in three hours flat. "Oi would be careful, maister. Keep your speed below sixty until it settles in."
"He'll do that alright," muttered Mark.

28

A MOVE TOO FAR

Mam had moved – at last. She had finally succumbed to the advice of the Social Services. Not a flat this time, but a two-storey council house. On the ground floor, Cecil had all the necessary facilities close at hand and on the same level: a bathroom, a toilet, a bedroom, and easy access to the front door.

But Mam wasn't happy tonight.

"Don't you think this house is better than your flat, Mam?"

"Not really, Den, I just can't settle. I'm too old for new tricks. Give me my old place. I knew where everything was there. This going upstairs to bed – it's peculiar. Plus, in the kitchen everything is in the wrong place. The cooker's where the sink should be, the bench is too small. I hate the place."

"What about you, Cecil?"

"Oh, it's better for him, I suppose," Mam conceded.

"M-much better, Joan. All on the level for me, everything handy. I c-can even go for a little shuffle along the s-street with my Zimmer for company."

"You'll miss the little car though, Cec. Pity you had to give it up."

"W-well, you know I had to, Den. That d-day my hands failed me on the c-controls halfway up Dunsmuir Grove. G-god! It was a good job I hadn't gone far and that little l-lad was passing."

I laughed. "You always seem to have a little lad around to send for help, Cec. Where do you keep these lads who know where Dover Road is?"

Cecil laughed. "I p-pull them out of hat."

"So you've got your wheelchair now, Cecil."

"Yeah, Joan. Don w-wheeled me along to the little park yesterday."

Shaking her head, Mam got up to poke the fire. "By, it always feels cold in here."

"But you've got central heating now. So how's that?"

"It might be me I suppose. Where's Mark and Anna, Joan?"

"Oh, Mark's supposed to be doing his homework for his O-levels, but I bet he's watching High Chaparral. He's says it's a pity we haven't got a colour telly. Mind, he seems to sail through his exams. Anna's at dancing class. We'll pick her up on the way home."

"Colour telly! The kids today have big ideas. They want everything as soon as it comes out. There wasn't even such a thing as a *wireless* in my day."

"Aye, Mam. Things were 'ard in Edwardian toimes. They were that."

Mam smiled and brandished the poker. "Stop scoffing, Den. Times *were* hard." She turned to Joan. "Did Anna enjoy being in that show at the Little Theatre? I would have gone if I'd felt up to it."

"Cinderella? She didn't have a main part, but she had fun. She's still only ten. I think they're talking of doing Pinocchio next year."

Cecil laughed. "She m-might be the star!"

"No, no, Cec. One, she hasn't got a big nose, and two, the niece of the big chief of the dancing class will get the top role."

"What's that?" It was Don, who'd just come in wearing the full regalia of the Northern Omnibus Company. He threw his cap into a corner and hung his overall in a cupboard.

"D-don't be nosey, D-Don," laughed Cecil.

"Have a good day, Don?"

"A busy one, Den. It's a rotten turn, this one to Jarrow. Very first trip you catch the pensioners with their bus passes. They make you late for the rest of the day."

"It's a free ride for them after half-nine, isn't it?"

"Aye, Den. So what happens, eh? I drive out of the bus station at 9.35. So guess what? At every blooming stop there's dozens of doddery pensioners taking ages to get on the bus. I'm blooming sure they're just out for the run. Who would want to go to Jarrow at that time in the morning, eh?"

"Who would want to go to Jarrow at any time, Don?"

"Good question."

Joan laughed, "I know what you mean about the oldies, though, Don. Pension days in the post office – open the door at nine o'clock and

Castle on a Cloud

jump out of the way. If you don't you'd get killed in the rush. I think they worry we're going to run out of money!"

"What a terrible time these people have, Cec, these people who work in post offices or on the buses."

"It's alright for you, Den."

"I wouldn't say that, Don. The problems we have with chemists."

"Aye, Den, the world would be a better place if there weren't any customers."

Chemists? Some good, some bad. Some paid their bills on time. Too many didn't. So what happens? Ivor is told by Head Office -'Your debtors' ratio is lousy'. So Ivor leans on me. So what do I do? So I pressurise Gerry and Les – our sales reps. But Gerry and Les are more interested in their commission on sales promotions than getting money in to pay that commission.

Solution? End of each month I go visiting chemists in my newly acquired Ford Cortina; old, but smart, easy on the oil, but with a mysterious hole in the floor. Unluckily for Joan it's at the passenger side. But as I say, I go dunning chemists, wielding a big stick. A metaphorical big stick. And a pen. A real pen. To encourage customers to sign their names on cheques. It worked – to a degree.

Otherwise, things weren't going too badly at Pharma. The new computer system was bedding in well. The rubber stamped orders were despatched to the computer centre daily; inputted into those big wardrobes; and miraculously transformed into neatly printed invoices. OK, there was the occasional blip; a chemist could find he was charged for 100 packs of penicillin instead of 10, cost say, £500 instead of £50, but that was the exception. Just caused by some poor girl at the Computer Centre with twitchy fingers. 'We're homing in on that problem, we'll solve it', Tony Higgins had said on one visit. 'Solve it? When?' I'd said. 'Mad Charlie Tompkins, he with the six shops, gave me a sore ear yesterday. I'll tell you what. You tell him you're homing in on it. He'll be tickled pink'.

I was harsh on Tony, but on balance, this computer thing was a vast improvement on what had gone before.

"Teleprinters, Paul," said Ivor, one morning.

"Aha?"

"You've heard of teleprinters?"

"They're the things you see on the telly on a Saturday afternoon giving the scores?"

"I suppose so. I saw that one come up on the screen on Saturday – Newcastle 0 Sunderland 3."

"Don't rub it in, Ivor. Anyway, what about teleprinters?"

"We're getting two with a direct line to the Computer Centre. We'll control our own input. Snag is, we'll need an office. Your office fits the bill."

"Hang on, where do *I* go?"

"You go in the empty office next to Claude's."

"Does that mean I'll be ABM?"

"Of course not, you silly bugger. But I do believe the bosses are coming round to the ABM concept again."

"What's going on?" It was Claude, no longer able to contain his curiosity. I'd spent the morning walking back and forth transferring my goods and chattels into my new office. Every time I'd passed his door I had spied his thin face peering through the glass, trying to solve this puzzler. Now he'd buttonholed me as I carried a bunch of files.

"Going on, Claude? What do you mean?"

"You know damn well what I mean. You're moving into the next door office, aren't you? I'm going to bone Jones; I've had eyes on that office for years."

"Ee, I'm sorry, Claude, but I have more reason to have it, and don't they say that possession is nine points of the law, anyway?" I laughed.

He slumped visibly. "You're not going to be ABM!"

"I'm working on it," I teased.

But, Claude, ABM? Not a chance, thank God, not so long as Ivor was boss.

"Ah, that's my phone Claude; we'll have to continue this discussion some other time, eh?"

I dropped the files on the desk and picked up the pristine handset. "Yes?"

"Mr Potts? I've been trying to get you. I didn't know you'd moved office. I have a message, your Mam's ill. She's at home but could you go to see her?"

I was there in ten minutes. Cecil, looking distressed, was sat in his wheelchair in the living room. "What's up, Cec? Where's Mam? What's happened?"

Castle on a Cloud

"I'm glad you've c-come, Den. She's had a s-stroke, a mild one, the doctor said. Don w-was on an early shift but when Mam didn't come d-down, I shouted up as b-best I could. There was no answer. So I struggled next door with my Zimmer and got Mrs Sloane. She went for the doctor. He's arranging for a nurse to c-come in."

"I'll go and see her."

She was sat up in bed; one side of her face was vaguely distorted. She opened her eyes, gave a pitiable one-sided smile, and tried to speak. I bent nearer and held her hand. It felt cold and lifeless. Her speech was slurred but I made out, "No hospital, Den."

"No, Mam. No hospital."

"Even this place better, Den."

Her eyes were drooping. "There, Mam. Go to sleep."

"Aye."

The doctor came again that night, Joan and I were there. So, of course were Don and Cecil. He explained that Mam may in time recover her full faculties. In the meantime, he would arrange nursing care. Cecil, too, would have help.

Days passed with little change in her condition. When Don was at work, Cecil sat alone downstairs and his mam lay alone upstairs. When Don was at home, he was their intermediary. We visited regularly and at last saw gradual improvement. Soon, she began to sit up, eat, even read a little, but as yet with no possibility of managing the descent to the living room and have Cecil's company.

One evening, we took Mark and Anna to see their uncle and their grandma. We turned into Mam's street. "I'll race you to Grandma's," shouted Anna, dashing off and leaving Mark still on the back foot.

"Cheat!" shouted, Mark, running in pursuit.

Anna disappeared into the house, with Mark close behind. That was no surprise. The door was always unlocked. What was startling, however, was that within seconds they reappeared.

"What's wrong?" I asked.

"There's no one in, Dad," said Mark.

"Uncle Cecil's not there and his wheelchair's empty," added Anna.

"Don't be daft," said Joan.

Curious now, we went into the living room. Yes, there was his vacant wheelchair. I explored further.

"He's not in the bathroom, Joan."

"Listen, Paul. I can hear voices, what's happening?"

I took the stairs two at a time. "Cec, what are you doing on the floor?"

He was sat, back against a chair, by the bed. Mam was raised on her pillow and seemed remarkably bright.

"How did you get up here, Cecil?" added Joan, as Mark and Anna pushed between us to get a better view of their uncle on the floor.

"On my b-bottom, stair by stair. I just w-wanted to see Mam, Joan. We've had a ch-chat."

Mam smiled. "He's marvellous, isn't he? Struggling up here. I could hear this bumping and thumping. I wondered what had happened. Then he appeared. It's made me feel much better just to see him."

"You're a stubborn beggar, Cec," I laughed. "How long did it take you to get up here?"

"Oh, about h-half-an-hour, maybe more."

"On your bottom, Uncle Cecil!" marvelled Anna.

"Yes, on his bum, love," said Mam. "My, it's good to see both of you as well. I'm having a good day."

"I think. I'd b-better start the return journey, Den."

"I'll give you a hand in a minute."

Mam eased herself up further, "Bye, love. It was a treat to see you, and now I've got another treat with Mark and Anna, here. Next time I'll come down to see you!"

But there was no next time. Just a next day – it was the very next day that I got the call. A second stroke. A massive stroke. Mam was dead. She'd seen her poor lame son, she'd seen her grandchildren. Hopefully, the manner of her going was one of contentment.

She'd had mixed fortunes; a loving husband and a special father to her bairns, but he had died when she was scarcely forty; she'd borne four boys, but one was now in a mental hospital, and another bitterly handicapped; she'd married again, but only to become a widow for the second time. Then the disappointment of another of her sons who had married in a Protestant church.

The day of the funeral saw a gathering of mother's kinsmen and women. Aunts, uncles and cousins that I'd never seen since my teens. So much older, so much greyer. Catholics all. As an apostate, I would probably never see them again. So be it. At the graveside, I looked around the mourners; the relatives who had boycotted my wedding; Uncle Joseph and his miserable wife, Ruth; Posh Aunt Sally; snooty

Castle on a Cloud

Cousin Delilah; the others. I hadn't craved to see them again. I hadn't missed them. These people or Joan? I looked at my wife and took her hand. She squeezed gently – a token of comfort at the graveside. Somehow, I believed that I'd got the best of the bargain.

Don was deep in conversation with Delilah. I took hold of Cecil's wheelchair. Joan placed a hand on his shoulder. "Shall we go, Cecil?"

Cecil fumbled and struggled with his handkerchief, his feeble hands shaking. He tried to wipe his eyes.

"Here Cecil, let me," said Joan, softly.

29

IT HAD TO HAPPEN

The funeral was over, the kinspeople had vanished into the shadows. Not one of them had asked how Don was going to manage, but he coped in his a tuppence-ha'penny way. His boss was helpful in allowing him to work constant middle-shifts, starting late morning, finishing early evening. That arrangement meant he was there to help Cecil to both get up and to go to bed. Joan and I visited regularly; Social Services organised a midday meal; but best of all for Cec was the priceless daily help solace and companionship of Sister Alice and Brother John. This young pair, novitiates from the local Catholic priory, were warm-hearted, and always thoughtful of his needs. Their conduct matched the stoical outlook of Cecil himself, and almost succeeded in filling the gap in his life left by Mam's demise.

But they could not halt his gradual deterioration.

That Christmas we entertained a shrunken family. Now, there was no Gran, no Grandma, and no Stephen around. Stephen was still living in his own little world with his mucker, Harry. They'd be having a big party at Stanningley and Santa would surely come to a Stephen now lost in a time warp.

Santa didn't come to Dover Road anymore, well he wouldn't would he? Not to a fifteen-year-old Beatle fan, or to an eleven-year-old sophisticated miss; and certainly not to an old Grandad from York.

My brothers came down in a taxi on Christmas Day. A special taxi with wheelchair access. We celebrated the day with our second 'Turkey Christmas', but it was a pathetic bird when compared to the whoppa that had landed on Ma Davidson's doorstep two decades earlier.

Elderly Grandad and tired, work-worn Don snoozed through the

Queen's Christmas message; perked up when time came for Christmas cake and mince pies; became positively chirpy at the appearance of ham sandwiches and Newcastle Brown. Joan had spent a deal of time in the kitchen; Mark, Anna, Cecil and me had ploughed through the games in Anna's Big Compendium; Ludo, Dominoes, Lotto; until Cecil opted out of Tiddleywinks. "I can't t-tiddle any more, Anna."

That was when Grandad and Don were awoken with a cacophony of raucous laughter.

"What was that?" asked Grandad. "Aa do believe Aa was dreamin' abowt aeroplanes. Aa thowt that noise was that Concorde thing."

"Aye, fancy travelling faster than the speed of sound!" said Don, "but I suppose that's no surprise – they say they'll be landing on the moon next."

"No good'll cum of it awl, Don. It's agenst the laws of nature. Just like that doctor in South Africa givin' that fella a new 'eart. Muckin' about like that. No, no," he said, shaking his bald head.

"I w-wish they'd muck about w-with a cure for MS, all the s-same." said Cecil, wistfully.

"Aye, that's different, lad. Now that wud be somethin'. But swoppin' 'earts! It meks me shudder. They'll be swoppin' giblets next."

"Dad!" laughed Joan. "Let's change the subject, let's have a sing-song."

'Good idea!' was the general response.

Mark was the lone dissenter. He hunted through his pile of presents and had soon buried his head in a new football annual.

"Aa'll 'ave to look at that there book, Mark, whilst Aa'm 'ere," said Grandad. "We're goin' t't match tomorrow, Cecil. Pity thee can't come, these days."

"I might s-see it on Match of The D-Day, that's if they have one on Boxing Day. They m-might not – it's a Tuesday; Sunderland they p-play, don't they?"

"Aye. Mind, they doan't play football like the owld days, Cecil. There's too much passin' back, tha knows."

"That's called tactics, Grandad," piped up Mark, suddenly taking an interest.

An interest that just as quickly subsided, when:

"CUM BACK, LIZA, CUM BACK, GIRL."

"L-listen, is that H-Harry Belafonte?"

No, it was Don, wide awake, now that a sing-song was in the offing.

Castle on a Cloud

"I hope you're not going to hog the floor, Don." I laughed.

"SIXTEEN TONS AND WHAT DO YOU GET? Fold your arms or I'll fold them for you."

It seemed that he was uncertain of the song he should open with, or perhaps he wondered whether he should lead in with Robert Mitchum impressions. There was a third possible explanation – was this just his trailer to the delights in store for us?

Meantime, we'd have to wait with bated breath – Joan had something to say: "Before anyone sings, I've got a surprise," she said, then mysteriously disappeared into the front room.

A hush descended over the assembled company, even Don was silent, as we waited for her return. The hold-up was brief. Back she came carrying a box-like object. She placed it on the table and opened the lid with a "Hey Presto!"

Grandad arose from the settee with a kind of creaky alacrity, keen to have a nosey. Anna, Mark, Don and I also gathered around the curious artefact. "What have you been up to, Joan? What the heck is it?"

"Well, Paul Dennis, I've surprised you, haven't I? It's a tape-deck. I got it from our old emporium on Coatsworth Road."

"What's a tape deck, Mammy?"

"I know, what it is, and I'm not having any. It can record people's voices," said Mark. "Nobody's going to hear me singing."

"Who'd want to?" taunted Anna.

"I had this idea," said Joan, ignoring the interruption "Why don't we record our voices for posterity?"

"Posterity might not want to hear them," laughed, Mark.

"I think it's a good idea," said Don, "COME MISTER TALLYMAN."

"'Od your 'orses, Don," laughed Grandad. "Age before beauty."

Joan plugged the machine into a nearby socket and fiddled with the knobs. I was impressed; she seemed to know the drill. "Testing, testing." Her enunciation also, in that mellifluous way of hers, was spot on.

Then she played it back; "TESTING, TESTING."

"That's a bit loud," said Mark.

"But what a voice!" I laughed.

"Right," said Don, "let's get cracking; Grandad, then me. We'll go down from the oldest, eh?"

"Aye," said Joan's aged parent, "Aa've got me song sorted out. Is the thing ready, Joan? Do Aa 'ave to bend over the contraption?"

"No, Dad, the microphone will pick you up. I'll switch on. Just go ahead."

"Ahem, ahem, huh, huh. Ladies and gentleman, George Speed is going to sing. Are you *sure* it's ready, Joan?" She nodded.

'Right, ahem.
When Aa went down to the lower arcade
That's a place for children's toys
Where you can buy a dolly or a spade
For good little girls and boys
Said a little wee voice to me."

"You've missed a bit, Dad."

"Aa know, Aa know. Where was Aa? Aye, 'ave got it."
And when Aa passed a certain stall
Said a little wee voice to me
Aa'm a dolly marked one and nine
An' Aa ride on a tin gee-gee
An' Aa ride on a tin gee-gee.
"Aa don't know any more, love."

"Encore, encore. G-good song."

"Play it back, Mammy," said Anna, clapping.

"Let's see, there, that's it. Listen to this."

"Ahem, ahem, huh, huh. Bzz, bzz. Ladies and gentlemen, George Speed is going to sing. Are you *sure* it's ready, Joan?"

"Right, ahem."

When Aa went down to the bzz arcade
That's a crackle for children's toys
Where you can bzz a dolly or spade
For bzz little girls and boys
Said a little wee voice to me."

"You've missed a bzz Dad."

"Aa know, Aa know. Where was Aa? Aye, 'ave got it."
And when Aa passed a certain stall
Said a little wee voice to me
Aa'm a crackle marked one and nine
An' Aa ride on a bzz gee-gee
An' Aa ride on a tin gee-gee.
"Aa don't bzz any more, love."

"Encore, encore. G-Good s-song."

Castle on a Cloud

"Play it back, Mammy. (Clap, clap, clap.)"
"Was that me? I sound funny!"
"Well, you do sound funny," laughed Mark. Then panicked, "It's not still on is it?"
"Y-you never know," said Cecil.
"The sound isn't all that good on it, Joan."
"Well, what do you expect for one pound ten?"
"Is that what it cost? By, that's a bargain. I suppose we can just ignore the buzzing," I said, quickly trying to atone for my carping criticism. "It's you next then, Don."

But Grandad hadn't finished. He now decided to be Master of Ceremonies. "It now gives me great pleasure to introduce my great friend, Donald Potts. Let's have a round of applause for Don. Oh, look Joan, he's dropped his nuts."

No, Don, hadn't dropped his nuts, it was poor Cecil who, in a fumbling attempt to clap, had knocked a saucer of his favourite snack – salted peanuts – onto the floor.

"Never mind, Cec, I'll get you some more."
"It's a good j-job it wasn't my b-beer, Den!"
"Do you know all this kerfuffle is on tape?" I laughed.
"Niver mind," said Grandad, anxious to resume his duties. "Let's get on with the show. What are you goin' to sing, Don?"

"Well, I'm in a bit of a quandary, Mr Speed. I don't know whether to sing, I KILLED NOBODEE BUT ME 'USBAND, SIXTEEN TONS, or do a Robert Mitchum."

"What's a Robert Mitchum, lad?" asked Grandad, naively.

"Well, like, 'OK, PUT ME IN CURSTODY, PUT HIM IN CURSTODY, PUT US ALL IN CURSTODY, WHAT DOES THAT PROVE? IT ONLY PROVES YOU'VE GOT A BIG GAOL!'"

"We'll settle for Sixteen Tons, Don," I laughed. "That might be shorter."

Don's turn over, Joan sang sweetly – Sing a Rainbow – I wondered if the rainbow was near that castle on a cloud.

Cecil, his voice losing its power, but helped by a discordant chorus, did his best with Island in the Sun. Me? It had to be And I Love You So. (For posterity.)

"Right, Mark, It's your turn."
"No chance, Dad."
"Spoilsport, spoilsport," cried Anna.

"It's you then, Anna."
"I'm not singing, Mam."
"Spoilsport, spoilsport," cried Mark.
"I'll tell some jokes, instead."
"Right, are you ready, Anna?"
"Hu-hu: I say, I say, I say. Why do bees hum?"
"WE DON'T KNOW, WHY DO BEES HUM?" we chorused.
"Because they don't know the words!"
"That joke was terrible," piped up Mark.
"Ah, ha. Your voice is on the tape. Your voice is on the tape. Here's another. What do you say to a deaf policeman?"
"WE DON'T KNOW, WHAT DO YOU SAY TO A DEAF POLICEMAN?"
"Owt you like, he cannot hear ye!"
Well, nobody could cap that. Joan closed the lid of the machine. "There, your voices are all in the box."
"You m-mean like a vent-ventriloquist's dummy?"
"More like six ventriloquists' dummies!" said Mark, laughing.

"Say that again; you think it would be useful, if I, as the Branch Accountant with experience of your computer systems, could initiate fellow accountants in other branches? Explain the purpose of all the reports that you're able to generate here in the Computer Centre? But aren't they self explanatory?"

I was in Pharma's Manchester Computer Centre. Tony Higgins had given me a quick tour of the set-up whilst Ivor remained in the office in discussion with Tom Williams. It had been a quick tour, when you've seen one black shiny wardrobe you've seen them all.

Now I was back in Tom Williams' office. Just the four of us there; Tom, Tony, Ivor and me. "Well," replied Tom, "Not everyone is as bright as you, Paul."

"Don't be smarmy, Tom," I laughed. "But which branches are you thinking of, and how long would I spend in each?"

"Well," butted in Ivor Jones, who had driven me to Manchester in his brand new Ford for this meeting. Driven like a madman, ignoring any pretence of running-in the car.

"Tom assures me that he's thinking of the branches in the north – a couple of days in each."

"Like which?"

"Well," said Tom, "Just the ones that will be coming on-line in the next twelve months. Lancaster, York, Paisley, Perth."

"Paisley? Perth? They're not north they're another country!"

"All part of Pharma," laughed Tony Higgins.

"Tom's been telling me that it's been cleared with Head Office," said Ivor, "You'll get an appropriate rise."

"It's beginning to sound better by the minute. And the reports?"

"Well," said Tony. "You've had them all in the branch this last three months. Listings of sales by customer, with six months history; debtors' lists, summary of sales by product, line values by product group, order values, sales by van run, etcetera, etcetera; and I know you've been analysing them for Ivor. The next step will be using this information to produce branch budgets. You'll be able to guide these other branch accountants, set them on the right path."

Well, well. I'd had these computer screeds plonked on my desk for a few months now. OK, some I'd found worthwhile, some I thought were just useless bumph. I'd have to examine the latter again, try to find some benefit that could be gleaned from them; other than waste-paper salvage. No worry there; for an extra two hundred or so a year, I'm sure my fertile imagination could come up with uses for even the most puerile report that would convince my fellow accountants. Yes! Yes!

"For the next half-hour, Paul, you can go next door with Tom and go through the printouts with Tom, confirm between the two of you the purpose of each one. [Oh! I might get one or two of the dodgy ones expunged today. That's even better.] Come up with any other ideas that these lads can put into motion," said Ivor.

"Then we'll go for a bite," said Tom.

"A bite?

Where would we get that? The office canteen? Not quite.

In Tom's car we twisted and turned through the streets of Manchester. It seemed a long journey to find an eatery.

"We'll park here," said Tom, as we came to a halt.

"Just down the lane," said Tony.

A mysterious narrow lane. A Chinese restaurant. We entered. A busy Chinese restaurant. Full of Oriental diners. Just a sprinkling of white faces; men in dark suits with briefcases by their chairs, incongruously waving chopsticks whilst in earnest discourse.

"Not many people know about this place; very authentic cuisine. Tony discovered it," said Tom.

"Have you eaten Chinese?" asked Tony.

"I once had a packet of prawn crackers at the Hoppings on Newcastle Town Moor. Does that count?" I queried.

"Hoppings?" asked Tom, puzzled.

"The annual fair. Biggest in the country. You must have heard of it." Tom looked at the ceiling and shook his head.

There were Chinese lanterns hanging up there, and, hanging on the walls, colourful fans and mystical eastern paintings. Was I being fanciful or could I sense the aroma of joss sticks floating in the air?

A smiling Chinese fellow appeared from nowhere. Not your usual Chinese fellow, this one didn't have his hands up his sleeves. "Ah! Meester 'Eegins! Your usual table?"

"Yes, Chung Lee, and you got my order for the Four Star, eh? Good. How's the wife these days?"

"Ah! The meeses is, how you say? Hunky dory? Velly hunky dory, Meester 'Eegins."

"Like your food, eh, Chung?" *Chung* laughed; *I* wondered. Wondered whether these computer chappies spent most of their lunchtimes in this place. Wondered even more when, at the table, I glanced at the menu. Extensive; expensive. Very extensive; very expensive. Much more varied, much dearer than that fish and chips bistro we'd taken the kids to on rainy days in Scarborough.

Ivor too, picked up the bill of fare. His eyebrows, which even in repose had the look of inverted Vs, became positively elevated.

"No, no, Ivor," said Tom, "put that down, we're having the Four Star Banquet. Only the best is good enough for you lads from our pilot branch. This meal will set you on your way home."

"Who ratifies your expense account, Tom?" asked Ivor.

"Well, this is Tony's hospitality. You see I sign Tony's expenses claim and I'll pass this one with a clear conscience. This is a big thank you for the way your branch has cooperated with our boys."

"Aaah, I see, said Ivor.

I'd never seen the like.

OK, I'd been to a Chinese Restaurant before, but that was in India. Yes, India. Just a pokey little place in Darjeeling, it was. I'd had mixed grill. Didn't fancy the Chinese stuff. No choice now. Had to eat it. Rude not to.

But I did have a choice: Sesame Prawn Toast, Barbecued Spare Ribs,

Castle on a Cloud

Spring Rolls *and/or* Crispy Seaweed – Crispy Seaweed!?; Crispy Duck *and/or* Crispy Duck; Deep Fried Chicken in Lemon Sauce, Sweet and Sour Pork Hong Kong Style, Fried King Prawns in Szechuan Sauce *and/or* Deep Fried Crispy Shredded Beef (Hot and spicy).
  Or a mixture – a bit of each.
  No, no. I didn't have a bit of each. I don't like anything hot and spicy for starters. No, that's not right. I don't mean for 'starters', I mean I don't like hot and spicy things, full stop.

Joan, Mark and Anna were all sat glued to the telly when I got home.
  "Hello," I said, taking off my jacket, expecting a warm welcome. Surprisingly – just perfunctory 'Hellos'.
  I sat down on the settee beside Joan; she offered her cheek for a kiss. Big deal. "Miss me, love?"
  "Shh." Then, "You've been drinking."
  "Just a pint."
  "Shh. We're watching this new thing. It's a scream."
  "What new thing?"
  "Quiet, Dad," said Mark between chuckles. "It's called Dad's Army."
  Humph. I'd accompanied a would-be Monte Carlo Rally driver halfway across the country, had the meal of a lifetime, secured a big rise, yet couldn't get a word in edgeways because of the darned telly. And here was me bursting to tell everybody about my day. What was so good about this programme anyway?
  Mmm, there were some funny characters in this thing, all the same. Home Guard, eh? I remember them. Wartime, eh? I remember that. It took me back a bit. 'We're doomed!' wasn't that the chap who was in The Thirty Nine Steps? 'Don't panic.' – Clive Dunn? He was in Bootsie and Snudge.
  "Ha, ha." OK. It was funny, this thing. What was it? Dad's Army?
  And that signing-off tune by the brass band – Who Do You Think You're Kiddin', Mr Hitler? Bud Flanagan sang that during the war, didn't he?
  As the song faded, Joan slipped her hand in mine. "Did you have a good day, love? You're late, I was worried about you."
  "Oh! You talk do you! You didn't seem worried when I came in."
  "I'm sorry, but you must admit the show was comical." She patted my thigh. "You've had a long day, pet. Are you hungry? Do you want something to eat?"

"Not today, possibly not tomorrow."
"You're not well?"
I reached for my jacket, pulled out that menu (I'd snaffled it when we left the restaurant), and flourished it. "Look at that – I had that Four Star Banquet."

Nosy Mark and Anna rushed up behind the settee and peered over Joan's shoulder. "The Four Star! Did you have all of that, Daddy?"

"Most of it," I laughed.

"No wonder you don't want anything to eat! And look at the price. That would keep the four of us for a week!"

"I didn't know you liked Chinese, Dad."

"I do now."

I'd told Joan about the day; about the proposed visits. "You'll be away overnight?" she'd said. "I won't like that. All alone in bed."

"You'd like to hear that I'm getting two-hundred pounds a year rise, though?"

"You're not! That's great love. Mind, you deserve it."

We were not late to bed. It had been a long day.

"Are you reading your book, pet?"

"Not tonight, Joan, I'm exhausted."

"I'll put the light out, then."

All was silence. A gentle silence disturbed only by the rhythmical sound of our breathing. For a moment Joan's breathing ceased, then recommenced. She was thinking! She turned; her back to me; but soon swivelled again. Her arm came around me. I knew the signs; in a moment she would speak. "Paul."

There it was! I snored sleepily – a pseudo snore.

"Paul, I know you're not asleep."

"Mmm? I'm nearly. What is it?"

"I've been thinking."

"Oh, no!"

"This rise. We've talked about a house. We need three bedrooms. Now we can do something. We can afford a bigger mortgage."

"Mmmm." I yawned.

"Sunday. Why don't we go up Low Fell and see what's what. See the area we fancy. We should start looking, don't you think?"

"Mm Mm. If you like. If you like."

"Paul." Her hand squeezed my thigh.

Castle on a Cloud

"What now?"
"You're nice. Are you *really* tired?"

We left the car in the Jolly Miller car park on the main Low Fell road. The pub had closed – it was nearly three o'clock – but a scattering of cars were still parked. We cut through the back to a modern estate and wandered down the hill.

"Look at the white mist rising in the valley, Joan. Isn't it strange?"
"Never mind the mist, love, we sussing out houses. Oh, look! *There's one for sale.*"

Long accustomed as I was to a world of terraced houses and flats, it was not surprising that each and every semi-detached dwelling seemed appealing. But I was determined to be a prudent buyer; not to be carried away by Joan's mounting enthusiasm, rather to make a careful appraisal of the pros and cons every step of the way.

"Yes, Joan, but I believe they'll be overlooked in the back garden."
"There's one for sale on the other side."
"That's better. But wait. Their garden's facing north."
"Is this what you're going to be like all the time?" she asked. A trifle huffily, I thought. "Let's try the next street."
"Cheltenham Gardens, that's a lovely name."
"God! We're not buying a house because it's got a nice-sounding address. Mind, the houses on the right seem to have a good outlook at the back. Looking over the green hills."
"The road's a bit steep, Paul."
"Now who's doing the carping?"
"Anyway," she said, as we walked up the street. There aren't any 'For sale' boards."

I stopped outside one house and took her arm. "Look at that," I said, pointing at the front window. "Look!"
"What? My God! He's putting a notice in the window."

We'd both caught a glimpse of the wording – 'For Sale. Apply Within.' Unbelievable. An old fellow was engrossed in his task, fumbling with Sellotape as he struggled to attach the home-made sign to the windowpane.

"Let's ring the bell," I said. "Find out about it."
"Do you think it's fate?" she asked.
"Don't jump the gun. And don't be too enthusiastic, right?"

After a wait of a minute or two, it was the old chap who opened the door, his equally ancient wife (or mother?) hovered behind.

"We've come to enquire about the house."

"Well, I'll go to the foot of our stairs! Margie!" he gasped, turning to his wife. (Margie? *Must* be his wife.)

She was a frail, bent old soul. "What did you say, Algie?" she quavered.

"The house, Margie. They've come about the house!" he shouted.

"By, that's quick. The Good Lord must have sent them. That notice of thine has done the trick, Algie."

He looked puzzled. "No, Margie," he bellowed. I've still got the notice in my hand. Blast this Sellotape"

"We just wondered whether we could have a look around," I laughed.

"Aye, of course, come in," he said, shaking his head in wonderment.

We looked alright. A spacious lounge, a dining room. Upstairs, three bedrooms, a bathroom, separate toilet. Downstairs again through the kitchen and into the garage. A garage!

Then out through a small conservatory leading to the garden.

The garden. Joan's main reason to move. My eyes alighted on the pleasant outlook across to the hills. Today, the valley between was covered with that mysterious white mist. Then I heard Joan squeal with surprise. She was pointing to the bottom of the garden, beyond the lawn.

A willow tree. A small willow tree, a young willow tree, but a willow tree, nevertheless.

The willow tree, the garden, and below, that mystic white mist. A castle on a cloud!

Was it Prudent Paul now, or The Grand Panjandrum?

No contest. "How much are you asking? I asked, turning to our escort.

"Four thousand one hundred."

I gave a crazy laugh, "Don't bother to put your notice in the window. Let's shake on it, eh? Then I'll put things in motion."

Joan said not a word, just smiled. She'd waited twenty years for this moment.

Printed in the United Kingdom
by Lightning Source UK Ltd.
108810UKS00001B/157-255